Tao Qian and the Chinese Poetic Tradition

Michigan Monographs in Chinese Studies, no. 66

《寄淵明》

天遣斯文一貫窮
游雲飛鳥過長空
丹心四海求經國
傲骨無儔棄囿籠
霜月汗鋤明素志
孤松芳菊嘯清風
百年飄跡人間世
影落南山照晚紅

To Yuanming

Heaven sends this scholar to a fate of adversity—
A roving cloud, a flying bird traversing the vast sky.
An ardent heart ranging the four seas, he seeks to help his motherland;
Proud bones with no companion, he leaves the fettering cage.
The frosty moon and sweaty hoe illumine his innate sentiments;
The lone pine and fragrant chrysanthemums hum to him in the fresh breeze.
A lifetime's drifting tracks through the human world,
His shadow falls on the southern hills, as they gleam in the evening sun.

Tao Qian and the Chinese Poetic Tradition

The Quest for Cultural Identity

Charles Yim-tze Kwong

Center for Chinese Studies
The University of Michigan

Center for Chinese Studies
104 Lane Hall
The University of Michigan
Ann Arbor, Michigan 48109

Cover design by Heidi Dailey
Cover art by Suk-ling Poon

Printed in the United States of America on acid-free paper
5 4 3 2 1

Library of Congress Cataloging-in-Publication Data
Kwong, Charles Yim-tze, 1958–
Tao Qian and the Chinese poetic tradition : the quest for cultural identity / Charles Yim-tze Kwong.
p. cm. — (Michigan monographs in Chinese studies ; no. 66)
Includes bibliographical references and index.
ISBN 0-89264-108-8 (alk. paper). —ISBN 0-89264-109-6 (pbk : alk. paper)
1. T'ao Ch'ien, 372?–427—Criticism and interpretation. 2. Chinese poetry—History and criticism. I. Title. II. Series.
PL2665.T3K96 1994
895.1'124—dc20 94-39652
CIP

Contents

Acknowledgments

This book first took shape during my study at Yale. I must begin by thanking Professors Kang-i Sun Chang, Ying-shih Yü and Yu-kung Kao for their valuable guidance and advice during the dissertation stage of my work. Substantial revisions have been made since then; I am grateful to the two readers for the Center for Chinese Studies, and to Professors Jo-shui Ch'en, Victor Mair, David McCraw, and especially Hans H. Frankel, for reading different drafts of the manuscript and making constructive suggestions. A special note of thanks goes to Professor Kang-i Sun Chang for being constantly supportive throughout the process.

The names of authors to whom I owe an intellectual debt are given in the notes and bibliography, but I would like to mention Professors James R. Hightower and A.R. Davis, whose pioneering translations of Tao Qian's writings have greatly faciliated my own translations, and Professor Chia-ying Yeh, who has shown me how analytical criticism is as much a matter of the heart and spirit as of the mind. I am also grateful to Professor Martyn K. Whyte, the Center's Director of Publications, for his enthusiasm and encouragement; to Walter Michener, the Center's editor, for his cheerful patience and indispensable professional support; and to the editors of *Chinese Literature: Essays, Articles, Reviews,* for permission to reprint certain paragraphs (some modified) in two articles of mine previously published in the journal: "Naturalness and Authenticity: The Poetry of

Tao Qian" (1989) and "The Rural World of Chinese 'Farmstead Poetry' (*Tianyuan Shi*): How Far Is It Pastoral?" (1993). In addition, I wish to thank Tufts University for a summer faculty fellowship and two research awards, and the National Endowment for the Humanities for a summer stipend, all of which have facilitated the completion of this book.

Every writer brings to his work different thoughts and feelings. This book owes much in spirit to my mother, who seems only to understand her duties but not her rights; to my father and my brother Luke, both sensitive poets who have inspired me as a practising student of classical Chinese poetry; and to those ancients whose visions of life are a part of my sensibility. Above all, I have received ungrudging help and constant inspiration (including the cover sketch) from my wife Suk-ling, who is a student of various Chinese arts and an embodiment of some of the best in Chinese civilization.

Abbreviations

Works most frequently cited have been abbreviated according to the list below:

A — *Lunyu* [yizhu] 論語[譯注] *(Analects of Confucius)*. trans. Yang Bojun 楊伯峻. Hong Kong: Zhonghua shuju, 1984.

D — *Tao Yüan-ming: His Works and Their Meaning*, 2 vols. Davis, A. R. Cambridge: Cambridge Univ. Press, 1983.

H — *Tao Yuanming yanjiu ziliao huibian* 陶淵明研究資料彙編, 2 vols. ed. Dept of Chinese, Beijing Univ. and Beijing Teachers' Univ. 北京大學北京師範大學中文系, Beijing: Zhonghua shuju, 1962.

HS — *Han shu* 漢書, 12 vols. Ban Gu 班固. Beijing: Zhonghua shuju, 1962.

HT — *The Poetry of T'ao Ch'ien*. Hightower, James R. Oxford: Oxford Univ. Press, 1970.

JS — *Jin shu* 晉書, 10 vols. Fang Xuanling 房玄齡 et al. Beijing: Zhonghua shuju, 1974.

L — *Laozi* [jiaoshi] 老子[校釋]. ed. Zhu Qianzhi 朱謙之. Beijing: Zhonghua shuju, 1984.

M — *Mengzi* [yizhu] 孟子[譯注], 2 vols. trans. Yang Bojun 楊伯峻. Beijing: Zhonghua shuju, 1960.

Mn *Doctrine of the Mean (Zhong Yong* 中庸*)*. In Zhu Xi 朱熹, ed. *Sishu* [zhangju jizhu] 四書[章句集注]. Beijing: Zhonghua shuju, 1983.

QTS *Quan Tang shi* 全唐詩, 25 vols. ed. Peng Dingqiu 彭定求 et al. Beijing: Zhonghua shuju, 1960.

SJ *Shi ji* 史記, 10 vols. Sima Qian 司馬遷. Beijing: Zhonghua shuju, 1982.

SP *Shipin* [zhu] 詩品[注]. Zhong Hong 鐘嶸. ed. Chen Yanjie 陳延傑. Beijing: Renmin wenxue chubanshe, 1980.

SS *Song shu* 宋書*,* 8 vols. Shen Yue 沈約. Beijing: Zhonghua shuju, 1974.

SX *Shishuo xinyu* [jiaojian] 世說新語[校箋]. Liu Yiqing 劉義慶. ed. Yang Yong 楊勇. Hong Kong: Dazhong shuju, 1969.

TYJ *Tao Yuanming ji* 陶淵明集. ed. Lu Qinli 逯欽立. Beijing: Zhonghua shuju, 1979.

WD *Wenxin diaolong* [yizhu] 文心雕龍[譯注], 2 vols. Liu Xie 劉勰. trans. Lu Kanru 陸侃如 and Mou Shijin 牟世金. Jinan: Qilu shushe, 1982.

X *Xunzi* [jijie] 荀子[集解], 2 vols. ed. Wang Xianqian 王先謙. Beijing: Zhonghua shuju, 1988. Numerals refer to chapter and line numbers as printed in the Harvard-Yenching concordance.

XLJ *Xie Lingyun ji* [jiaozhu] 謝靈運集[校注]. ed. Gu Shaobai 顧紹柏. Henan: Zhongzhou guji chubanshe, 1987.

XQH *XianQin Han Wei Jin Nanbeichao shi* 先秦漢魏晉南北朝詩, 3 vols. ed. Lu Qinli 逯欽立. Beijing: Zhonghua shuju, 1983.

Z *Zhuangzi* 莊子. Numerals refer to chapter and line numbers as printed in the Harvard-Yenching concordance.

ZJ *Zhuangzi* [jishi] 莊子[集釋], 4 vols. ed. Guo Qingfan 郭慶藩, Beijing: Zhonghua shuju, 1961.

Introduction

Poetry is art embedded in history and culture. While the immediate focus of this book is on Tao Qian (365–427),[1] the poet's writings are placed within literary, intellectual, and socio-political contexts developed over the preceding two centuries, and related to longstanding philosophical and aesthetic ideals from the pre-Qin period. Comparisons are drawn from the Western literary tradition as occasion arises, with the mindfulness that perspectives independently formed in China and the West cannot be facilely transferred from one to the other. Relating close reading to wider cultural-historical factors and to cross-cultural literary phenomena, the study attempts an integral interpretive approach.

My discussion consists of two main parts. Part I moves from an overview of the Wei-Jin (220–420) ethos to Tao's lifelong quest for a personal and cultural identity; the complex artistic world revealed in his work reflects a dialectic search for a social and natural ideal informed by Daoism and Confucianism. More importantly, these visions constitute both a thematic macrostructure and a stylistic underpinning of his art. Analysis in Part II of its main aspects and its variations in tone, rhythm, and language to express different experiences shows Tao's art to be in essential unity with his life and ideals. Indeed the artistic process, in crystallizing a poetry of naturalness and simplicity, becomes a symbolic parallel to the poet's existential quest.

A number of authors, forms, and literary trends are introduced in a series of comparisons that highlight the artistic, historical, and cultural distinction of Tao's poetry in the Chinese lyric tradition.

To interpret Tao's poetry is also to discuss his life and poetic personality, first because they are so interfused with his work that a sense of them, as constituted from his writings, will in turn shed light on individual texts. Moreover, such a sense also enhances interpretive validity in being part of a wider evidential framework that may be the best antidote to selective reading based on a small number of texts and loaded theoretical premises. Third, Tao's life and identity form part of his poetic legacy that is revitalized by successive generations of readers, and that became a source of artistic inspiration to later poets as they tried to emulate him. No doubt the relationship between an author's work and life is no simple determinate question, not least because that life includes things he did *not* do: apart from empirical experience, the creative process is sparked yet not totally dictated by his conscious and unconscious intentions and impulses, nor does the import of the resultant work correspond exactly with them. Still, in both conception and praxis, much of Chinese lyricism remains an expressive record of thoughts, feelings, and life experiences. In Tao's work such autobiography is approximate because much of his known identity comes from his work; incomplete since it gives no comprehensive account of his life; and poetic in that pieces based on life experiences are blended with expressions and compositions of imaginative idealism, which may be fictional to the critic but are a real and deeply felt part of the poet's life, and so must be included in an extended sense of the autobiographical. Now fictional elements in poetic autobiography may point to a number of meanings and functions; suffice it to say that their presence does not always mean self-conscious role-playing or defensive image-building—just as such attempts do not always involve fictional fabrication. Indeed, while the postulation of self-image construction implies an act of manipulation and distortion and ultimately a certain authorial insincerity, the possibility is always there—especially if the poet's sensibility is of a visionary or idealistic cast—that the empirically fictional elements in his work may be experientially and expressively authentic. From recognizing the autobiographical nature of Tao's work, it does not follow that he is consciously engaged in a sustained attempt to write his autobiography. Only textual evidence will determine whether a particular poet writes first to express his sentiments,[2] or to promote himself to his readers.

The question of lyric authenticity is one of several wider issues, illustrated by Tao's poetry and partly indicated by the chapter headings, interwoven into this study. More generally, my discussion is predicated on the belief that literature is best appreciated not as an autonomous verbal entity but as the fruit of a temporal, cultural activity. Indeed, as the crystallization of a personal vision founded on cultural ideals, of a writer's sentiments (private and public) and experience in his encounter with history, great literature becomes fully intelligible only in light of the larger values, institutions, and personal and historical circumstances in which it is embedded. Since writers are situated within a literary and cultural tradition, the spirit and taste of the age as well as a web of historical conditions, there can be no rigid distinction between what lies within and outside a text, but rather a mutualistic relation between cultural-historical study and formal analysis. A full contextualization of the text beyond its formal boundaries—synchronically and diachronically—will enable it to be understood in a more meaningful and aesthetically profound way, one that is true to the irreducible complexity of history and culture itself.

To recognize the necessity of cultural-historical understanding for literary interpretation is not to see the relationship between them as a simple one. For a text far removed in time, any historical context supplied is but approximate, for the factors constituting it—material and nonmaterial, coeval and past, personal or otherwise—cannot be recovered in totality. Moreover, there are always specific traits about the spirit of a writer's age that are superimposed on the more permanent, deep-seated elements of the culture's value system, so that the dynamic between them must be carefully examined. Above all, no context can be rigidly determinative of textual meaning, for no cultural-historical activity needs to be confined within the orientations directing the culture of a given period. The author's response to historical realities is both individual and mediated by contemporary and time-honored ideas, just as his understanding of these ideas is filtered through his own and the larger historical situation. No neutral transmitters but renovators of culture, great artists do not just affirm but extend cultural boundaries by testing them against the contingencies of history. To the extent that great literary works always reinterpret inherited principles and standards which may be paradoxical and conflicting themselves, the understanding of history and culture is partly dependent on the literary work. Establishing the links and roots of a text cannot substitute for close reading, because a text is cultural not so much by reference to the world beyond as by virtue of what it has internalized and renewed.

Yet while falling short of completeness and total objectivity, the contextual restitution need not be arbitrary. Since interpretation begins and ends with the text, one can start with information it contains—quotations, topical references, language recalling prior usage or shared by contemporary discourse. Guiding literary and philosophical orientations within the cultural framework should be heeded, and spiritual values infusing the lyric impulse as heartfelt sentiments and lived experience elucidated. In the case of Tao, my study shows how his cultural heritage of interlocking and sometimes conflicting value-orientations generates a spiritual-aesthetic order along with a set of models and imperatives that are tested against a shattering reality. As with all great artists, his poetic sensibility and technique are not confined by the period ethos and trends in which he existed. Writing becomes a way of negotiating experience as he interacts with his cultural matrix; and in the living continuity between the venerable past and the afflicting present, the dynamic between the contingencies of history and the search for lasting truth, is to be found the individual vitality of Tao's poetry that cannot be explained in purely formalistic terms.

Lyric poetry is primarily expressive rather than didactic. In the work of an idealist like Tao, though, one finds ample support for the ancient Chinese perception of the cultural function of literature, whose embodiment of values and ideals gives it a heuristic resonance beyond "artistic" bounds. While not as emphatic about this function as Spenser, when he declares the purpose of *The Faerie Queene* as one of "fashion[ing] a gentleman or noble person," Tao surely sees art in a similar light when he writes "If I do not transmit [the Way as Confucius did], how will later generations hear about it?" (*TYJ* 106). The perception and reception of a poet's work can thus become testimony to its cultural significance. Largely ignored for three centuries by a readership of different tastes, Tao's poetry transcends and perpetuates its historicity by being constantly revitalized in subsequent periods. But its elevation from neglect to eventual canonicity represents more than a reversal of collective critical verdict: underlying the stabilized judgment of posterity are values and ideals which also help insure the poetry's continual capacity to invigorate the culture that fostered it. At least since Song (960–1279) times, Tao's poetry has remained living testimony to Daoist and Confucian visions of existence that have always spurred literati with a higher sense of ideal; as a reservoir of images, archetypes, and topoi repeatedly invoked and applied to new situations; and as a stylistic and generic touchstone by which to measure works it inspired. The function of literature as a cultural conveyor is especially clear from the often aesthetic-cum-spiritual response of later readers to Tao's poetry, since the artistic ideal and model of wisdom it exemplifies are essentially similar. In this light, our appreciation of the total significance of Tao's art does depend on our understanding of the poet's entire culture.

In sum, this book attempts to show how the study of literature, history, and ideas can be integrated to yield a sense of the complex whole of both literature and culture. Beyond its immediate task of appraising Tao's art, the discussion offers a glimpse of what may be called the quintessential spirit of the Chinese poet, one that continues to imbue the ways in which he envisions the world, the goals of existence he strives to enact, and the aesthetic ideals he tries to attain. A full substantiation of this proposition calls for more evidence than the present study can offer, but Tao's embodiment of this spirit certainly points the way in which many larger literary questions may be considered. To the poet's existential and artistic quest we shall now turn.

I

The Poet within the Wei-Jin Ethos and Classical Ideals

1

The Spirit of the Age

The Han dynasty (206 B.C.–A.D. 220) saw the institution of a new sociopolitical and intellectual order. The question of the self and its destiny, keenly debated in Daoist and pre-Qin Confucian thought, was largely suspended after Confucianism was established as the state ideology in 134 B.C. Instead, Han thinkers turned their attention to a comprehensive organization of collective life: regimentation of the individual found definitive expression in the "three bonds and six rules" of human relationships,[1] and the systematic formulation of elaborate *li* (rites and rules of propriety) for their enactment. But after three centuries of Confucian supremacy, the social and intellectual climate showed signs of ferment in the latter half of the second century A.D. The legitimacy of the three bonds was increasingly challenged by radical members of the elite class, reflecting an erosion of ritualistic collectivism if not a complete disintegration of the social framework. This was paralleled by a spiritual rediscovery of the individual as the natural being upheld in classical Daoism, with an affirmation of the authentic self who would feel, think, and express himself truthfully according to the free flow of his spirit.[2]

With the notions of individuality and freedom resurgent toward the end of the Han, Chinese thought easily took a sharp turn after the fall of the dynasty. That swing did not occur suddenly, for the philosophical discourse that dominated the Neo-Daoist movement[3] of the third and fourth centuries was audible among intellectuals and Imperial Academy students in the last years of the Han. With the court eunuchs' relentless persecutions of vocal dissidents following the great *danggu* purges of 166 and 169, many terrorized literati withdrew from the heated "pure criticism" of political *qingyi* to the witty "pure conversation" of philosophical *qingtan*, just as interest shifted from Confucian classical scholarship *(jingxue)* to the "abstruse learning" *(xuanxue)* of metaphysical speculation on the substrate of being. The persecution intensified under the dominion of the Wei (220–66) and the Sima family which supplanted it, so that for the social elite, survival often necessitated a flight from political involvement to an intellectual sanctuary that seems disjoined from worldly matters.

But beyond a fugitive pull drawing many literati to Neo-Daoism, there was a deeper quest for a macrocosmic vision that would answer the inner needs arising from their recent self-discovery. For instance, Liu Shao's (early third century) postulation of four categories of principles encompassing the cosmos *(daoli)*, social institutions *(shili)*, morality *(yili)* and feelings *(qingli)*,[4] reveals a spirit trying to redefine itself in relation to the surrounding world. Not only was such fundamental inquiry missing in Han Confucian scholarship—which had by then petrified into pedantic and fragmented textual analysis—but it would be difficult to find adequate treatment of all such issues in classical Confucianism itself, whose main concern is one of erecting a moral order through sociopolitical realization. It is in Daoism, with a central principle of naturalness or spontaneity *(ziran)* extending from ontological nonbeing *(wu)* and cosmological "non-action" *(wu wei)* to innate existential freedom *(xiaoyao)*, that the awakened individual found the resources for spiritual exploration. No wonder one focal issue in Neo-Daoist thought concerns the dialectic between *ziran* and *mingjiao* (the teaching of names).

In point of fact, this question has been raised in *Laozi* and *Zhuangzi*. Laozi[5] says "Dao models itself on *ziran*" (*L* 25), while Zhuangzi[6] advocates "according with the natural way of things" and "doing nothing [artificial]" (*Z* 7/11, 16/7). The term *mingjiao* does not appear in either text, but Laozi writes "once institutions arose there were names *(ming)*" (*L* 32), which Ch'en Yin-k'o rightly notes may be identified with the same character in *mingjiao*,[7] the Confucian moral and socio-political codes concocted after the decline of the simple, wholesome Dao (*L* 18, 28). The ridicule of Confucian norms comes even sharper from Zhuangzi, who sees them as a baneful "storehouse of schemes" usurping Nature (*Z* 7/31), akin to a halter around a horse's head or a string through an ox's nose (*Z* 17/51–52). Taken in its full dimensions, the conflict between *ziran* and *mingjiao* involves no less than divergent ontological, cosmological, and existential visions, with no room for reconciliation.

For many of the Wei-Jin elite, however, the intellectual debate was fraught with social and political meanings variously related to and interpreted by different individuals. When Wang Bi (226–49) writes "All being *(you)* originates from nonbeing *(wu)*" and "the nature of the myriad things lies in spontaneity," or "to model on naturalness means to model after a square while within a square and after a circle while within a circle,"[8] he also offers philosophical legitimacy to the non-aristocratic Wei's forging of a dynasty from scratch, as well as supplying a justification for Cao Cao's (155–220) pragmatic policies.[9] Meanwhile, for Ruan Ji (210–63), Xi Kang (223–62) and others caught in the transition from the Wei to the Western Jin (266–316), espousal of *mingjiao* or *ziran* amounts to a gesture of political allegiance to or protest against the Sima faction—the latter at the risk of one's life. The dispute translates into a choice between serving *(shi)* and reclusion *(yin)*: as Ch'en Yin-k'o notes, supporters of the Sima clan embraced *mingjiao*, while those loyal to the Wei upheld *ziran* in defiant withdrawal.[10] With the two doctrines thus remaining at odds on a political level, the ambiguity of the dialectic is shown through those who were forced out of reclusion to serve the Jin, and who would thus feel easier about their change of heart if the opposite teachings could somehow be squared. At the same time, beyond the psychological factor at work in some lies a broader consideration shared by most of the leading Neo-Daoist thinkers and *qingtan* participants, in that the ambiguity of the *ziran-mingjiao* discourse is inherent in their social background. On the one hand, an appeal to the *ziran* of spontaneous feelings can always justify one's individual expression, disregard of propriety, or sensual indulgence—even though that chosen conduct of "nonconformity" may itself be stylized and ritualized. On the other hand, since most of the Neo-Daoist elite came from aristocratic families, a total championing of *ziran* would undermine hierarchical distinctions and threaten their social, political, and economic privileges. Not surprisingly, one "natural" solution was to regard certain practices and institutions as *ziran*,[11] to synthesize the opposite doctrines into a single construct that makes *ziran* its metaphysical basis and *mingjiao* its sociopolitical application. The tendency is already discernible in Wang Bi's comment on Laozi's statement on names:

> When the uncarved block [*pu*, symbol of primordial naturalness] was dispersed . . . there were officials and rulers. When institutions and regulations, officials and rulers are initiated, it is *impossible not to* establish names and statutes by which to determine superior and inferior.[12]

With *pu* posited as its basis, political order takes on a sense of naturalness and logical necessity. A similar bent is even more evident in Guo Xiang's (d. 312) commentary on *Zhuangzi*. Now it is a moot point as to how much Wang's and Guo's philosophy might have been influenced by their own situation, though it may be noted that both served and were not known for moral rectitude.[13] Yet what is interesting here is the familiar but scanted fact that Guo has incorporated into his commentary the views of Xiang Xiu (221?–300?), one of the "Seven Worthies of the Bamboo Grove" and among those who, giving up reclusion to serve the Jin, would have needed a doctrinal justification for their conversion from *ziran* to *mingjiao*. In this light, it becomes especially relevant to note that "Xiang-Guo," starting from a different metaphysical postulate that Dao is literally nothing (*ZJ* 6/1:248), see everything producing itself (*ZJ* 2/1:50, 6/1:224) as the necessary outcome of given conditions: "It is not by accident that we have our life; it is not by chance that our life is what it is" (*ZJ* 5/1:213). Moral codes and social institutions, categorically denounced by Zhuangzi, now come to be seen in terms of spontaneous generation and supersession (*ZJ* 14/2:494, 513–14). By this logic, "though the sage may be found in the court, his mind is no different than if he were amid hills and woods" (*ZJ* 1/1:28), since both are "natural" environments. The philosophical underpinnings of the unity of the two doctrines are complete.

Planting the roots of *mingjiao* in *ziran*, then, Neo-Daoist thinkers do not challenge the *raison d'être* of polity, though it should be a nonacting one in keeping with its cosmic prototype of *wu wei*.[14] As a story in *Shishuo xinyu* (A New Account of Tales of the World) illustrates, the new doctrine of *ziran-mingjiao* unity was making headway among the literati of the time:

> Since Ruan Xiu (c. 270–312) had a fine reputation, Defender-in-chief Wang Yan went to visit him, and asked, "Lao-Zhuang and the teachings of the Sage [Confucius]—are they the same or different?"
>
> Ruan replied, "Aren't they the same *[jiang wu tong]?"*
>
> The Defender-in-chief liked his answer and appointed him his aide, so in his day he was known as "the Three-Word Aide."[15] (*SX* 4/18)

Here *"jiang wu tong"* offers a "self-explanatory" rhetorical answer affirming the unison of *mingjiao* and *ziran*, serving and withdrawal; it points to the later Neo-Daoist outlook that gained popularity among elite circles in the course of the Jin, even though the political situation that had spurred the doctrinal debate and unification was gone. As Ch'en Yin-k'o demonstrates with quotations from Yuan Hong's *HouHan ji*, Guo Xiang's *Zhuangzi zhu*, Xie Lingyun's poetry, and Pei Xisheng's stone inscription essay for Xi Shao, the new creed exerted a pervasive influence on all facets of Chinese culture, from ethics and historiography to philosophy and literature.[16] The only difference is that pure conversation had turned into an intellectual game of wit;

indeed Neo-Daoism largely superficialized into an adornment of elite life that sought satisfaction in elegant bearing and gesticulation, in verbal expression feigning loftiness or profundity, or even in meticulous facial cosmetics by way of enhancing those attributes. This is why Ch'en comments that by the Eastern Jin (317–420) pure conversation only functioned decoratively to qualify one as a "reputed gentleman" *(mingshi)*; it "had lost real political meaning" and "had nothing to do with [the] actual life" of the literati, whether or not they believed in the unity of *ziran* and *mingjiao*.[17]

Ch'en's remark, however, is valid only insofar as the Neo-Daoist debate was no longer a soul-searching issue tied up with a grave existential choice. For regardless of its practitioners' degree of conviction, the themes of *qingtan* did affect the outlook of the Jin literati. Since pure conversation assumes a spirit beyond the bounds of worldly affairs, they were one in voicing a return to *ziran* (in its double sense of naturalness and Nature),[18] whatever their individual motives and sensibilities. This espousal of *ziran*, in turn, led to the hermit being seen as an embodiment of such loftiness, a perception variously supported by the key philosophical texts of the period. Laozi advises "retir[ing] when one's task is accomplished" (*L* 9), and his championing of quietistic, nonassertive values fits in much better with the recluse than with the courtier. Withdrawal may be no issue for the "true man" independent of externalities,[19] but for those "within the realm," it is easy to see how the advocacy in *Zhuangzi* for transcending humanistic confines, emptying the mind, and forgetting everything readily translates into some form of detachment from the world. There are also hexagrams in *Yijing* attesting to the superior virtue of retirement: the top line of #18 *gu* reads "he does not serve kings and princes but pursues loftier goals," while the top line of #33 *dun* affirms "comfortable retreat" *(feidun)* as "advantageous in every respect."[20]

Not surprisingly, hermits quickly became objects of reverence among the Jin elite, even though reclusion was often a fashion of easy pleasure. If Xi Kang's refusal to serve led to a charge of treason and his execution in 262, the eremitic idea regained enough legitimacy in early Western Jin for Yu Jun (d. 273) to memorialize to the first emperor that, while court literati are like the ruler's "legs and arms, heart and backbone," those in mountains and forests can advance social morals by stopping avarice and strife through their examples. This is why hermits have always been honored since the time of the former sage-kings: "Though their sense of rectitude bade them leave the world [of action], their virtue accorded with that of their lord; though their conduct departed from that of the court, their merit equalled that of governing" (*JS* 50/5:1392–93). Indeed not a few considered reclusion superior to serving. Pan Ni (c. 250–310), for one, contends in his "Anshen lun" (Treatise on Settling One's Life) that the affluent official is "no match in honor" for the hermit peaceful in slender means, that the meritorious minister "cannot compare in loftiness" to the wise man who understands the truth of Nature (*JS* 55/5:1509). Similarly, Xie Wan (fl. 371) champions *ziran* over *mingjiao* in his "Baxian lun" (Discussion on Eight Worthies), using four pairs of contrastive examples to prove that "the reclusive is superior and the serving is inferior" (*SX* 4/91, n.1): Qu Yuan and the fisherman who advised him to drop his vain messianic effort,[21] Jia Yi and Sima Jizhu who told him a diviner's life is worthier than an official one (SJ 127/10:3216–20); Gong Sheng and the old man of Chu who, at the former's funeral, disowned him as a disciple for getting embroiled in politics (*HS* 72/10:3085); Xi Kang and Sun Deng who foresaw his doom.[22] Also becoming popular during the late third and early fourth centuries was a type of "invitation to hiding" *(zhaoyin)* poem, which customarily "described either a visit by the poet to some carefree recluse, or the poet's own longing to go into retirement."[23] Criticism of reclusion as "neglecting the regulation of key human relations" and "forgetting the duty of relieving one's soverign" was but a minority voice.[24]

In fact, hermits were held in such high esteem that the term was grossly abused, so that anyone not serving at court could count himself a recluse. Even the extravagant Shi Chong (249–300), who revelled in his Jingu Gardens after being removed from office upon the fall of his political associate Jia Mi, styled himself one living in *feidun*.[25] On the positive side, though, the hermit Zhai Tang (272–344) was said to have kept bandits off his grounds by force of his lofty name (*SX* 18/9, n.1). And the ardent Chi Chao (336–77) would provide an allowance and a residence for a *bona fide* recluse (*SX* 18/15).

Meanwhile, the honor conferred on eremitism led to the custom of summoning hermits to court, and Liu Bei's (160–223) soliciting of Zhuge Liang (181–234) became as much a prototype for rulers as it did for the literati. The lesser Jin counterpart to Zhuge Liang is Xie An (320–85), who had originally lived in retirement and fended off "persistent stringent orders from the court" (*SX* 25/32), until his younger brother's dismissal from high military office persuaded him to restore the waning prestige of his family.[26] One day Huan Wen (312–73), whom Xie was serving as assistant at the time, received a gift of medicinal herbs that included one variously called *yuanzhi* (far-reaching aspirations) and *xiaocao* (small grass). Huan asked Xie why it had alternative names, but before Xie could reply, He Long jumped in with an answer: "That's very easy to explain. In reclusion it's 'far-reaching aspirations'; out in public life it's 'small grass.'" Xie was extremely abashed (*SX* 25/32). No doubt aware of the circumstances behind Xie's emergence, He was probably just his usual humorous self; but his remark testifies to the political capital (increased by every refusal of office) accrued to a summoned hermit, who enjoyed far more respect and attention from the ruler than an average minister could command. Indeed Jin rulers not only looked on prominent recluses with fond indulgence—as Emperor Jianwen (r. 371–72) did on Xie An (*SX* 7/21)—but paid tribute to them through persistent offers of appointment. Less noted, but no less real, was the rulers' belief that an exaltation of hermits also meant an elevation of themselves, for the "search and promotion of secluded hermits" was supposedly emblematic of a "wise king ordering the world." A decree of Emperor Xiaowu's (r. 393–97) attests, "From the deep valley flows the song 'Tether the horse, keep it tied';[27] in hamlets and gardens are ranged processions offering appointments" (*JS* 94/8:2459), while Huan Xuan, just before his brief usurpation of the Jin throne, installed a Huangfu Xizhi in the country and commanded the latter to turn down his offer of high office (*JS* 99/8:2593–94).

The fact that withdrawal served as a shortcut to office certainly casts doubt on the motive of many whose "bodies may be amid rivers and seas but [whose] minds remain with the palace towers" (Z 28/56), and whose eremitism was no matter of principle or protest. One Zhang Wei, recognized by Ruan Xiu as nursing an ulterior motive when he became a hermit, acquired an office but was implicated in an intrigue (*JS* 49/5:1366). Another hermit, Fu Yuan, failed to meet the lofty standards laid down by Chi Chao, who accordingly refused to carry through his promised bequest (*SX* 18/15). Even the Buddhist monk Kang Sengyuan (fl. c. 300–350) was lured from retreat by his rising fame (*SX* 18/11). Unlike the modest contentment of a few true hermits of relatively humble origin,[28] reclusion among the Jin elite involved nothing of the physical risks or hardships described in "Zhao yinshi" (Summons for a Recluse) in *Chuci* (Songs of the South), let alone the starvation of Bo Yi and Shu Qi; it was an escape from official duties and political intrigue to the relaxing milieu of a country estate.[29] Ruan Yu, Wang Xizhi, and Xie An, to name but a few, all lived literally in *feidun*.[30] Socially revered, politically gainful, and materially comfortable, reclusion seemed an ideal course of action underpinned by the doctrine of *ziran-mingjiao* unity.

At the same time, the proposition also legitimized a more active form of political expediency, support for which was again sought in Laozi and Zhuangzi. The former was by legend a custodian of imperial archives at the Zhou court, exemplary of the wise man who "buries himself among the people" (Z 25/34). From the scorning Bo Yi who opts to starve in the wilderness (Z 8/23–26) to escapist anglers among rivers and lakes (Z 15/4–16), the hermit is for Zhuangzi ultimately misguided in his move, for over-attachment to an idea of purity renders one no less a victim of conventions than the mean worldling; eremitism is no issue for the "true man" who remains unfettered amid the world (Z 15/19–22), as Zhuangzi himself did as a minor official of Qiyuan. The validity of this point notwithstanding, Laozi and Zhuangzi could preserve their spiritual autonomy because they were far from the center of the political web and its sure entanglements; this is why Xie Lingyun (385–433) writes in his *Shanju fu* (*Fu* on Dwelling in the Mountains) that while wilderness and court make no difference in the mind, "in practice living in the mountains is quite distinct from the fetters of the marketplace" (*XLJ* 318). All the same, the unity between *shi* and *yin* was claimed early on by Dongfang Shuo (c. 161–87 B.C.), who as Emperor Wu's Court Gentleman considered himself a "court recluse" *(chaoyin)*: "Within the palace one may find refuge from the world and preserve oneself. Must it be in remote hills and thatched huts?" (*SJ* 126/10:3205). Dongfang lauded Liuxia Hui for maintaining his equanimity even while thrice dismissed from office, and he was not alone in seeing the latter as a *chaoyin*.[31] Continuing in this tradition, Wang Kangju (fourth century), citing Laozi as a paragon, asserted that "petty recluses hide amid hills and groves; great recluses hide in the court and cities" (*XQH* 2:953).

The claim of unity between *shi* and *yin* thus became the perfect solution for those who desire both worldly success and a lofty name. If Xin Mi confirmed even as he declined office that worthies and superior men remain so whether at court or in the wilds (*JS* 94/8:2447), Deng Can justified his switch from *yin* to *shi* by arguing that "reclusion can take place at the court and in the city, for it lies basically with me rather than anything else"(*JS* 82/7:2151). The opposite conduct of Xin and Deng and the identity of their pronouncements well illustrate the moral ambivalence of the doctrine of *ziran-mingjiao* unity, not only because of its all-accommodating position but because it legitimizes a complete *disunity* between "spirit" and action, the former always able to claim its lofty independence and so exonerate one from responsibility for one's conduct. Early in the Western Jin, Fu Xuan (217–78) had already warned that "Emperor Wen of Wei admired complete freedom *(tongda)*, so everyone thought little of keeping his integrity" (*JS* 47/5:1317–18). Fu's criticism was reiterated in the Eastern Jin by Wang Xizhi (309–c. 365), who noted how easily any remark by the ancients (here Confucius) can be twisted to serve ulterior motives: "The so-called thorough understanding *(tongshi)* just means advancing and hiding as the situation requires,[32] and deeming it farsightedness" (*JS* 80/7:2102).

No doubt Wang was responding to the widespread abuses of the doctrine of *ziran-mingjiao* unity. For instance, it gave Wang Yan (256–311) the licence to champion the primacy of nonbeing, to hold an eminent office in idleness so that his subordinates also "saw dereliction as loftiness" (*SX* 26/11, n.1), to act shrewdly for self-interest though never for public good—all without theoretically contradicting himself (*JS* 43/4:1236–68). It enabled high officials to do nothing in the name of "letting the mind roam freely beyond worldly affairs," to wallow in sensual pleasures while "leaving no traces by which they might be incriminated" (*SX* 6/10).[33] In extreme cases it led to the nonconformist eccentricities of the so-called "Eight Free Spirits" *(ba da)*, who "had no transcendent mind but merely found an excuse for self-indulgence" (*SX* 23/13, n.1), with nude drinking parties and imitation of the Bamboo Worthies.[34] It permitted even the Buddhist monk Zhu Fashen (286–374) to sail in and out of "vermilion gates" and claim he was but among "mat doors" (*SX* 2/48). Above all, it allowed not only double dealing but a double standard in its application to oneself and to others. While scorning Shan Tao for being "neither courtier nor hermit" (*JS* 56/5:1544), Sun Chuo could claim to have "seen the truth of 'stopping in contentment'" in his early reclusion (*SX* 2/84), then proceed to a string of key posts at the capital, all the while disdained for his "corrupt conduct" (*SX* 9/61).[35]

This is why, while an absolute follower of Zhuangzi should be independent of circumstances, most real Jin hermits kept out of politics. "His body lodged amid dusty profanity but his mind dwelling beyond the world," Guo Wen remained unswayed even as he stayed at Wang Dao's court residence for seven years,[36] but he was the exception that proves the rule. Most "retreated from the world to preserve their truthfulness" (*JS* 94/8:2427), the more humble ones earning their livelihood by farming;[37] some fled into mountains whenever appointment decrees came,[38] while others lived hermetically and eventually vanished.[39] Meanwhile, for most of the social and political elite, the credo of *ziran-mingjiao* unity was always at hand as a conscience-salving device by which one may cling to the privileges of conformity while enjoying the self-indulgence of "naturalness," or switch freely between serving and withdrawal without ostensibly contradicting oneself. Its psychological utility goes a long way toward explaining why, as Zhu Xi (1130–1200) said, "though Jin and (Liu) Song people might talk about being lofty, every one of them wanted an official post. Engaging in pure conversation on the one hand, they grabbed power and riches on the other" (*H* 1:75).

2

The Dilemma of Engagement or Reclusion

It is in light of the ethos outlined above that Zhu Xi placed Tao above his contemporaries (*H* 1:75). The key issues of the period are traceable in his writings, but they are filtered through a sensibility deeply at odds with his age. For instance, while he might have shared the Neo-Daoist premise of *ziran-mingjiao* unity in conception, his outlook is rooted in time-honored cultural ideals:

或擊壤以自歡	One may delight himself with the *jirang*[1] game
或大濟於蒼生	Or bring great benefit to mankind.
靡潛躍之非分	Neither hiding nor leaping[2] ill-fits his nature,
常傲然以稱情	For he always nobly suits his feelings.

(*TYJ* 147)

Daoist natural equality and Confucian political order, spiritual freedom and social concern, are not mental subjects to Tao. What is to Guo Xiang a philosophical question and to the later Pure Conversationists occasion for light witticisms is embedded in the poet's "nature" and "feelings"; *ziran* and *mingjiao* are one because they form the two sides of his being. Moreover, for him the meaning of *mingjiao* reaches beyond dynastic loyalty to the calling laid down by Confucius for all *shi* (literati), that of "bringing peace to the people" (*A* 14/45). The poet's sense of mission can be seen in his reverence for the "earnestly-striving old man of Lu [Confucius]," who "mended and patched [his age] to make it wholesome" (*TYJ* 99). Family tradition also seemed to have inspired Tao with the same personal and social ideal: from his "meritorious and virtuous" great-grandfather, the "valorous [Duke of] Changsha" who "did no wrong when enjoying favors" and "retired after completing his mission," through his "dignified" grandfather who kept "straight and square [even] in the provinces" and "brought harmony over a thousand *li*," to his "humane" father who, "finding his track among winds and clouds [i.e., officialdom]," "showed neither anger nor elation" (*TYJ* 28). Hagiographical or not, such panegyric reveals the models Tao wishes to follow.

"A man of humanity is sure to possess courage" (*A* 14/4), and find "bringing peace to people within the four seas . . . his delight" (*M* 7A/21). Both veins are present in the poet's "reminisce[nce of] my youth and prime," when "with valiant aspirations reaching beyond the four seas, / I raised my wings, and thought of distant flight" (*TYJ* 117). That imaginative flight is given a concrete course in "After Ancient Poems" #8:[3]

少時壯且厲　In my youth I was spirited and bold;
撫劍獨行遊　Stroking my sword, I went wandering alone.
誰言行遊近　Who says I wandered only nearby?
張掖至幽州　[West] from Zhangye [and north] to Youzhou.

(*TYJ* 113)

Beyond the "spirited and bold" optimism manifest in both excerpts, the course of his winging spirit reveals more than a personal heroic dream. With the Eastern Jin controlling only the territory south of the Yangzi River, several abortive attempts had been made to retake the northern lands (wherein lie Zhangye and Youzhou) under foreign rule;[4] Tao's great-grandfather Tao Kan was one who "directed his efforts at the Central Plains" (*JS* 66/6:1773). Not only does the poet's "distant flight" show a similar direction—from his southern home in

Chaisang to the far north and west—but its expanse across the "four seas" echoes the social commitment voiced by Confucius and Mencius (*A* 20/1; *M* 1A/7, 7A/21). Add to this background the inspiriting drama of 383 (while Tao was in his "youth and prime") when the outnumbered Jin troops defeated Fu Jian's invading army and recovered six commanderies,[5] and the poet's "valiant aspirations" clearly point to sentiments of a public character.

But such sentiments reflect only one side of him. For he is also inclined to the quiet music of Nature, especially in contrast to the din of worldly affairs: "Since youth I have failed to fit the worldly tune, / From the first my nature loved mountains and hills" (*TYJ* 40). Given his sense of social duty, Tao would never have followed Zhuangzi in mocking the Confucian vocation as a harmful interference with Nature that "violates the Way with the mind" (*Z* 6/9–12). But he does aspire to the free spirit of Zhuangzi's true man, who embraces all reality with pacific magnanimity and spontaneous delight (*Z* 2/34). The mystical proportions of the true man are absent in Tao's writings, but the following description, as will become clear in due course, fits in well with the Daoist side of his ideal:

> The true man of old did not chafe in want or brag of achievements, or scheme about affairs. . . . Knowing neither to love life nor to hate death, . . . he accepted [what was given] gladly, and forgetting [distinctions], returned to [a natural state]. . . . He is in accord with all things and no one knows his limit. . . . His bounty extends to ten thousand ages, but not for any [partial] love of men. . . . At ease in his uniqueness but not insistent, capacious in his vacuity and not ostentatious, . . . he rested in his virtue relaxed. (*Z* 6/4–16)[6]

Yet such a state of being Tao can locate only in the past, and nostalgically he tells his sons how, with "trees joined in shade" and "the season's birds changing their songs," he would "repose in the cool breeze" and "call myself a man of the remote times of [sage-] Emperor Fuxi" (*TYJ* 188). For alas,

> Since the time when the truthful ethos had receded and gross deviousness held sway, people in the villages have lost the virtue of honorable withdrawal, while in the marketplace and court men spurred thoughts

> of easy advancement.[7] Righteous literati who aspired to the Way "hid their jade" [*A* 9/13] in their prime, while those who purified themselves and distilled their virtues labored vainly to the end of their lives. (*TYJ* 145)[8]

Inherent in the poet's visualization of "remote times" is a sadness that an irresolvable conflict now exists between "hiding" and "leaping" where once there was none.

For Tao's age was one when "no high official came from a humble family and no low official from a prominent clan,"[9] when the existence of the state hinged on the support of large gentry clans *(shizu)* that virtually monopolized power and privilege. It was hard enough for a talent of humble birth to enter the hierarchy at all; Tao Kan's mother had to cut her hair to provide a meal for a visiting official, who thus felt obliged to recommend her son for a minor post (*JS* 66/6:1768). Family need and a sense of calling did spur the wavering poet to begin public service as Regional Libationer, but his misgivings about the times were soon more than confirmed for him to resign shortly afterward:

疇昔苦長飢	In the past I was afflicted by continual hunger;
投耒去學仕	Throwing down my plough, I went like others to serve.
將養不得節	I had not found a way to support my family;
. . . .	. . . .
志意多所恥	I was much shamed by my sentiments and goals.
遂盡介然分	So fulfilling my rightful destiny,
拂衣歸田里	I shook my robe and returned to the farm.

("Drinking Wine" #19, *TYJ* 98)

A drama of inner conflict generated by practical need and a dual longing is condensed into these lines. It is revealing that while social concern is always part of Tao's "sentiments and goals," the reminiscing voice is marked not by spirit but by regret. The sense of mission is apparently submerged beneath the "shaming" service experience of Tao, who at this poetic moment can only count his slender means and breadwinner's duty as the motives for his sojourn in officialdom.

His half-heartedness is indicated by the words "went like others," and if indeed he "threw down his plough" to serve, it would seem that he had been engaged in farming since youthful days, though not with decided commitment.

Yet while the *shi* lives as a "fish stranded on earth" (*Z* 6/22–23), his active sympathy remains with his stranded fellows; it is in part a resilient idealism that gives Tao's poetry a vitality largely lost since the "inspired power" *(fengli)* of Jian'an (196–220) verse. The latter's fundamental power lies in its square realism, compassionate social concern and positive attitude to life, coupled with a resolve to amend the age and establish a deserved name.[10] Witness these lines from Cao Cao's "Bu chu Xiamen xing" (Walking out of Xia Gate) and "Duange xing" (A Song in Short Meter):

老驥伏櫪　The fine old horse lying in the stable
志在千里　Still yearns to gallop a thousand *li;*
烈士暮年　The noble man may be waning in years,
壯心不已　But his lofty aspirations never cease.

(*XQH* 1:349)

山不厭高　I mind not the height of the mountains
海不厭深　Nor the depth of the seas.
周公吐哺　As the Duke of Zhou spits out his food,[11]
天下歸心　All in the realm turn their hearts toward him.

(*XQH* 1:354)

The bold will combining personal heroism and social idealism, undaunted by age or difficulties and conquering mountains and seas, is representative of the Jian'an voice at its most inspirited. But even this pales a little beside the visionary ardor of Tao's "Trees in Bloom":

先師遺訓　The Former Master's bequeathed teaching—
余豈云墜　Would I ever abandon it!
四十無聞　If at forty he is unknown
斯不足畏　He is not worthy of respect! 4

脂我名車　Grease my famed carriage,
策我名驥　Whip up my famed coursers:
千里雖遥　A thousand *li* may be far,
孰敢不至　But how dare I not go!

(*TYJ* 16)

Such inspired lyricism was almost "unknown" in the two centuries after Cao's songs, and all the more notable because while Cao's heroism stems from military success, Tao's buoyancy persists despite a lack of accomplishment. The short four-character line, though generally viewed as having less lyric potential than the five-character form, captures perfectly the vigorous pulsing rhythm of the poet's outburst of idealism. The poem is even more dynamic than Cao's partly because of its interjectional note, which lifts its tempo and raises its intensity and so accentuates the force imparted by the lyric form. But the effect is also due to Tao's heightened sense of social mission, as shown in his invocation of Confucius (ll.1–4, from *A* 9/23) and allusion to Xunzi (ll.7–8, from *X* 1/44). The optimism here offers a striking contrast to the chagrin in "Drinking Wine" #19—one that corresponds to the discrepancy between vision and reality; the coexistent states of mind form a complex, counterbalancing response to public service as the poet alternates between being inspired by ideals and disheartened by experience.

From some of Tao's dated poems, indeed, one sees how the pattern of hope, engagement, disillusionment, and withdrawal had to be repeatedly enacted before he could accept the futility of involvement in an adverse age. In 399 he joined the establishment of Huan Xuan, but two years later obtained leave of absence to return home. His mother's death soon afterward gave him the opportunity to resign, but when Liu Yu led a punitive force in 404 against Huan, who had usurped the throne in the previous year, Tao reentered service as adjutant to Liu before quitting again after a short while. Thus remembering the Master's words that "If at forty he is unknown / He is not worthy of respect," the poet left the farm lane for the "main road" of officialdom (*TYJ* 71) to translate ideal into action.

One poem, "Written as I Passed Qu'e while Beginning My

Service as Adjutant to the Defense Army General" (probably Liu Yu), epitomizes Tao's vacillation between conflicting sentiments:

弱齡寄事外
委懷在琴書
被褐欣自得
屢空常晏如
時來苟冥會
踠轡憩通衢
投策命晨裝
暫與園田疏
眇眇孤舟逝
綿綿歸思紆
我行豈不遥
登降千里餘
目倦川塗異
心念山澤居
望雲慚高鳥
臨水愧游魚
真想初在襟
誰謂形跡拘
聊且憑化遷
終返班生廬

When young I found resort beyond the world's affairs;
I placed my heart in my lute and books.
Wearing coarse clothes,[12] happy and contented;
Often empty,[13] but always at peace.
The time came, as chance would have it,
When I let go my rein and rested in the main road.
Throwing down my staff I ordered my luggage for the morning;
For a while I was parted from my farmland.
Far, far, the lone boat goes;
Endless, endless, thoughts of return meander.
Isn't my journey a distant one?
I've climbed up and down for over a thousand *li*.
My eyes grow weary of the strange rivers and roads;
My heart yearns to dwell amid hills and vales.
Gazing at the clouds, I feel mortified by the high-flying birds;
Looking down at the waters, I feel shamed by the gliding fish.
From the first the true ideal was in my breast—
Who says one is bound by externals?
For now I'll just follow the turn of things;
In the end I shall return to Master Ban's hut.[14]

(*TYJ* 71)

Like others that relate to his official life, this poem tells not of Tao's service but of his longing to leave it. The line between "the world's affairs" and "lute and books" is gently but clearly drawn at the outset, by a poet who, speaking not as a breadwinner, would embrace a meager, peaceful life with past worthies for company. For now he has reentered public service, but his submission to "chance" "for a while" shows a hesitant state of mind. Faced with a reality that promises little chance of fulfillment, his aspiration to "bring great benefit to mankind" finds expression as a brief spark of spirit and anticipation (l.7), but quickly sinks into weariness and a wish to break the bondage of office. The lone boat becomes both a parallel and a contrast to the poet, pointing to his loneliness even as he is supposedly partaking in a common cause, and sending him in a direction opposite to that of his heart. Nature, meanwhile, aggravates his dejection by "shaming" him with its silent admonition. Deepening the poem's lyric sense, the self-questioning lines underscore his inner doubt about the current course and his determination to withdraw to "the true ideal." A similar sentiment can be found in other poems as well, such as one he wrote during his brief service under Huan Xuan:

久游戀所生	After prolonged journeying I pine for her who bore me;
如何淹在茲	Why am I lingering in this place?
靜念園林好	Silently I think of the joys of the garden and woods;
人間良可辭	The human world can well be left behind.

(*TYJ* 74)

There may be some argument about the date of these two poems,[15] but none about their regretful and nostalgic note.

In an acrimonious attack on the poet, Okamura Shigeru calls him a "self-serving," "unscrupulous," and "glaringly nasty opportunist" who shifts positions in order to "get along in the world," "an extremely hard-boiled utilitarian rare even in his age."[16] It is true that Tao served under the two key figures in the last years of the Eastern Jin, except that on both occasions he withdrew while their power was on the rise. His voluntary dissociation from Liu Yu is especially revealing of his basic motive in seeking office: not desire for personal preferment, but faith in his ability to help amend the times. As Confucius says, "to govern *(zheng)* is to rectify *(zheng)*" (*A* 12/17).

Not that the *shi* should always serve, of course, for the fulfillment of his ideal is contingent on the moral Dao being politically operative. The Master himself acknowledges a potential necessity to "live in reclusion in order to attain one's purpose": "Emerge when the Way prevails in the empire, but hide when it does not" (*A* 15/11, 8/13). The latter soon became the only option left for Tao, who must have known how Eastern Jin politics was plagued by unceasing power struggles,[17] and witnessed for himself the ruthless ambition of

Huan Xuan and Liu Yu: the former briefly proclaimed himself emperor before being crushed by a collective force led by Liu, who in turn was to assassinate the restored Emperor An in 418, topple the Jin two years later, and dispose of the last Jin Emperor Gong.[18]

In terms of his humanistic sentiments, then, public service was Tao's first commitment, if only it were morally possible. But officialdom entails compromise even in the best of times, let alone one when "the truthful ethos had receded and gross deviousness held sway." Out of need he held a brief final office as Magistrate of Pengze (*TYJ* 159), but it only aggravated his shame in "enslaving himself." While Confucius could still search from state to state for a virtuous ruler, Tao is forced to retreat as the only way to preserve his integrity. Echoing the Madman of Chu's song to the Master—"the past cannot be helped, but the future may still be won back" (*A* 18/5)—the poet listens to his inner voice in the key decision of his life:

歸去來兮	Let me return!
田園將蕪胡不歸	My farmstead will soon be overgrown with weeds: why not return?
既自以心為形役	It was I who made my heart my body's slave;
奚惆悵而獨悲	Why should I be dismayed and grieve in solitude?
悟已往之不諫	I realize the past cannot be helped,
知來者之可追	But I know the future may still be regained.

("Return Home" *fu*, *TYJ* 160)

While Tao is extremely reticent about his political experience, the basic facts of Eastern Jin history—the incessant power strifes he witnessed while serving under Huan Xuan and Liu Yu, the landowners' exploitation of tenant farmers and northern immigrants,[19] which led to the massive rebellion of Sun En between 399 and 402[20]—suffice to shed light on his chagrin in an ethos so contrary to the Confucian ideal. In all the poet likens himself to "a bird frightened" by the "wide snare" of politics, who "thus flees emolument and returns to farming" (*TYJ* 147).

But to withdraw in dejection is to return in delight. As he writes in the first of his "Returning to Live on the Farmstead" poems,

少無適俗韻
性本愛丘山
誤落塵網中
一去十三年
羈鳥戀舊林
池魚思故淵
開荒南野際
守拙歸園田
方宅十餘畝
草屋八九間
榆柳蔭後簷
桃李羅堂前
曖曖遠人村
依依墟里烟
狗吠深巷中
雞鳴桑樹巔
戸庭無塵雜
虚室有餘閑
久在樊籠裏
復得返自然

Since youth I have not fitted the worldly tune;
From the first my nature loved mountains and hills.
By mistake I fell into the dusty net,
And was gone for thirteen years.
The fettered bird yearns for the old woods;
The pond-fish longs for the former deep.
Opening up some waste land by the southern wilds,
I abide by rusticity, and have returned to my farmland.
My homestead covers a few acres,
My thatched house several rooms.
Elms and willows shade the rear eaves;
Peaches and plums range before the hall.
Hazy, hazy, the distant villages;
Soft, soft, the smoke from hamlet lanes.
Dogs bark in hidden alleys;
Cocks crow atop mulberry trees.
Within my doors there is no dust or clutter;
In my empty rooms there is leisure to spare.
Long have I been in the confining cage;
Again I have managed to return to Nature.

(*TYJ* 40)

While leaving a formal analysis until later (in chapter 6), I shall examine the poem's movement in relation to the poetic spirit, which Stephen Owen sees as that of a "misanthropic recluse" "obsessively . . . defensive of his values and acts," explaining "his revulsion at our values" and scornful "rejection of us and our world."[21] The poem begins with a sketch of Tao's disposition and its deflection by his long venture into the world. Cast imagistically in terms of a contrast of "mountains and hills" with "dusty net," this double sense of exile and confinement—no conventional gesture in light of the historical facts mentioned above—is extended by the images of the fettered bird and pond-fish, but its very expression as a yearning impels the poem forward even as it casts a nostalgic glance. For indeed the poem's center of gravity lies not in the regrettable past but the cherishable present emerging in lines 7–8; disjunction from politics gives way to unity with Nature, and the poet's "abiding by rusticity" shows a firmness of purpose that plants his life on solid ground. Then in a cinematic shift, the poem's focus moves to his farm life, and we follow his spirit from field to thatched house amid the lively trees. The lack of meticulous description in the manner of Xie Lingyun means we are following no detached observer of a poet, but one whose inner vision unfolds the objects and scenes drawn into the flow of his consciousness during the moment of experience.[22] As the poem takes a "hazy, soft" turn blurring the still, "distant" village and the rising, closer smoke into one, that turn also reflects the affectionate spirit's meandering from the visual to the aural plane, enveloped by Nature's music in a melodious harmony. No random mixture of contents as in stream-of-consciousness descriptions, this lyric flow carries along elements of a coherent picture of existence, showing that it is one internalized in the poet's being. Self-expressive in its peaceful vitality, this picture speaks eloquently for the poet's spirit, as it merges into a sense of wholeness almost reminiscent of the undifferentiated chaos *(hundun)* in *Zhuangzi* (Z 7/33–35). It is only in the last four lines that Tao returns to a more contemplative mood.

The poem reflects the state of one contented in his simple life. Just as Tao merely touches on "worldly tune," "dusty net," and "confining cage" as the experiential background of his return, so he admits his "mistake" without any presumptuous self-justification. The summary statement of his nature and discomforting experience, his modest and mellow tone, all reflect the inner calm of one eager neither to censure a relinquished past nor to elevate himself by harping on his lofty detachment from the world. Whereas "Li sao" (Encountering Sorrow) is marked throughout by a chord of divisiveness between the poet and his enemies, "Return" #1 is notable for a pervasive ambience of unity. Like the true man who perceives without condemning (Z 33/66), the poet simply follows his heart and resolves his discord with the times by disengaging himself. His reclusion may be seen in the broad tradition of moral protest established by Bo Yi and Shu Qi, except that his tone is not one of defiance—which is irrelevant in the peaceful embrace of Nature. With no proclamation of his sole integrity in a corrupt world in the manner of Qu Yuan (c. 340–278 B.C.),[23] the voice is not that of an injured ego tinged with sour grapes, but bears out Wolfgang Bauer's remark that true seclusion is "quite often aimed not at the preservation of the ego but rather at its final dissolution in the cosmos and nature."[24] Writing no *zhaoyin* verse as the Western Jin poets did, he does not get "literary" about his choice; the truth of his lyricism comes from a depth of feeling coupled with the poem's graceful movement and soft tone, which convey the serenity of a spirit singing its natural tune.

Not that this tune is fanciful, for its lyric ease is rooted in a practical-minded honesty:

人生歸有道	Human life returns to the Way,
衣食固其端	But food and clothing are indeed its beginnings.
孰是都不營	How can one not provide for these
而以求自安	And yet seek peace for oneself?

(*TYJ* 84)

While in truth the *shi* "worries about the Way and not poverty" (*TYJ* 77, from *A* 15/32), Tao interprets the Master's words situationally. For if the volatile multistate polity in Confucius's age gave him hope to "work toward a goal which he knew cannot be realized" (*A* 14/38), the ethico-social ideal has become "far off and unattainable" in the poet's time (*TYJ* 77), and the once-rejected reclusion of Changju and Jieni (*A* 18/6)[25] a much more realistic option (*TYJ* 25, 76). Besides, while the Master could afford not to encourage farming (*A* 13/4)[26] but to focus on the Way, Tao knows he must "set his mind on lifelong toil" (*TYJ* 77). Again drawing support from the past when the sage-kings did farm work—"Shun ploughed with his own hand; / Yu also sowed and reaped" (*TYJ* 25)[27]—he decides to pursue the same as a practical and honorable course of action: "Surely one must earn his own clothing and food; / Hard ploughing will not let me down" (*TYJ* 57).

This note of relative optimism can be heard in a number of poems written in the early days following Tao's withdrawal. "I do not complain that spring work is hard," he writes in self-reliance, "But often fear failing in what I cherish" (*TYJ* 85). As manual and spiritual cultivation proceed together amid rural fellowship, daily life becomes the stuff of poetry: "After farm work each returns to his home; / In our leisure we always think of each other" (*TYJ* 57). The common sources of their joy and anxiety are conveyed in "Return" #2:

相見無雜言　When we meet there is no idle chatter,
但道桑麻長　Only talk of how mulberry and hemp have grown.
. . . .　. . . . .
常恐霜霰至　Often I fear the coming of frost and hail,
零落同草莽　When [my crops] would wither with the weeds.

(*TYJ* 41)

Mingling with his fellow farmers and sharing their language and sensibility, the earthly recluse in Tao's poems is no kin to the "hidden hermit" who lives in the fairyland Penglai in Guo Pu's "Youxian shi" (Wandering Immortals Poem), who "takes magical herbs" in Lu Ji's "Zhaoyin shi" (Invitation to Hiding Poem), who dwells among "caves without [housing] structures" in Zuo Si's same-titled poem (*XQH* 2:865, 1:691, 1:734). The fragrant plants and jadelike springs on which these rarefied, semi-immortal souls of *zhaoyin* verse subsist are conventional symbols; the frost and hail descending on the poet-farmer's fields are no literary device but real threats to his livelihood. So are the weeds in "Return" #3:

種豆南山下　I planted beans below the southern hill;
草盛豆苗稀　The weeds flourish, but the bean shoots are few.
晨興理荒穢　At dawn I rise to clear away the weeds;
帶月荷鋤歸　Bringing along the moon, I return shouldering my hoe.
道狹草木長　The path is narrow, the plants and trees tall;
夕露沾我衣　The evening dew soaks my clothes.
衣沾不足惜　Having my clothes soaked is no cause for pity,
但使願無違　Only let my wishes not be betrayed.

(*TYJ* 42)

While #2 describes Tao's life in relation to his neighbors, here the focus narrows to his own work. The poem also complements #1 well: Nature is exacting as much as delighting, and the contemplative poet appreciating rustic life as a whole is also the active novice farmer handling natural and human objects of labor. In the foreground is no longer the light mood of self-sufficiency but the anxiety of struggle, not the idyllic charm and quiet of the farmstead but the trouble of productive planting and the toil of protracted work. Feeling his cherished land as he walks home after another long day, the poet cannot but reflect on his "narrow path" and face the trial of will brought by his new life, not only because it is toilsome but because it is no more immune than public service from the reality that effort does not ensure effect. The firm answer that comes in the last couplet is convincing in being a tested and considered conclusion; we empathize with him as he reaffirms his faith, tired in body but refreshed in spirit, knowing from the hoe on his shoulder that he is "not betraying his wishes."[28]

Blending a vibrancy of spirit with a sober understanding of his choice, the "Return" poems range in mood from the buoyant delight of #1 to the dark pessimism of #4:

久去山澤游	Long have I left roaming hills and lakes,
浪莽林野娛	Unrestrainedly enjoying woods and country.
. . . .	. . . .
徘徊丘壠間	Lingering among the grave mounds,
依依昔人居	I brood on the dwellings of men past.
井竈有遺處	Of wells and hearths, the sites remain;
桑竹殘朽株	Of mulberry and bamboo, rotten stumps survive.
. . . .	. . . .
人生似幻化	Human life is like the changes of an illusion,
終當歸空無	Ultimately returning to blank nothingness.

(*TYJ* 42)

Recording a visit to a deserted village, the poem is striking for its steady descent from initial merriment through broodiness to an "ultimate" sense of "nothingness." The latter is prompted not by any preexisting thought but by the overwhelming images of both human and natural desolation, which keep Tao "brooding" and "lingering" until existence (including his own) is seen at its most meaningless, in terms of inevitable decay and formless illusiveness. This "anxiety and unsureness" about his identity, which Owen thinks Tao hides beneath a deceiving "surface role" marked by "georgic bliss" and "calm dispassion of . . . mind,"[29] is thus laid bare from the first as part of a spectrum of sentiments voiced in Tao's work, often within the same poem. In fact, it is partly this balance of expression that lends authenticity to his music of harmony: "I delight in the affectionate words of my family; / And take pleasure in lute and books to disperse my cares" (*TYJ* 161). That music is often more touching in bearing a note of sadness:

悵恨獨策還 Sadly I return alone, leaning on my staff,
崎嶇歷榛曲 Up and down the thicketed winding path.
山澗清且淺 The mountain brook is clear and shallow;
可以濯吾足 It will serve to wash my feet.
漉我新熟酒 I strain my newly ripened wine,
隻雞招近局 And to a single chicken treat my neighbors.
日入室中闇 As the sun sets the house turns dark;
荊薪代明燭 Thorn firewood takes the place of bright candles.
歡來苦夕短 Happy we are, but regret that night is short;
已復至天旭 Already dawn has come again.

("Return" #5, *TYJ* 43)

Relating Tao's sparetime activity as in #4, this poem is an inversion of the former in its shift of mood and setting. In #4 the poet goes outdoors only to witness the depressing side of Nature and human existence; here he experiences the healing power of both as he heads home and steps inside. The change is swift and marked as he is brought out of the introverted solitude of his walk to enjoy the clear brook, no longer "brooding" and "lingering" in his sadness. As the poem moves indoors in line 5, the restoration of spirits continues amid the genial company of neighbors; the modest arrangements of the party underline the poet's hospitality and the substantiality of their delight. That domestic companionship is important to Tao's resilience is also reflected in other poems that refer to his literati friends: "In company we appreciate unusual writings, / Together we thrash out uncertain meanings" (*TYJ* 56).

Reading the "Return" poems especially as a whole, one is struck by the poet's honest description of rustic life as he experienced it from various sides, and not according to some stock notion of reclusion that might enhance any self-image. This translates into a distinct touch of artistic authenticity quietly validating the poems' theme from different angles—that of return to Nature also as a return to human nature and natural existence. What they show is that while marking the practical death of his social idealism, Tao's retreat is also a liberating entry into currents of life that enable him to translate understanding into action, longing into reality. The total experience of earning his keep—from communion with Nature and domestic joy to rural concerns and impoverishing natural disasters—constitutes a baptism that deepens his art and insight into life.

For all is not smoothness and calm. On the most immediate level, indigence gradually adds a darker hue to Tao's poetry and life: "I have never deserted my work, / Yet in cold and hunger I often eat chaff" (*TYJ* 119). So does his family, and the poet faces up to the "inner shame" of his failed duty as a father, that in refusing to compromise his integrity he has "made [them] all suffer cold and hunger" (*TYJ* 188, 187). As his circumstances become increasingly reduced toward the later years of his life, he describes how

夏日抱長飢	On summer days I bear continuous hunger;
寒夜無被眠	Through winter nights I sleep without a cover.
造夕思雞鳴	Toward dusk I long for the cock to crow;
及晨願烏遷	At dawn I wish the sun would move away.

(*TYJ* 49–50)

The poet's response to time, usually more cultural and philosophical in nature, is reduced here to biological terms. Time becomes painfully slow when all it promises ahead is an extension of hardship, and begging for food dislocates his sense of being: "Hunger came and drove me out, / But I did not know where to go" (*TYJ* 48). A note of self-query has crept into his writings, often heard as an invocation of the Master's words about standing "firm in adversity" (*A* 15/1):

不賴固窮節	If not for the virtue of firmness in adversity,
百世當誰傳	Who would be passed on for a hundred generations?

(*TYJ* 87)

誰云固窮難	Who says staying firm in adversity is hard?
邈哉此前修	Ah, remote are those former worthies!

(*TYJ* 127–28)

斯濫豈攸志	Is "going to excess" what I want?
固窮夙所歸	To be firm in adversity was early my resolve.[30]

(*TYJ* 107)

This pattern of self-directed interrogatives is evident again as he reflects on the times: "As principle mine is shamed by 'thorough understanding';[31] / Yet what I preserve—is it something shallow?" (*TYJ* 76). Far from leading to a loss of faith, however, his self-query and typically modest manner mask an inner tenacity unbroken by material distress:

豈不實辛苦	Isn't it hard enough in reality?
所懼非飢寒	What I fear is not hunger or cold.
貧富常交戰	Poverty and riches are ever at war,
道勝無戚顏	But when the Way prevails there is no sad face.

(*TYJ* 126)

These lines reflect the more tangible sense of struggle and loneliness present in his later writings. Reminding himself that many who "left behind a name" of immortal honor[32] "suffered privations throughout their lives" (*TYJ* 93), he is sustained by the lasting virtue to which their "rectified" names attest: "How can I find solace for my heart? / I rely on all those ancient worthies" (*TYJ* 123).[33] In the reiterations of "firmness in adversity" which his inner dialectic generates, what we feel is not tedious theorization or self-glorification, but a resolve that needs to be fortified in face of chronic hardship. In the words of the *Great Learning*, one must "renovate oneself day after day."[34]

And destitution is not the major affliction for the poet. For all his delight in Nature and affection for his family and friends, his poetry expresses an indelible loneliness in the recesses of his being:

春醪獨撫　　The spring wine I hold alone.

(*TYJ* 11)

偶影獨遊　　Accompanied by my shadow, I stroll out alone.

(*TYJ* 13)

慨獨在余　　Sadness is singularly with me.

(*TYJ* 14)

What Wordsworth calls "that inward eye / Which is the bliss of solitude"[35] is also its melancholy; in the above lines it is the word *du* (singularly alone) that stands out. After all, taken reluctantly by the idealistic *shi* while awaiting better times, the eremitic choice entails a sense of loss and anxiety stemming from an undying hope for social fulfillment before time expires.[36] Tao's fellow farmers cannot be expected to understand his broader sentiments, and his literati friends do not seem to share the same idealism or compunction about serving in a dark age. In a poem to Yin Jingren on the latter's departure for duty, Tao observes how "Speech and silence naturally make different stands, / We knew well we had to be parted." Their divergent paths are described not without a touch of irony: "Fine talents do not retire from the world, / Those among rivers and lakes are mostly poor and humble" (*TYJ* 63–64). Genial friendship offers no lasting relief from the solitude that makes him yearn for a kindred spirit *(zhiyin)*: "Where is he whom I can set my mat near / And talk of everything in my life?" (*TYJ* 12).

In fact, apart from lyric moments of immersion in the quiet harmony of Nature,[37] Tao's spirits seldom consist of unadulterated joy, as even his legendary drinking illustrates. One easily recalls the moment of relish in "Return Home *fu*" when he first tasted the nectar of freedom after his permanent withdrawal (*TYJ* 161), or those scenes where the relaxing wine[38] after work forms an integral part of his contentment:

盥濯息簷下
斗酒散襟顏

Having washed my hands and feet, I rest beneath the eaves;
A measure of wine relaxes my bosom and face.

(*TYJ* 84)

日入相與歸
壺漿勞近鄰

When the sun sets we return home together,
And to a jug of wine I treat my near neighbors.

(*TYJ* 77)

But "delight and sadness are mingled" even during the calmer years of early reclusion (*TYJ* 13), as his "inner heart burns" at the thought of death that would annihilate his idealistic hopes (*TYJ* 83). If the Gentleman of the Five Willows is carefree in his drinking, Tao resorts to it partly as temporary solace for a frustrated purpose:

清琴橫床
濁酒半壺
黃唐莫逮
慨獨在余

The clear lute lies across its stand;
Cloudy wine half fills the jug.
The [days of sage-rulers] Huang [di] and Tang [Yao] cannot be reached:
Sadness is singularly with me.

(*TYJ* 14)

And as his visionary ardor comes to sag under the weariness of a battered spirit, what once enhanced his happy moods in earlier times turns into an anaesthetic:

中觴縱遙情
忘彼千載憂

Amid drinking we let go our ranging feelings,
And forget those worries of a thousand years.

(*TYJ* 45)

汎此忘憂物
遠我遺世情

I float [the chrysanthemums on] this care-dispelling thing,
Drifting far my feelings that have left the world behind.

(*TYJ* 90)

While he knows drinking only "shortens his life" (*TYJ* 37) and once tried to give it up (*TYJ* 101), he continues to rely on the "care-dispelling thing" to "drive out a hundred cares" (*TYJ* 39), "put aside" the threat of death (*TYJ* 81), and consign himself to oblivion.

For sobering up always means a return to his multitude of concerns, including the bleak world which he has formally left but cannot forget altogether. His mixed feelings reflect the inner conflict inherent in reclusive life, precisely because they lack the ambiguity of motive often underlying similar gestures made by the Jin elite. After all, the eremitic choice is felt most acutely not by Zhuangzi's disinterested disciple[39] but by one caught in the dilemma of serving in unworthy times. Sadly Tao watches his country roll on amid the turmoil of political supersession:

種桑長江邊	They planted mulberry trees by the Yangzi's bank,
三年當望採	In three years expecting to pluck their leaves.
枝條始欲茂	But just when the twigs and foliage were about to turn lush,
忽值山河改	Suddenly the hills and rivers happened to change.

("After Ancient Poems" #9, *TYJ* 114)

As Hashikawa Tokio notes, there are *fu* pieces written by Western Jin poets on the mulberry tree which associate its planting and thriving with the rise of the dynasty (*H* 2:246). Moreover, it is clear that when Tao writes "Shanyang returned to a lesser kingdom" (*TYJ* 102) in the atypically obscure "Shu jiu" (Telling of Wine), he is drawing an analogy between the deposed Han Emperor Xian (demoted to Duke of Shanyang) and the Emperor Gong ousted by Liu Yu. That such lines may point to loyalist sentiments is also corroborated by the absence of Liu-Song reign titles in Tao's work[40] and the studied vagueness of some other "Ancient" poems[41] reminiscent of Ruan Ji's (210–63) "Yonghuai shi" (Singing of My Heart) verses, which do invite a political reading. Although the later (Song) claim that Tao changed his name from "Yuanming" to "Qian" (hide) after the dynastic change (*H* 1:96,98) remains disputable (*D* 2:174), it is not without reason that a whole line of critics, from Shen Yue (441–513) and Xiao Tong (501–31) to Zhen Dexiu (Song), Song Lian (Ming), and Yun Jing (Qing), have come to see Tao's reclusion as a gesture of loyalty to a dynasty his ancestors had served.[42]

This does not mean his political sentiments are just loyalist ones. For if he refused to recognize the Liu-Song, he was disillusioned enough with the Jin to have "hidden" fifteen years before Liu Yu usurped the throne, and his Peach Blossom Spring utopia is closed to the Eastern Jin society against which it is set (*TYJ* 166). There is no need to claim for Tao a prophetic clairvoyance about an imminent dynastic change in the manner of Yun Jing (*H* 1:218); as Liang Ch'i-ch'ao and Yeh Chia-ying observe, overstating the loyalty case results in reductive perception.[43] Not only are Tao's poetic contemplations consistently wider in perspective than a dynastic one, but his political ideal is clearly oriented toward all humanity, as seen in his wish to "bring great benefit to mankind" and his visionary yearning for predynastic sage-rule:

愚生三季後	Born in a time after the Three Dynasties,
慨然念黃虞	With deep feeling I think of [sage-rulers] Huang [di] and Yu [Shun].

(*TYJ* 65)[44]

Doubly tormented by the conditions of the age and his inability to help "mend and make it wholesome," he longs for the return of a more fulfilling epoch when true worth was recognized by wise rulers, when everyone lived in the peaceful harmony of *zhen* (*TYJ* 24).

Zhen, or truthfulness, is what Yeh Chia-ying rightly sees as the essence of Tao's spirit.[45] As Fukunaga Mitsuji notes, quoting Gu Yanwu (1613–82) and Duan Yucai (1735–1815), the word is not found in the Confucian classics, being distinctly Daoist in philosophical origin.[46] It is used in *Laozi* and *Zhuangzi* to describe Dao, *de* (*L* 21, 41; *Z* 28/27, 7/3), and human nature (*L* 54, *Z* 17/53, 16/16), as epitomized by the true man mentioned above. One may thus add that truthfulness is truth as well, for human nature is seen to be rooted in a higher source that is also the operational principle of the universe. And because the ontological, cosmological, and existential are one, truthfulness is no mere subjective attitude: *zhen* is to be truthful to an "objectively" present Dao, though it is its existential fulfillment that is stressed. On the other hand, since recognition of Dao is not detachable from the subject as physical measurements can be, that "objective" truth is not of a positivist kind, nor what Mou Zongsan (borrowing Bertrand Russell's terms) calls an "extensional truth," but an "intensional truth"[47] immanent in the world.[48]

According to Horie Tadamichi's tabulation, the word *zhen* occurs ten times in Tao's work.[49] As the following excerpts show, *zhen* is both character and ideal, truthfulness and intensional truth:

悠悠上古	Far far off in remote antiquity
. . . . .	. . . .
抱朴含真	[People] embraced simplicity and embodied truth.

(*TYJ* 24)

真想初在襟	From the first the true ideal was in my breast—
誰謂形跡拘	Who says one is bound by externals?

(*TYJ* 71)

天豈去此哉	Is Heaven removed from here?
任真無所先	Setting free the true annuls all preferences.

(*TYJ* 55)

The single "thread running through" (*A* 4/15) the lines is clear. Living in an age of "gross deviousness," Tao yearns for a past "truthful ethos" when people "embraced simplicity and embodied truth." Longing to recover "the true ideal . . . from the first within my breast," he knows that "setting free the true" will remove all external fetters causing disquiet and conflict. The coupling of "embracing simplicity" with "embodying truth" recalls Laozi's and Zhuangzi's similar advice to rid oneself of cleverness and desire and embrace simplicity (*L* 19, *Z* 9/10), the "uncarved block" (*L* 28, *Z* 9/13).

The import of *zhen* in Tao's poetry, however, is a wider one. In placing his ideal within a wholly Daoist framework,[50] Fukunaga overlooks the Confucian Dao of humanity which the poet equally cherishes. As we have seen (in chapter 1), sheer "truthfulness" without a basis of "truth" is subject to easy abuse. Just as the doctrine of *ziran-mingjiao* unity handily justified political ambition, the pretext of being true to one's nature legitimized the sensual indulgence of the "Eight Free Spirits" and their kind, as Ying Zhan (274–326) pointed out: "Since the Yuankang reign (291–99) the classics were slighted and Daoism prized. The broad uninhibitedness of Abstruse and Empty *(xuanxu)* learning was taken for freedom, and the clear temperateness of Confucian precepts was considered vulgar" (*JS* 70/6:1858). In contrast to such excesses, Tao's *zhen* is one that entails moral goodness *(shan):*

結髮念善事 僶俛六九年	Since my hair was bound I have thought of good deeds, And striven studiously for six times nine years.

(*TYJ* 49)

夫履信思順 生人之善行	To honor faithfulness and remember one's natural duties[51] Is the good conduct of living men.
. . . .	. . . .
原百行之攸貴 莫爲善之可娛	If one seeks what is valuable in the hundred forms of conduct, Nothing can delight more than doing good.
. . . .	. . . .
澄得一以作鑒 恒輔善而佑仁	Purely obtaining the one [Way] to be a mirror,[52] Heaven ever aids goodness and supports humanity.

(*TYJ* 145–48)

Coming straight from Confucius himself (*A* 7/23), this moral perception of man and Heaven is a far cry from Laozi's naturalistic view that "Heaven and Earth are not humane" (*L* 5).

In fact, Tao's work clearly shows Daoist naturalism and the Confucian moral Way fused into a total outlook and vision, though more by sensibility and experience than by deliberate eclecticism:

養真衡茅下	I'll nourish truthfulness under my humble thatch roof,
庶以善自名	So as to make good my name.

(*TYJ* 75)

羲農去我久	[Fu]xi and [Shen]nong have long left us;
舉世少復真	In the present world few return to the true.
汲汲魯中叟	Earnestly striving was the old man of Lu [Confucius],
彌縫使其淳	Mending and patching [his age] to make it wholesome.

(*TYJ* 99)

These excerpts serve as illuminating intertexts: the Daoist sage-rulers and Confucius are brought together just as to "nourish truthfulness" is to "make good one's name," a goal echoing the Master's own in "rectifying names" (*A* 13/3) in order that human life measure up to its name. The same unity is shown in the remark "To embrace simplicity and maintain quietude / Is the superior man's abiding essence" (*TYJ* 145), where "maintain quietude" (*L* 16, *Z* 11/36) and "embrace simplicity" are wedded to the paragon of the *junzi*. That Daoist and Confucian values form a total ideal is best seen in Tao's visualization of Nature, as exemplified by the playful "Stopping Wine" where every line contains the word "stop" *(zhi):*

坐止高蔭下	My resting stops beneath the high shade;
步止蓽門裏	My stroll stops inside the rustic gate.
好味止園葵	My favorite food stops with garden mallows;
大歡止稚子	My great delight stops with my young sons.

(*TYJ* 100)

Just as familial joy is blended again with Nature's delights, so every *zhi* suggests both the Daoist free spirit (*Z* 3/6) and the "firmness in adversity" that "stops" "going to excess" (*A* 15/1); Nature becomes an amalgam of naturalistic and moral meanings for a poet who sees in it his deepest convictions. Indeed even the posthumous title his friends gave him, *Jingjie* or "serene integrity," is reflective of his two sides: "his grace in joyously letting life come to its end; his principles of honesty and self-mastery" (*H* 1:1–2). Revealingly, this state is in line with a quintessential Neo-Daoist standard, as succinctly formulated by Xi Kang in his "Shisi lun" (Discourse on Release from Self-Interest): "On the spur of the moment one would give free rein to the heart—and the heart would meet with goodness."[53]

Far more than an escape from the world in order to stay unsullied or preserve one's life, Tao's reclusion represents a quest for *zhen* and *shan* intensified by a devious age. But the loftiness of vision defines the depth of its grief, and Tao's spirit remains weighed down from independence by his Confucian sentiments, for peace is never complete until it is realized for all humanity. The inner harmony he attains at lyric moments is an unstable enclave which reality lies in wait to submerge,[54] and his joyous freedom coexists with an anguished sense of helplessness as time and tide ever recede away. Chronic poverty has worn down his physical vitality, and prolonged frustration has sapped the radiance of a youthful optimism: "Gradually the years and months slipped by, / This heart is partly gone" (*TYJ* 117). The idealistic expression that underlies the elevating resonance of his verse takes on a heightened poignancy, as six out of twelve "Miscellaneous Poems" lament the pitilessness of time in washing man and his purpose away:[55]

人生無根蒂　Man's life is without root and base,[56]
飄如陌上塵　Drifting like dust on the path.
分散逐風轉　Scattered and driven by the wind,
此已非常身　This is no longer his original form.
落地爲兄弟　All who are born to earth are brothers;
何必骨肉親　Must they be blood relations?
得歡當作樂　While we can be happy we should make merry,
斗酒聚比鄰　And gather near neighbors for a measure of wine.
盛年不重來　The prime of our lives does not come again;
一日難再晨　No one day will dawn a second time.
及時當勉勵　Strive hard while you have time;
歲月不待人　Years and months wait for no man.

(#1, *TYJ* 115)

In sentiment and expression this verse recalls several of the "Nineteen Ancient Poems" which grieve over the rush of time and the transience of life; Tao's beginning lines partly echo a couplet in #4: "Human existence is a lifetime's sojourn, / Darting by like windblown dust" (*XQH* 1:330). There is a deepened poignancy in Tao's poem, however, where the human plight is not just temporal but spatial as well: the rootless plant, stalkless leaf and pathway dust form a string of ever-diminishing and devitalizing images of man, helplessly "drifting . . . , scattered and driven" at the mercy of capricious "winds" (from fate and chance to war and politics) until he is "no longer his original form." While "hills and rivers have no season of change, / Plants and trees hold to a constant rule, . . . / Man alone is not like these," the poet writes in "Body, Shadow, and Spirit" (*TYJ* 35); there is a unique amplitude for suffering in an existence neither permanent nor regular and renewing. Yet one can also find unity and support in this common human condition, and the poet moves not down a pessimistic spiral but to a recognition of universal fellowship (ll. 5–6). Perhaps this is why, in a note of companionship absent in stock *carpe diem* statements, lines 7–8 advise "gathering near neighbors" for enjoyment rather than any "splendid feast" in the manner of the "Ancient Poems." Pondering on the irretrievability of time and youth, the poet comes to yet another perturbing but ardent conclusion, his idealistic resolve to "strive hard" strengthened even if all is doomed. If the poem's preponderant negatives (five in all) represent an indictment of life for all it has denied him, they do not ultimately negate his heart, for the affirmation in line 9 is couched in the imperative. As Cao Cao says, "The noble man may be waning in years, / But his lofty aspirations never cease" (*XQH* 1:349).

What one sees in this poem is a spiritual and emotional cadence that ends higher than it begins. Indeed, it is characteristic of Tao that the attrition of harsh experience never sinks him into despair:

精衞銜微木	Jingwei[57] carried small twigs in her mouth,
將以填滄海	In order to fill up the blue sea.
形夭舞干戚	Xingyao[58] brandished shield and battle axe,
猛志故常在	His valiant aspirations remain ever alive.

(*TYJ* 138)

His humanistic commitment continues to buoy him up with a resilient hope against reality, as the dialectic in "Miscellaneous Poems" #2 illustrates:

白日淪西河	The white sun sinks into the western river;
素月出東嶺	The pale moon rises from the eastern range.
遥遥萬里暉	Far, far-reaching, its beams of myriad miles;
蕩蕩空中景	Vast, vast, its radiance in the sky.
風來入房戶	A wind comes through my bedroom door;
夜中枕席冷	In the night pillow and mat grow cold.
氣變悟時易	As the air changes I realize the season is shifting;
不眠知夕永	Sleepless, I feel the night is so long.
欲言無予和	I wish to talk, but there is none to answer;
揮杯勸孤影	So I raise my cup and urge my lonely shadow.
日月擲人去	The sun and moon cast off man and leave;
有志不獲騁	My aspirations are not given free rein.
念此懷悲悽	Thinking of this, my heart is grieved;
終曉不能靜	Through dawn I can find no repose.

(*TYJ* 115–16)

Another paradigm of Tao's simple, direct style, the poem begins with an autumnal moonlit scene purifying in its limpid radiance and inspiring in its boundless expanse. As the focus moves from far to near, entering the room with the wind, we see Nature taking on an opposite coloring with the word "cold": the whiteness of the sun and moon turns desolate, and the beauty of the empyrean panorama is shrouded in the grief of a spirit hemmed in by circumstances. As he lies helplessly bearing the wind's corrosive chill, the night's slow passage, and the season's turn, he is reminded of his vanishing prospect to fulfill his social aspirations. Initially evoking spatial amplitude, the sun and moon return in a dark echo as markers of time (l. 11), whose principal meaning to the poet is embodied in the poem's four negatives. "Cast off" and without an understanding friend, he can only turn to his shadow and wine which fails to numb him to repose; the vivid image of the ironic troika only underlines his loneliness.

Finding "some conscious tradition" in *zashi* of expressing "general themes and broad reflections on life," Davis traces a line of "'Melancholy Thoughts at Night'" from "Ancient Poems" #19 through the "Zashi" (Miscellaneous Poems) of Cao Pi (186–226), Fu Xuan (217–78) and Zhang Hua (232–300) to Tao's poem (*D* 1:125–28). Certainly all five share a general mood and atmosphere evoked through such universal components as the moon, wind, cold, long night, loneliness, and sleeplessness. Tao's poem remains nonetheless individual, free of certain specific elements in the quoted precedents that smack of formulism: putting on clothes and pacing, gazing about ("Ancient" #19, Cao, Fu) and noticing constellations (Cao, Fu, Zhang). More substantively, the import of the first four lines is anything but melancholy; tradition never remains intact when filtered through the vision of a great artist. For while the gloomy human veil spread over the pristine luminosity of the natural view is readily discernible, more remarkable in this context are the flowing spaciousness of the spectacle and the dynamic energy bobbing beneath its ostensible stillness—indicated by words like "sinking," "rising," "far-reaching," "vast" and "radiance"—that call to mind the capacious spirit of the High Tang:

青海長雲暗雪山
孤城遙望玉門關

Across Qinghai unbroken clouds darken
snow mountains;
From afar the lone fortress looks upon the
Jade Gate Pass.[59]

明月出天山
蒼茫雲海間
長風幾萬里
吹渡玉門關

The bright moon rises above the Heavenly Ranges,
Among the vast, misty sea of clouds.
The unbroken wind sweeps on for myriads of
miles,
And blows past the Jade Gate Pass.[60]

Tao's mood is not as confident as that of Wang Changling (c. 698–c. 757) or Li Bai (701–62), but the magnificent view is clearly a natural correlative to a winging spirit. Tao may be seen by Zhong Hong (459–518) as the paradigmatic recluse-poet (*H* 1:9) and put in the dynastic histories in the category of hermits,[61] but Zhu Xi rightly sees him also as "one wanting to do something [for humanity]," and feels his poetry is as "valiant" as it is "calm" (*H* 1:75, 74). Indeed, from his youthful "valiant aspirations reaching beyond the four seas," through the middle-age dejection expressed here, to what "remains ever alive" in the waning vitality of old age, the poet's quest is infused with the same visionary ardor that engenders its hope and its anguish. To the last a *nil desperandum* life force defines the idealist with his undying sense of mission.

3

Peach Blossom Spring and Visions of Utopia

It is, indeed, this *nil desperandum* spirit that lies behind Tao's crystallization of his utopian vision in "Peach Blossom Spring," a two-part composition with a prose narrative followed by a poem. The former relates a stray fisherman's accidental discovery of a hidden society some time "during the Taiyuan reign [376–96] of the Eastern Jin":

> The fragrant flowers were fresh and beautiful; fallen petals lay in rich profusion. . . . Where the [blossoming peach] grove ended at the stream's source there stood a hill, in which there was a small opening. . . . At first extremely narrow, . . . it opened out into a broad, level plain where houses and huts stood neatly, with rich fields and lovely ponds, mulberries, bamboos and the like. The field dykes crisscrossed; chickens and dogs could be heard from farm to farm. . . . White-haired elders and children with hair in flowing tufts were all happily enjoying themselves. When [the people] saw the fisherman, they were greatly surprised. . . . Then they invited him to their home, setting out wine and killing a chicken to prepare a meal.[1] . . . They said their ancestors fled from the troubles of Qin times . . . [and] asked what dynasty it was now; they knew nothing of the existence of the Han, let alone the Wei or the Jin. (*TYJ* 165–66)[2]

The fisherman left after a few days, and later tried in vain to return with an official whose very identity threatened its self-contained peace. The account ends with the utopia remaining hermetic, and the poem takes over:

嬴氏亂天紀	When the Ying [Qin] upset Heaven's order,
賢者避其世	Worthy people shunned their world.
黃綺之商山	Huang and Qi left for Mount Shang;
伊人亦云逝	These people['s ancestors] also went away.
往迹浸復湮	Their parting tracks were gradually buried;
來逕遂蕪廢	Their trodden paths became overgrown.
相命肆農耕	They bid one another to work hard at farming,
日入從所憩	And at sunset go home to rest.
桑竹垂餘蔭	Mulberry and bamboo overhang with ample shade;
菽稷隨時藝	Beans and millet are planted in season.
春蠶收長絲	From spring silkworms long threads are gathered;
秋熟靡王稅	On the autumn harvest no royal tax is levied.
荒路曖交通	Overgrown roads have obscured traces of traffic;
雞犬互鳴吠	Cocks crow and dogs bark at one another.
俎豆猶古法	Their ritual vessels still follow ancient designs;
衣裳無新製	Their clothes display no new fashions.
童孺縱行歌	Children freely run and sing;
斑白歡遊詣	Gray-heads joyfully wander and visit.
草榮識節和	When grass grows lush they realize the season is mild;
木衰知風厲	When trees wither they know the wind is harsh.
雖無紀曆誌	Though they have no calendar to mark time,
四時自成歲	The four seasons naturally form a year.
怡然有餘樂	Contented in their ample happiness,
于何勞智慧	Why should they bother with knowledge and cleverness?
奇蹤隱五百	Their extraordinary course was hidden five hundred years;
一朝敞神界	Then one day their heavenly land was disclosed.
淳薄既異源	Since the pure and the mean have different roots,
旋復還幽蔽	Soon their world returned to seclusion again.
借問游方士	May I ask you who wander within the realm,
焉測塵囂外	Can you fathom what lies beyond the dust and noise?

願言躡輕風 I would like to tread the light breeze,
高舉尋吾契 And fly high to seek my fellows. 32

(*TYJ* 167–68)

Just place Tao and his fellow farmers into Peach Blossom Spring, and one immediately knows that his social ideal is a simple agrarian model based on experience. On an obvious level, the prose account and the poem combine to convey the implications of the portrait. Here the voice is less personal than universal, the main subject not personal sentiments or any individual worthy but society as a whole. Sealed from the vicissitudes of history, the inhabitants have preserved their ingenuous mode of life in which all work readily and harmoniously. Founded on freedom, equality, and amity extended naturally to an unknown visitor—there being no stranger in the Confucian and Daoist ideals united again—the land is free from war, malice, oppression, even the taxation impoverishing Tao's rural community, hence from moral and especially political affliction: as Wang Anshi (1021–86) writes in his "Taoyuan xing" (Song of the Peach Spring), no ruler-subject tie exists on top of the filial bond (*H* 1:26). Not only does "spatial" (social) distance cease to exist, but history's temporal course is replaced by Nature's timeless cycle now running undisturbed. Yet the poet's endorsement of such a hermetic community only underlines the remoteness of what should be universally accessible, and it is not without a twinge of sadness that he ends by expressing a yearning to join the realm.

It is this open wish that brings into relief the relation between the work's complementary parts, in no way repetitive but variant in focus, structure, and means of expression. Dramatically constructed with the fisherman's "witness" testimony as its main linking thread, the prose is a succinct narrative of the discovery and eventual sequestration of the Peach Blossom Spring community, enlivened by vivid description of its charming layout and vital sights that make up a blessed environment. The account is told objectively by an impersonal narrator, who nonetheless stresses toward the end the community's fugitive nature and ultimate seclusion. The verse, on the other hand, comes from a single, more personal and interpretive voice that treats Peach Blossom Spring not as physical setting but as natural social order. The poem begins by narrating the community's refugee origins (ll. 1–6), but soon turns to an admiring description of the basis on which it functions and endures—from its tax-free agrarian economy (ll. 7–12) to its general mode of life and pre-calendric culture (ll. 13–24)—before commenting on the fisherman's fruitless encounter (ll. 25–30) and culminating in a direct yearning for the ideal (ll. 31–32). In short, while half of the portrayal gives an alien's external glimpse of the utopia with emphasis on its inaccessibility, the other half conveys the inner substance of the ideal along with a personal wish to seek it despite its insulation. In fact this central ambiguity is presaged in the prose itself: after all, why is a utopia squarely down-to-earth in character so inaccessible—a point underlined by the account's formal resemblance to the Six Dynasties *zhiguai* (recording anomalies) stories, which often stress the disjunction between mundane reality and the other world?[3] As we shall see later (in chapter 5), Tao's work runs counter to the fantastic flavor of these stories, but here he seems to be using the *zhiguai* form to express his doubts about the realizability of the ideal. The tension between visionary longing and historical consciousness explains the presence of two voices, one that finds utopia in nothing more exotic than a sublimation of everyday reality, and the other which gauges its chance in the contemporary milieu. And while the historical voice has the last word in the prose, it is the visionary one that takes the poem to a crescendo, yearning for a society where the *shi* will not be "born out of his time," where "hiding" and "leaping forth" make no real difference for the feelings (*TYJ* 147). In such a society, the dilemma that has long agonized humanity will not be solved but *dis*solved. What the lyric voice registers is a hope that the ordinary ideal which has turned almost other-worldly might still be realizable, if only a more innocent form of social organization could be found. The one ending on a subdued and the other on a romantic note, the two parts give contrastive rings that attest to the complexity of the poet's sentiments.

It is remarkable that Tao should come up with such a "stunted" utopia. After all, his vision of universal happiness all but leaves out the virtuous rulers of the Three Dynasties placed in the age of "Lesser Prosperity" *(xiao kang)* in *Liji* (Book of Rites), among whom are King Wen and the Duke of Zhou so admired by Confucius. If anything, the poet's repeated evocation of such legendary sage-rulers as Fuxi, Shennong, the Yellow Emperor, Yao and Shun,[4] points in sentiment to the higher ideal of "Great Unity" *(da tong)*:

> When the great Dao was in operation, the world was a common one. The worthy and talented were selected, faithfulness was upheld and affection cultivated. Thus men loved not only their own parents nor fostered only their own children, but ensured that the aged were provided for, the able-bodied employed, and the young brought up. Widowers, widows, orphans, the childless, disabled and diseased were all well cared for. . . . [Assets] need not be kept to oneself . . . nor need [effort] be exerted for one's sake. Thus schemings ended rather than grew, robbery and disorder never occurred, so that outer doors need not be closed. This was called "Great Unity."[5]

It is only that Peach Blossom Spring reflects a different spirit and scale. For while bearing Daoist influence, *da tong* is still a Confucian ideal in which all are taken care of by an active government led by a moral elite. Tao, however, discredits "knowledge and cleverness" in echo of Laozi's warning that "when knowledge and cleverness appeared there emerged great deviousness" (*L* 18), and visualizes a social structure even more primitivistic than Laozi's predynastic "small state with few people" (*L* 80). The poor, tottering livelihood of Tao and his neighbors despite their conscientious labor must have prompted him to seek the roots of their plight, so that while even "The Gentleman of the Five Willows" refers to legendary sage-rulers, "Peach Blossom Spring" comes to deny all forms of political organization.

The discrepancy between Tao's social vision and the model he delineates also raises the question as to how far he was persuaded that peace and harmony are feasible only in a small community. For his utopia is not without its philosophical and historical contexts. As another voice in the call for return to *ziran*, anarchist thought assaulting the *raison d'être* of political order emerged during the latter half of the second century and climaxed over the next two centuries,[6] spurred by widespread suffering under rapid dynastic succession. Two statements, from Ruan Ji's "Daren xiansheng zhuan" (Biography of the Great Man) and Bao Jingyan (fourth century), will serve as a clear index:

> For without rulers everything fell into place; without officials every matter proceeded in order. . . . With the institutions of rulers oppression arose; with the appointment of officials robbery came about.[7]

> In remote antiquity there were neither rulers nor subjects. People dug wells for drinking and tilled fields for food. At sunrise they got up, at sunset they rested. They lived freely without restraint, broadminded and self-fulfilled. They neither competed nor schemed, and there was no glory or disgrace.[8]

No mere attack against the overextension of polity in the manner of Laozi—who still affirms rule by *wu wei* (*L* 57, 63)—these are denunciations of sociopolitical organization as the origin of oppression, inequality, and strife; the Confucian framework is discarded for Zhuangzi's natural order where people left alone "will not overstep their nature and sway their virtue" (Z 11/2). Bao's community is pervaded by an atmosphere of "vacuity, serenity, mellowness, quietude and non-action," the "basic characteristics of Heaven and Earth and the ultimate of *Dao* and *de*" (Z 13/4–5) that are also the attributes of Tao's utopia. Inspiration for the poet might also have come from *Liezi*:[9] in the state of Huaxu "there are no teachers or leaders . . . [and] the people have no cravings or lusts," while in Zhongbei, where "everything is but natural," "the people are gentle by nature and compliant with the course of things, neither compete nor contend, . . . are never arrogant or jealous, . . . and no one is ruler or subject."[10] In its classless spirit and apolitical configuration, Peach Blossom Spring is less akin to Laozi's formulation than to those of Zhuangzi, *Liezi*, Ruan, and Bao.

Moreover, there is a historical relevance about "Peach Blossom Spring"; Ch'en Yin-k'o has supplied extensive evidence of the widespread existence of cloistered refugee settlements since Wei times, prompted by wars, famines, and pestilences ravaging a country already under chronic unrest (*H* 1:338–46).[11] Keeping this in mind as a backdrop, one may add facts more immediate to Tao himself. In a memorial submitted to the throne in 411, Liu Yi, then Commander-in-Chief of the Jiangzhou area (wherein lay Tao's home), stated that

> Since the times of Huan Xuan, things have reached such a shattered state that . . . [people] are fleeing to other places, not shunning those that are deeply secluded. (JS 85/7:2208)[12]

There seems little doubt that these were personally witnessed conditions which intensified Tao's social yearning, and it is no accident that one of his poems (*TYJ* 110) praises Tian Chou (c. 169–215), a righteous, heroic recluse-patriot who became the enlightened ruler of a northern frontier outpost.[13] Perhaps partly based on such settlement models, depoliticized by Daoist egalitarianism and freed from the fantastic elements found in Huaxu and Zhongbei, Peach Blossom Spring is the result of Tao's social vision and personal experience blended with current philosophical ideas and historical realities. If Ruan and Bao offer discursive criticism of the present through the past, Tao brings that retrospective ideal into the present, vivifies it with details distilled from his rural life, and in so doing offers the first graphic crystallization of social idealism in Chinese literature.

There are other issues in "Peach Blossom Spring" to be examined in Part II. Meanwhile, it will be instructive to explore a little, with reference to pastoral literature, how far the work reflects a universal longing for a golden age of innocence and happiness. In Western literature the golden age was first referred to (the term itself was not used) in Hesiod's (eighth century B.C.) poem "Works and Days," which gives an account of successive human races marked by continuous moral and physical decay. The first species, however, was the golden race, who lived "at peace" in a natural order

> Untouched by work or sorrow. Vile old age
> Never appeared, but always lively-limbed,
> Far from all ills, they feasted happily.
> Death came to them as sleep, and all good things
> Were theirs; ungrudgingly, the fertile land
> Gave up her fruits unasked.[14]

Free from the cares of ordinary humanity and the afflictions of history, life is marked by spontaneous plenty and festive peace where death follows ever-youthful life (while it lasts) as a repose. The myth was continued in later Greek and Latin versions, most notably in Ovid's (43 B.C.–A.D. 17) *Metamorphoses* where Hesiod's golden race became the more familiar golden age, with the history of races collapsed into that of a single race and the process of gradual decay polarized into a contrast between then and now. But Ovid's description follows Hesiod's model in the main:

> In the beginning was the Golden Age, when men of their own accord, without threat of punishment, . . . maintained good faith and did what was right. . . . The peoples of the world [knew only their own shores, and] untroubled by any fears, enjoyed a leisurely and peaceful existence, and had no use for soldiers. The earth itself, without compulsion, . . . produced all things spontaneously, and men were content with foods that grew without cultivation. . . . It was a season of everlasting spring.[15]

If anything, Ovid makes it clearer that "golden" life proceeds in a clime of "everlasting spring."[16]

Meanwhile—a little earlier on, in fact—the myth took on a more defined shape through integration with pastoral conventions in the *Eclogues* of Virgil (70–19 B.C.), whose Arcadia was created during a period of civil wars almost as a sanctuary from the violence of history. Pastoral poetry itself began with Theocritus's (first half of third century B.C.) *Idylls*, which well illustrate the genre's readiness to accommodate the myth. In a nutshell, pastoral life is one of leisure and plenty, as seen in Idyll 7, where the poet and his friend join a farming family for "The Harvest Festival":

Larks and linnets were singing, a dove made moan,
And brown bees loitered, flitting about the springs.
The tall air smelt of summer, it smelt of ripeness.
We lay stretched out in plenty, pears at our feet,
Apples at our side and plumtrees reaching down,
Branches pulled earthward by the weight of fruit.[17]

"Stretched out in plenty" in a land of ripeness and chime: such is the bright mood of the lush Theocritean world, of a Sicily experienced in boyhood and idealized through a memory projecting from the Alexandrian court.

Even from this cursory view of the early pastoral, it is clear that ample common ground exists between it and the golden age myth for an easy conflation, with pastoral serving as the setting for a happy innocent world. This is best exemplified by Virgil's fourth eclogue, in which a prophecy about a golden age "born afresh" blends with pastoral depiction at its most idle and bountiful:

Earth untilled
Will pour the straying ivy rife, and baccaris,
And colocasia mixing with acanthus' smile.
She-goats unshepherded will bring home udders plumped
. . . .
Soft spikes of grain will gradually gild the fields,
And reddening grapes will hang in clusters on wild brier,
And dewy honey sweat from tough Italian oaks.[18]

What is more, when Virgil announces "the great succession of centuries" in which the "iron age" will be replaced, he also adds an inspiriting hope for regeneration to a pessimistic view of the present. One legacy of Virgil's pastoral is that as the product of nostalgia for an ideal past and longing for a similar future, it is not so much a type of poem as an outlook that may serve "to insinuate and glaunce at greater matters."[19]

Thus despite a physical form too pretty to convince one of its reality, the golden pastoral landscape bears a deeper symbolic meaning than its silken contours might suggest.[20] Class distinctions blur in

Theocritus when the poet joins the farmers, while by allowing Meliboeus to voice his hardship,[21] Virgil implies criticism of those who have caused it. Ovid's golden age is one of social justice and righteous conduct: what automatic plenitude provides is a basis for virtuous leisure, an absence of avarice and hence of evil. Latent or overt, the invocation of a superior rustic alternative is bound to carry a questioning of the existing society which the poet wishes to change. An irresolvable tension between the realistic and imaginary elements often exists in formulations of the golden age, but what it establishes is an absolute material order and a parallel spiritual autonomy that ensure harmony between man and Nature. Indeed some degree of pristine egalitarianism is usually present in socially serious pastoral of later times.

In Elizabethan pastoral, for instance, the alternative society proffered is one that minimizes division and inequality within a harmonious hierarchy. In its depiction of a manor house, Ben Jonson's (1573–1637) "To Penhurst" suggests a social outlook of "hospitalitie" that combines simplicity and elegance; rising through the scale from plants and animals to "ripe" pretty girls, the lord of the manor and the king, the description puts each element in a place befitting the just proportions of a social "edifice."[22] The image of a fair happy society also appears in Shakespeare's (1564–1616) *As You Like It*, whose main issue is the perversion of social relationships and whose structural principle is their restoration. It is in the congenial pastoral setting of Arden that wrongs like Oliver's maltreatment of Orlando and Ferdinand's usurpation of Duke Senior's place are righted, and natural human ties given the chance to develop. The play portrays an order whose underlying basis is care by the superior and loyalty of the inferior, a mutual bond integrating Celia and Corin, Orlando and Adam, Duke Senior and Orlando.

In his yearning for a society where *mingjiao* and *ziran* can be naturally united and human nature freely realized, Tao also shares this broad "pastoral" sentiment. After all, the visionary nature of the golden age is what underlies its great malleability to accommodate longings of different times and places, enabling it to be located on both ends of the temporal scale. Where the lost past at which the idealist glances back points him to a renewable ideal in the future, nostalgia becomes the wellspring of ardor and optimism.[23] That is why, like the Master who often looks back to Yao and Shun, King Wen, and the Duke of Zhou (*A* 6/28, 9/5, 14/45, 15/4), Tao frequently evokes the halcyon days of the legendary sage-kings. The nostalgia has its archaic elements; it is as though the poet were driven by a sordid reality to a compensating retreat within a visualized ideal. Yet it would be a mistake to dismiss this feeling as a reactionary longing for an obsolete model, based on a regressive view of history that sees only decline from a vanished age. For it is part of the Confucian vision that history is a cyclic process of growth and decay (*M* 2B/13) imparting both hope and regret. This complex of sentiments gains depth in light of the Chinese tradition of euhemerization, where myth takes on the validity of historical experience, and conceptual formulations the concrete shape of "real-life" paradigms. Actual or not, the pristine model is believed in good faith to be a realized and therefore realizable ideal.

Such, too, is the sentiment behind Peach Blossom Spring. But to what extent is it a pastoral world? While reflecting a critical response to a historical reality not broadly unlike that of Virgil's Arcadia, Tao's utopia is modest in conception and down-to-earth in daily operation, less literary invention than a distilled version of his farm life. No strain of personal escapism exists as it sometimes does in pastoral: if Don Quixote's idyllic fantasy after the failure of his chivalric heroism is another false move that also indicates a shrinking of vision from the social to the personal,[24] Tao's golden age remains universal in outlook. True to the humanistic temper of Confucianism and Daoism,[25] the age of sage-rulership he often evokes is conceived in attainable terms that feature no mythical pantheon of gods mingling or associated with men, as with Hesiod, Virgil, and even Ovid's world of justice. The inhabitants of Peach Blossom Spring live in sufficiency untrammelled by institutional setups, but not in a domain of effortless, self-producing plenty wrapped in eternal spring. While sharing the universal longing for innocence and happiness, Tao predicates its fulfillment on work and self-reliance, reminding himself that even the sage-rulers Shun and Yu once labored as farmers (*TYJ* 25). Perhaps the realistic cast of his ideal helps to explain why euhemerization is a common process in the Chinese tradition: many of the "myths" and legends regarded as history are not different from the latter in essential nature. They represent what history should be.

Perhaps in one way, what "Peach Blossom Spring" presents is more utopian (if no less real) than that in socially serious pastoral. While *As You Like It* offers an ideological solution affirming the naturalness of the master-servant bond between Adam and Orlando, Peach Blossom Spring is a classless society in which all hierarchy is dissolved. Instead of softening tensions between the ruling and the ruled, or obscuring the harshness of socioeconomic organization by recasting the political structure and maintaining the validity of good government, it abolishes polity and class altogether in favor of absolute egalitarianism. Yet even this idealism remains close in its familiarity and reasonable in its commonsense flavor. While bearing a certain affinity and outward resemblance to the golden-age concept in Western pastoral, "Peach Blossom Spring" is best seen in the cultural context of the poet's vision, both in configuration and in the attitude behind its creation.

Here, in his chief utopian work, Tao's personal farmstead is transfigured by a poignant imagination into a luminous farmland "state" that shows up the darkness of his country. Both the idealism of "Peach Blossom Spring" and the gap between Tao's expansive spirit and his stunted utopia serve as an index of an age in which sanguinity has become almost impossible.

4

Mortality and the Meaning of Life

As Tao moves toward the evening of his life still alternating between his Confucian and Daoist sentiments, between self-containment and solitude, serenity and grief, his inner dialectic crystallizes into the philosophical dialogue in "Body, Shadow, and Spirit." As he states in the preface,

> Noble or humble, wise or stupid, there is none who does not strenuously cling to life. This is a great delusion. So I have set out in full the griefs of body and shadow, and made spirit explain the truth of naturalness to liberate them. (*TYJ* 35)[1]

"Strenuously clinging to life" is a delusion in face of certain death; and the body, addressing the shadow, advocates drinking and merriment:

適見在世中	Just now we see a man in the world;
奄去靡歸期	Then suddenly he is gone with no return.
. . . .	. . . .

我無騰化術　We have no arts to rise above Transformation;
. . . .　. . . . .
得酒莫苟辭　If you're given wine, don't carelessly refuse.

(*TYJ* 35–36)

Before tracing the poet's seesaw thoughts, it may be noted that contrary to popular beliefs and practices among the Jin literati, body, shadow, and spirit all reject the possibility of physical immortality, a notion that runs counter to Daoist thinking. For Laozi, "safeguarding life" (*L* 50) means preserving one's natural lifespan through meekness (*L* 52), moderation (*L* 55), humility (*L* 56), quietude, wisdom, and *wu wei* (*L* 16); instead of affirming immortals *(xian)*, he sees the return of all to Nonbeing upon decay and death (*L* 16).[2] In more dynamic terms, Zhuangzi maintains the dialectic unity of life and death in the cosmic flux (*Z* 17/47, 22/40); while he writes of a "spiritual man" subsisting on wind and dew (*Z* 1/29), he is referring not literally to an immortal but to a man of transcendental spirit, who has no "key to nourishing life" other than comprehending Dao (*Z* 3/5). Wei-Jin commentators of *Laozi* and *Zhuangzi* share much the same perception: Wang Bi comments (on *L* 13) "the fullness of life is bound to lead to death" (*L* 13), and perceives Laozi's advice to "concentrate one's vital force" (*L* 10) in terms not of breathing techniques but of the truth of *ziran*.[3] Similarly, Guo Xiang sees life and death as unceasing transformation (*ZJ* 17/3:587 n.11, 22/3:747 n.3), and consistently reads the "spiritual man" passage in symbolic terms (*ZJ* 1/1:28–30). In short, the issue of physical immortality does not arise in Daoist thought because immortality only exists in the sense of being one with the eternal Dao.[4]

This orientation in philosophical Daoism notwithstanding, there is no lack of religious Daoist statements endorsing the *xian* concept, particularly in the eclectic Ge Hong's (283–363) *Baopuzi*, which sums up beliefs among earlier literati and deeply influenced religious Daoism during the Eastern Jin. The book's inner chapters offer an encyclopedic reference on the arts of becoming a *xian*, including such life-prolonging ways as meditation techniques, breathing exercises, gymnastics, sexual hygiene, taking herbs, and above all the real keys—alchemy and elixirs:

> As for immortals, they nourish their bodies with elixirs and extend their lives through arts, so that internal diseases do not come to them and external ailments cannot enter them. Though they live long they do not die, and their aged bodies do not change. If one has the way, there is nothing difficult about [gaining immortality].[5]

Not only is immortality supposedly attainable, but there is a host of appurtenant magic powers acquired in the process:

> If one masters the essentials, things beyond the Eight Limits will be accessible as if they were within the palm and fingers; the distance of a hundred generations will feel like a contemporaneous moment. . . . One can elevate one's body among clouds and sky above, or submerge oneself in rivers and seas below. . . . One can plug one's ears and hear sounds a thousand *li* away, close one's eyes and see the future.[6]

As Ying-shih Yü points out, moreover, the idea of immortality also underwent a transformation during the Qin-Han period: entailing a reclusive, ascetic, and otherworldly transcendence of secular desires up to the early Han, it came to be viewed as a grander perpetuation of sensual pleasures attainable through drugs and elixirs.[7] Obviously this kind of *xian* became even more attractive to the worldling; and indeed *Baopuzi* mentions a new type of "earthly immortal,"[8] typified by a Mr. Baishi who allegedly lived over two millenia through sexual practices and elixirs, and who, revelling in wine, meat, and grain, refused to ascend to Heaven because it offered no human delights.[9]

Ludicrous as these notions of immortality and supernatural powers seem, not a few Jin rulers and literati had enough faith in them to try elixirs. Emperor Ai (r. 361–65), for instance, died of poison due to excessive intake of drugs (*JS* 8/1:208–9). As Ch'en Yin-k'o notes, many aristocratic families of the Six Dynasties period were hereditary adherents of the "Way of the Celestial Master" *(Tianshi dao),*[10] a religious Daoist sect active since the end of the Han and mixed with immortality fancies and alchemical practices by Eastern Jin times.[11]

Wang Xizhi's family is a famous case in point (*JS* 80/7:2103): while knowing that "life may be long or short in accordance with transformation but all must end in death,"[12] the calligrapher himself took drugs and searched for herbs and minerals supposedly conducive to immortality (*JS* 80/7:2101). Recluses were involved in similar practices, looking to occultists for help to learn the requisite arts.[13] Tao's own family, too, were by tradition followers of *Tianshi dao*:[14] his uncle Tao Dan is quoted as saying "the way of immortality can be aspired toward" (*JS* 94/8:2460). And as the poet inadvertently reveals in a sacrificial piece for his cousin Jingyuan, the latter was so much "roused in his mind" by thoughts of the "far-off celestial land" that, "abstaining from grain" and "plucking choice herbs" (*TYJ* 194), he was probably poisoned by potions and died just a little over thirty.

Despite being thus steeped in an ethos of religious Daoism, Tao himself sees the pursuit of immortality as a delusion:

運生會歸盡	The cycle of life must come to an end—
終古謂之然	From oldest times it has been stated so.
世間有松喬	Immortals Song and Qiao[15] were once in the world,
於今定何間	But now where are they to be found?

(*TYJ* 55)

自古皆有沒	From antiquity there has been death;
何人得靈長	What man has kept his soul forever?

(*TYJ* 137)

天地賦命	Heaven and Earth endow us with life;
生必有死	Birth necessarily comes with death.

(*TYJ* 187)[16]

Such remarks are in line not only with Zhuangzi's vision of cosmic transformation but with Confucian attitudes; in explaining mourning rites as a regulated catharsis of feelings, *Xunzi* and *Liji* state that the departed cannot return to life.[17] Facing the prospect of death honestly does not mean the poet is not preoccupied with it; his liking for chrysanthemums *(ju)* is linked to a belief that "*ju* [wine] can arrest the declining years." But what "the thatch-hut *shi*" fears is not so much death itself as "vainly watching the seasons pass" (*TYJ* 39); the threat of existential nothingness lies less in personal extinction than in the failure to do his duty.

It is thus based on a rejection of physical immortality that the dialogue between body, shadow, and spirit begins. What the body sets forth is the *carpe diem* sentiment familiar since the "Nineteen Ancient Poems" and the *yuefu* (Music Bureau) poetry of the Latter Han, as one excerpt from the former will illustrate:

人生忽如寄	Human life is brief as a sojourn;
壽無金石固	His age lacks the fixity of metal or stone.
萬歲更相送	A myriad years come and go,
聖賢莫能度	Sage or worthy—none can find a way out.
服食求神仙	Those who take drugs in quest of immortality
多爲藥所誤	Are mostly tricked by their potions.
不如飲美酒	Better to drink fine wine,
被服紈與素	And clothe yourself in soft and white silk![18]

This outlook gained currency during the Eastern Jin, partly due to Zhang Zhan's (fl. 310) commentary on *Liezi* which brought the "Yang Zhu Chapter" into the limelight. Now while Yang Zhu's original teachings are a matter of some doubt,[19] the message of the extant chapter is a hedonistic one: where life is brief and no lasting name can "moisten dry bones," it would be foolish to restrain desires with empty moral conventions. Instead, "acting as the heart prompts without betraying one's natural desires," it would be far wiser to "fully enjoy the merriment of our single life" with "a gorgeous house, fine clothes, choice food, and beautiful women."[20] As Yang Bojun notes, the "Yang Zhu Chapter" may serve to indicate the mores of the Jin literati who fashioned it as a doctrinal justification of their conduct.[21]

Rebutting the case for sensual indulgence in the face of mortality, the poet offers an alternative in the reply of the shadow, here without its negative connotations in Jungian psychology.[22] If wine can momentarily dispel worries, "establishing good" can achieve something more enduring:

身沒名亦盡
念之五情熱
立善有遺愛
胡爲不自竭
酒云能消憂
方此詎不劣

When the body dies the name also ends:
Thinking of this makes the five emotions boil.
Establish good *(li shan)* and there will be posthumous
    love;
Why do you not apply yourself?
Wine may be able to dissolve grief,
But is it not inferior to this?

(*TYJ* 36)

While the author of the "Yang Zhu Chapter" values "pleasure in life" over "name after death," and likens what he calls "striving for a moment's empty praise" to self-incarceration in "manifold prisons and multiple chains,"[23] there are others who regard a lasting name as an extension of one's transient life. A more profane motive is again seen in some of the "Nineteen Ancient Poems":

何不策高足
先據要路津
無爲守窮賤
轗軻長苦辛

Why not whip up your noble courser
And be first to command the key road and ford
    [to power, fame, etc.]?
Do not stay in poverty and lowliness,
Floundering forever in bitterness and sorrow!

(#4, *XQH* 1:330)

盛衰各有時
立身苦不早
. . . .
奄忽隨物化
榮名以爲寶

Waxing and waning each has its season;
How regrettably late I am in establishing myself.
. . . .
Swiftly we change with all things,
Let an honored name be our treasure!

(#11, *XQH* 1:331–32)

Despite a Confucian guise, this is a stance akin to the self-serving *mingjiao* seen in the Jin; and it is in thus construing the shadow's reply that Richard Mather sees it as one which "Tao cannot accept" either.[24]

For any attempt to erect "an honored name" for fear of oblivion is just another form of "strenuously clinging to life."

Yet while the shadow's argument seems a pragmatic one, what comes with a sure idealistic ring are the words *li shan*, showing that the shadow is concerned with a purpose standing at the heart of the *shi*. "Resting in the shade we seem sundered awhile, / but staying in the sun we are never parted," the shadow says to the body (*TYJ* 36); in the "light" of the humane ideal the "shadow" of duty will never leave the self. If Tao has any wish for "immortality," it is in the sense stated in *Zuozhuan*: that through virtue, meritorious deeds, and words whose inspiration for posterity transcends personal fate, he may help in the preservation of culture which Confucius sees as the responsibility of the *shi* (*A* 9/5). It is this goal, rather than "some fugitive reputation after death,"[25] which makes the idealist "hate not leaving a good name when he is gone" (*A* 15/20). A rectified name is meaningful not only in being a natural result of a self-sufficient effort, but because it perpetuates the work of *li shan* as a living moral force. That Tao is imbued with this cultural purpose is incidentally confirmed by the spirit's explanation: "Establishing good is always a source of joy, / But who is obliged to sing your praises?" (*TYJ* 37). The poet is against *mingjiao* only as practised by his contemporaries and in rejecting the regime of the day[26]—in feeling that he is born out of his time.

Still, the spirit comes along to explain the unity and equality of all in their "uniform transformation" *(hua)* in the cosmic flux (*Z* 12/1). With "all things com[ing] from . . . and return[ing] to [Dao's] organic process" (*Z* 18/45–46), anaesthetic abandon would hasten a natural course while hoping for a rectified name would be idle, especially given a historical milieu unpropitious most of the time. It is this perspective that constitutes a fundamental challenge to the Confucian commitment, for Zhuangzi's vision dissolves the problem that has prompted the body's and the shadow's response. Both frustration about the transience of life and questing for permanence miss the truth of Dao, for no hope or despair, joy or gloom, exists amid one's accord with the cosmic rhythm:

大鈞無私力　The Great Wheel exerts no partial force;
萬物自森著　The myriad things thrive of themselves.
. . . .　. . . . .
老少同一死　Old and young come to the same death;
賢愚無復數　Neither wise nor foolish is destined to return.
日醉或能忘　In daily drunkenness you may forget things,
將非促齡具　But does it not shorten your life?
立善常所欣　Establishing good is always a source of joy,
誰當為汝譽　But who is obliged to sing your praises?
甚念傷吾生　Too much brooding harms our life;
正宜委運去　It is just right to entrust yourself to Change.
縱浪大化中　Leap into the waves of the Great Transformation;
不喜亦不懼　Be neither delighted nor afraid.

(*TYJ* 36–37)

There is no question that Tao gives the spirit the final and most cogent word. But is the poem a debate that discredits the sensuality of "old *ziran*" Neo-Daoism and the pragmatism of *mingjiao* Confucianism in favor of a "new *ziran*" naturalness, as Ch'en Yin-k'o sees it?[27] Without disputing the historical evidence Ch'en presents, I am not sure the poem is best read as an essay in intellectual history that expounds Tao's position in the Jin philosophical polemic.[28] His personal tone marks not a rational debate but an internal dialogue, and the intellectual currents informing the poem are not separate but blended within the same sensibility: the shadow tells the body they do not stand apart, while the spirit reminds both that "Though I am of a different order from you, / We are born in mutual dependence" (*TYJ* 36). Yoshikawa Kōjirō is right in identifying all three voices as facets of the poet's personality,[29] though one must add they are not of equal importance. For the *carpe diem* sentiment is only occasionally seen in Tao's verse as a venting of his frustrated social idealism; besides, derived from "high shade" and "young sons" (*TYJ* 100), "a clear lute across the bench / [and] half a jug of unstrained wine" (*TYJ* 14), his delights are rooted in moral resolve and natural harmony rather than sensual and material gratification. On the other hand, the Confucian purpose is something he cannot discard, so that the poem is no linear "pilgrimage"[30] ending in a lasting repose in the spirit's wisdom.

Unlike the complete inner freedom of the true man who transcends the *shi*'s humanistic commitment, any tranquility the poet might have gained through this dialogue remains an unstable one.

In fact, in the dialectic between the shadow and the spirit may be seen Tao's dual perspective on the larger principles directing his destiny *(fen)*: a natural Dao devoid of ethical teleology, and a taxing Confucian Way that alternates between Heaven's moral decree *(tian ming)* and an unknowable Fate *(ming)*. No perception of the self as a servant for Heaven's purpose (*A* 7/23) can square with an acceptance of futility in face of the inscrutable,[31] but Tao knows it is between fate and moral decree that the realm of his existential endeavor lies. If personal destiny is at least partly shaped by one's merit, the limiting terms of existence can be taken in a self-exhorting spirit:

繁華朝起　　Their many flowers blossom in the morning;
慨暮不存　　But alas, by evening they are gone.
貞脆由人　　Firmness or frailty depends on man;
禍福無門　　Trouble and fortune follow no fixed path.

("Trees in Bloom," *TYJ* 16)

Recognizing Nature's laws yet affirming human effort, the poet transcends what may fetter the self to reflexive resignation, and seeks to honor the higher imperative he is enjoined to obey: "If not the Way, on what do we rely? / If not goodness, for what do we strive?" (*TYJ* 16).

But as the prolonged attritions of life sap the idealist's faith in a transcendental will—

積善云有報　　Accumulating good is said to lead to reward,
夷叔在西山　　Yet Boyi and Shuqi [starved to death] on West Hill.
善惡苟不應　　If good and evil find no retribution,
何事空立言　　Why vainly lay down such words?

(*TYJ* 87)

—it is Daoism that increasingly forms the mainstay of his spirit. Even earlier there have been moments when *tian ming* crosses over from "Heaven's decree" to "what Nature has ordained": "Just let me ride with Change and return to my end; / Rejoicing in *tian ming*—what more should I doubt?" ("Return" *fu*, *TYJ* 62). As time goes by, it is the cosmic flux of Nature that seems to be the ultimate truth of life:

遷化或夷險
肆志無窊隆

Change and transformation may bring smoothness or ruggedness,
But follow your sentiments, and there will be no ups and downs.

(*TYJ* 53)

形迹憑化往
靈府長獨閑

My bodily form passes on with Change,
But my spiritual core is always at ease.

(*TYJ* 82)

As an open expression of Tao's inner tensions, "Body, Shadow, and Spirit" offers little in its theme that has not been explored in his other writings. Far from appearing superfluous, the poem shows the need for faith and understanding in life to be renewed, as T. S. Eliot concludes about the human quest in *Four Quartets*:

> We shall not cease from exploration
> And the end of all our exploring
> Will be to arrive where we started
> And know the place for the first time.[32]

From first to last, indeed, Confucian and Daoist ideals alternate as an existential current charging the poet with antipodal sentiments. On the one hand is a constant reminder that

> "Not serving is to ignore one's duty. . . . Just in order to keep oneself unsullied, one upsets the most important of human relations. The superior man serves to do his duty. As for failing to put the Way into practice, he has known this reality all along." (*A* 18/7)[33]

On the other is a supramundane truth daily experienced in Nature, one that finds the altruistic *junzi* "throwing away his life in pursuit of [external] things" (Z 28/28). As "Confucius" is made to confess in *Zhuangzi*,

> "[There are those who] wander beyond the realm, and I travel within it. *Beyond and within can never meet*. . . . They come and go in life and death, knowing neither beginning nor end. Without attachments they stroll beyond the dust and dirt, wandering free and easy in nonaction." (Z 6/66–70, emphasis mine)[34]

The irony is that these outlooks not only meet but are fused in the same spirit. While "the humane man is peaceful in humanity *(ren)*" (*A* 4/2) despite adversity, Tao remains stirred by the call of public duty even as he "knows the Way cannot be put into practice" (*A* 14/38). But his social commitment is bound to render him vulnerable, for the fulfillment of his purpose depends on a convergence of historical variables beyond individual control. After all, not even the Master managed during his long itineracy to turn his vision into reality. There is a poignant sense in which inner peace remains fickle for the poet, because no society short of a utopia will coincide with his ideal. While he may find joy and strength "devoting his heart" to the moral Way (*M* 6A/6, 7A/1), his sense of duty is not dissoluble in the repose that comes from appeasing a private conscience. That personal serenity will always coexist with an anguish of having failed his vocation, and it is in the dynamic between these moods that Tao's life and poetry take shape. In spurring him toward a goal that ever eludes him, the poet's compassion becomes the root of a sadness which his pacifying rustic life can never quite relieve; it is only at moments of communion with Nature, wrapped in the harmonious unity and equality of all being, that he feels total peace in an ultimate abode. Visualizing the universe in moral or naturalistic terms defines the basic difference; discrepancy between ideal and reality determines the altruist's grief. And for the visionary who finds himself at home in Nature but drawn toward mankind, the vacillation between calling and quiescence is a multiple existential seesaw that never comes to rest.

II

Tao Qian's Poetic Art

5

Spontaneous Symbolism and Visionary Realism

Having examined Tao's work in light of his quest to fulfill cultural ideals, we may begin a more focused study of his art. Rooted in his earthy life and deep feeling for the world, the poet's artistic universe is marked by a vivid sense of empirical realism. At the same time, his visionary sensibility also promises a spontaneous mode of symbolism in which human and transcendental meanings are readily fused. Closely identified with his cultural heritage, Tao sees no firm line between history and legend, fact and fiction, for legend/fiction is what history/fact should be. Partly because of this enlarged, flexible sense of reality, he shows little interest in fine delineations of "formal verisimilitude" *(xingsi):* even "Peach Blossom Spring" contains no elaborate details beyond what suffices for a concrete portrait.

Tao's biographical writings will serve as a convenient starting point for our discussion. As we have seen, his eulogies of his paternal ancestors as models of virtue reveal more about his goals than about his ancestors. Another side of his personal ideal, so fitting genetically, is seen in his biography of his maternal grandfather Meng Jia:

> He never showed joy or anger on his face. He liked to drink heavily, but however much he drank he never became disorderly. When he had followed his heart and attained his wish he would become genially remote, as if no one were present. (*TYJ* 171)[1]

That such a character is what the poet aspires to be is even more evident in his "Biography of the Gentleman of the Five Willows":

> Tranquil and laconic, he coveted neither fame nor profit. Though fond of reading, he did not seek thorough comprehension of details. But every time some meaning flashed upon him, he would become so happy as to forget to eat. By nature he was fond of wine, but being poor he could not afford it too often. Knowing this, his relatives and friends would sometimes get together a drinking party and invite him. . . . When drunk he would withdraw, never making a fuss about going or staying. The walls of his house were bare, unable to ward off the wind and sun. His short coarse robe was torn and patched, his rice-basket and water-ladle were often empty; but for all that he was peaceful and at ease. Often he amused himself with writing, in which he would quite openly express his sentiments. Unmindful of gain and loss, he thus lived out his life. (*TYJ* 175)[2]

Perceptions of this composition raise a basic question about the approach to Tao's poetry. While Yoshikawa follows many traditional Chinese critics in taking the portrait as a reflection of the poet,[3] Davis sees in the "self-depreciating, self-assuring description" a "most successful [attempt] at creating a self-image," which he thinks is why Tao was so admired as a personality: "Because his self-image was so perfect a literary creation, it was easy for others to identify themselves with it." Davis maintains he is not suggesting insincerity, but that Tao is "projecting for the world a readily accepted image of himself" in that "a man can never be entirely one with his dramatization of himself, for this would be to ignore the element of art" (*D* 1:208–9, 3–4). Owen would go farther: Tao not only creates the "surface role" of a "self-satisfied farmer-recluse" that he is not, but does so in order to snub the world with contempt. What is more, fearing our detection of the "secret motives" behind his "deception" and the disunity between his self-image and his real state, he becomes "painfully self-conscious" and "obsessively . . . defensive about his values and acts," trying desperately to collapse his "doubleness" into the unified image of an "unsophisticated and unself-conscious" man, elevating himself at our expense so that we may admire him in our "shame." Rather than relating his actual farming life, his poetry represents both a self-mythologization and a defense: its "spontaneity" is a false impression calculated to "lull" us into accepting appearance for reality, constructed from "manipulation and distortion" in order to cast himself favorably in the eyes of "nameless, future readers of poetry of other places and other times," but which ultimately betrays itself if we are wary enough to "see through" him.[4]

Such statements are reflective of a critical bent that assumes a need to penetrate roles, personae, and manipulative strategies in order to unmask the artist's identity. This assumption is especially relevant to poets with a declared interest in the power of words,[5] or to poets editing their own works (not uncommon since the early ninth century), whose editorial selection, organization, and juxtapositions necessarily result in a more self-conscious and sometimes distorting presentation of one's life. But the contention that Tao created a self-image does not hold up as one moves across the spectrum of his writings. First, he neither "claims to be a naive and straightforward poet" nor "passionately desires that we recognize and always remember the calm dispassion of his mind"; what he conveys is not a "[constant] unity of self and role"[6] but both the unity and disunity of self and ideals, for mixed with his poems of peace and delight are others expressing inner doubt, anguish, and loneliness. Moreover, how could Tao have known that what he presented in his work would become a "perfect" or "readily accepted" image for later generations? In fact, had he been vainly intent on fabricating a favorable self-image, he would never have jeopardized it by expressing "vulgar" opinions and subjects that might be deemed unworthy of "the Former Master's bequeathed teaching." Where Confucius frowns upon Fan Chi's interest in husbandry and says "the superior man worries about the Way and not poverty" (*A* 13/4, 15/32), Tao writes not only of his daily farming concerns and privations but of his mendicancy (*TYJ* 48), describing actual experiences. The fact that Wang Wei (699–759) shows no sympathy for Tao's plight, and that some commentators try to allegorize "Begging Food" because they feel it beneath a poet to beg (*H* 1:16; 2:70), and that others have found it necessary to defend Tao's "farmer's words" or protest against them (*H* 1:9, 178–79, 184), amply attests to an honesty of expression independent of cultural-literary taboos and reader opinion. He admits to accepting the magistracy of Pengze out of economic need because it is a fact, and when he quits does not vehemently condemn the world like the exiled Qu Yuan. While Tao's poetry reflects a yearning for a kindred spirit to understand him, he makes no literary fanfare of his reclusion, neither writing *zhaoyin* verse as his earlier contemporaries did nor harping on his singular loftiness in a corrupt world.

What then does one make of the portrait? Noting the word *bu* (no/not) as the key to the composition, Qian Zhongshu relates Five Willows to what Confucius calls the "scrupulous," for "there are things he will not do" (*A* 13/21).[7] Indeed, what emerges from this negative mode of characterization is a man who prefers anonymous reclusion to active fame-angling, and who remains unfettered by worldly troubles and material pursuits. In this light, the traditional view becomes partly defensible on the literal level in that it recognizes the expressive nature of Tao's verse, and the character of Five Willows largely matches what is known about the poet, so that the portrait was regarded as a "true record" of himself not only by his contemporaries (*H* 1:5, 7) but by all his early biographers, from coeval Yan Yanzhi (384–456) to Shen Yue and Xiao Tong, who both wrote within a century of Tao's death. The fact that none of them duly appreciates his art reduces the chance of overpraise and enhances the credibility of their appraisal. Were the self-image argument to be taken on its own terms, one might contend that the poet's "self-portrait" is basically accurate.

But whether as "true record" or created "self-image," the portrait would be evaluated in narrowly autobiographical terms, when the issue of factual correspondence between author and subject is ultimately irrelevant. For judging from the range of moods laid bare in his writings, it is clear Tao knows and admits how far he is spiritually from Five Willows; and it is probably this self-knowledge that has prompted the portrait as a heuristic model for himself, just as Peach Blossom Spring is an artistic embodiment of his social ideal. Owen is right in seeing a "doubleness" in Tao, but it is not a matter of "an outward appearance concealing, dimming or distorting some true and hidden nature."[8] Like the poet, Five Willows is a Daoist-Confucian character: his serenity and freedom of spirit call to mind the true man (Z 6/1–20), his forgetting to eat amid contemplation Confucius (*A* 7/18), and his ease in poverty Yan Hui (*A* 6/11). If Tao is conscious of a discrepancy within himself, it is not between an external image of the self and its reality but between its reality and the ideal it aspires to be. In his transcendent obliviousness—he is even nameless like Zhuangzi's sage (Z 1/22)[9]—Five Willows becomes a paradigm of natural existence, a source of inspiration for the poet in moments of solitude. What Mather has observed of Tao's writings generally is especially pertinent here:

> All literary biographers have learned to be wary of taking at face value the elaborately constructed personae of writers who wish to be accepted in a particular guise that is often, in fact, largely a pose. But I do not think T'ao Ch'ien was posing. There is too much evidence even in his own account of very human frailty—moments of self-doubt and heroic whistlings in the dark—to dismiss what he is telling us as purposeful distortion.[10]

Like many fictional and historical figures of which Tao writes, Five Willows is a projection of inner yearning based on time-honored cultural ideals, a sustaining symbol as the poet turns inward for support in his rural life. To say that Tao's poetry "really cares little for farmers" is to overlook a key constituent of his material, emotional, spiritual, and artistic life in which he comes to experience Dao in the ordinary; to stress that it "speaks to and for our flurried world of carriage-riders and poetry readers"[11] is to relegate its primary lyric nature and its larger cultural function of inspiring self and posterity with noble sentiments and ideals. If it is impossible to record in poetry every detail of one's life, an expression of what is uplifting does not constitute a dramatization such as might be said of Qu Yuan. To see Tao as one "who effectively created his own legend during his own lifetime" (*D* 1:3) is to take the effect for the cause, for it was others who made a legend of him.

I do not mean to suggest that Tao is totally unself-conscious of his poetry, that he does not occasionally play with words,[12] that he has no interest in rhetoric or the effect his poetry has on others. What I maintain is that Tao's perception of poetry is much more as a document of experience lived and ideals aspired toward than as a work of "art," that his artistic praxis is fundamentally in line with his perception, and that therefore we should not ground our basic approach to his poetry on aspects and motives that are insignificant or nonexistent in him. The above discussion is part of the consistent evidence showing that in his creative impulse, Tao is not a poet cautiously weighing what to hide and what to reveal, but one who largely writes spontaneously in the light of his ideals and experiences. This is not to make of him an automaton of genius devoid of deliberating activity. For spontaneity is not only relative in that language and art must involve conscious ordering; in a higher sense it is the outcome of cultivation as well. Both Confucianism and Daoism recognize this paradoxical relationship in a broader spiritual context. Confucius, Mencius, and Xunzi all stress the necessity of assiduous practice to making *ren* a natural attribute of conduct, and the Master admits to having achieved spontaneity of action only at seventy himself (*A* 2/4). Laozi writes "The highest type of men who hear about Dao diligently practise it" (*L* 41), while Zhuangzi's discussion of "discarding intelligence" and "forgetting everything" (*Z* 6/92–93) suggests not a sage of original unconsciousness but one who progresses beyond common perception. Just as it takes prolonged assimilation for Cook Ding to elevate his skill to an effortless yet perfect rhythm where "perceptual cognition has stopped and the spirit moves at will" (*Z* 3/6), so learning, application, reflection, judgment, and organization of the means of one's chosen medium are all necessary prerequisites and accompaniments to the highest artistic achievement. It is only with cultivation that the natural genius can spring into spontaneous activity and acquire an almost independent life. As Zhu Guangqian notes, Tao's artistic spontaneity is the distillate of a refinement process infused with the wisdom of experience, rather than the naivety of simple-mindedness where consciousness has not reached full development (*H* 1:376). One can well apply to Tao what Coleridge says of Shakespeare: "[He was] no passive vehicle of inspiration possessed by the spirit, . . . [but] first studied patiently, meditated deeply, understood minutely, till knowledge, becom[ing] habitual and intuitive, . . . at length gave birth to that stupendous power."[13]

That power is also evident in the symbolic projection in Tao's "poems on historical subjects" *(yongshi shi)*,[14] in which narrative, discursive, and lyric elements are typically blended together. From early times history was looked upon as a guide to conduct; it is stated in *Liji* that "what [the Confucian] practises in the present age, later generations will take as their model."[15] Not surprisingly, *yongshi shi* came to fall within the ambit of *yonghuai shi* (poems singing of thoughts and feelings), for historical subjects offer ready nuclei on which one's sentiments may be condensed. Such topics necessarily impose on the poet the bounds of historical facticity, but within them he is free to highlight elements most resonant to himself. A case in point is that of Jing Ke, a knight-errant recruited by Prince Dan of Yan to assassinate the King of Qin (later First Emperor of Qin, r. 221–210 B.C.). At least two poets, Ruan Yu (d. 212) and Zuo Si (c. 253–c. 307), had written on Jing before Tao.[16] The surviving fragment (ten lines) of Ruan's poem does not reveal any authorial stance, but focuses on the sadness of the parting scene:

素車駕白馬
相送易水津
漸離擊筑歌
悲聲感路人

In white carriages harnessed to white horses,
They [Prince Dan and retainers] escorted him to the ford of River Yi.
Jianli[17] struck his lute and sang;
The mournful sounds moved passers-by.

(*XQH* 1:379)

Zuo's poem is of more interest in having an audible poetic voice:

荆軻飲燕市	Jing Ke drank in the market-place of Yan,
酒酣氣益震	When he got drunk his spirit became yet bolder.
. . . .	. . . .
雖無壯士節	Though lacking a hero's conduct,
與世亦殊倫	He is different in kind from the world.
高眄邈四海	His towering glance belittles the four seas;
豪右何足陳	Are the powerful clans [*haoyou*] worth mentioning?

(*XQH* 1:733)

Singling out Jing's bold spirit, the poem's narrow focus and "belittling" of *haoyou* show that Zuo is less interested in his subject than in using it to vent his anger at the aristocratic domination of society and politics in a class-riven age.[18] The "powerful families" that deny Zuo opportunity and recognition because of his humble origin are made an object of disdain as the lowly *shi*, invested in the form of Jing, towers above them. But what is most notable here is that Zuo does not quite grant a heroic stature to Jing, for this is what Tao confers on him.

Although Prince Dan's motive—hence Jing's purpose—in the assassination attempt is given in history as partly personal, Tao's poem quickly casts Jing's cause as a public one with the words "mighty Ying" (l. 2), for Ying/Qin invariably appears in Tao's works as the equivalent of cultural disorder.[19] If the poet sees Jing as "a superior man [who] dies for an understanding friend" (l. 5), this personal note also resonates with a larger meaning that is magnified in the ensuing description, its solemn hyperboles and mournful key elevating Jing to the status of a tragic hero:

素驥鳴廣陌	"The white horses neigh on the broad road;
慷慨送我行	With deep feelings they escort me on my way."
雄髮指危冠	His manly hair thrusts through his tall cap;
猛氣衝長纓	His valiant spirit charges his long cap-strings.
飲餞易水上	He drinks a farewell cup by River Yi;
四座列羣英	On four sides warriors are arrayed.
漸離擊悲筑	Jianli strikes a mournful lute;
宋意唱高聲	Song Yi sings a shrill song.

蕭蕭哀風逝	Soughing, soughing, the sad wind recedes;
淡淡寒波生	Swelling, swelling, the cold waves rise.
商音更流涕	Then with the *shang* notes tears flow fast;
羽奏壯士驚	With *yu* played the valorous man is roused.

(*TYJ* 131, ll. 7–18)

Transforming his subject with visionary ardor, Tao's symbolic instinct is in full action. While Sima Qian only mentions white robes and caps in the escort scene (*SJ* 86/8:2534), Tao adopts Ruan Ju's horses and makes them "neigh." The hyperbole applied to the escorts in *Shiji* is transferred to the hero (l. 9), and the dramatic force is amplified by an added detail where the bursting spirit charges even the cap-strings (l. 10). Enhancing history again as the poem moves to the parting scene, six lines of sound effects intensify the tragic aura and augment Jing's stature as an evil-removing hero.[20] Not only do the sounds blend into a congealed somberness representing the mood and words of the silent warriors, but Jing's original song-line—"Soughing, soughing the wind, / The River Yi is cold" (*SJ* 86/8:2534)—now broadens into a larger mournful atmosphere, with the wind and waves heaving empathically to deepen the effect. But the scene is not just gloomy: the water's chill also suggests a cold resoluteness within the hero, whose "roused" will seems to be "swelling" and "rising" with the waves. True to the poet's visionary sensibility, Jing is not painted in finite material strokes but felt through ambient effects serving as a foil to the hero, who is free to extend in the imagination as a model of righteous valor. This focus on his spirit and mission continues with the description of his journey:

心知去不歸	In his heart he knows that once gone, he will not return,
且有後世名	But that he will have a name in posterity.
登車何時顧	Mounting his carriage, he never looks back;
飛蓋入秦庭	Canopy flying, he sweeps along to the Qin court.
凌厲越萬里	Spiritedly he traverses ten thousand *li*;
逶迤過千城	Winding his way, he passes a thousand cities.

(Ibid., ll. 19–24)

The noble image further expands as Jing is linked to a tradition with which Tao is himself concerned. The certainty of death and immortality settles Jing's mind and fortifies his will, reflected in the "spirited" way in which he "flies" along in his carriage without looking back. But having brought him to such heights, how does Tao square Jing's heroism with his failure? "The despotic sovereign is stark terrified," the poet writes, injecting another strong beat that overshadows the brief couplet in which the vain attempt is told. The heroism is sustained to the end as the lyric voice comes in for the judgment:

其人雖已沒	Although the man has perished,
千載有餘情	His sentiments will linger through the ages.

(Ibid., ll. 29–30)

This triumphant vindication of transpersonal ideals clearly links the historical figure to the poet himself and his wish to leave behind an inspiring name through worthy achievement.

Placing the poem beside Jing's biography in *Shiji* (86/8:2526–38), Zuo Si's poem, and Tao's other works, it is clear that history has been recast not for any need of fictional embellishment, but in accordance with the subject's symbolic significance in the poet's vision. Indeed, whether he writes in narrative or lyric form, employs autobiographical, historical, natural, mythical, or fictional materials, his voice is usually audible in empathy with his subject. Just as "Peach Blossom Spring" ends with an express wish to "seek my fellows," so his praise of a lofty poor gentleman ends with a personal request:

願留就君住	I'd like to stay and live with you,
從今至歲寒	From now until the year turns cold.

(*TYJ* 112)

Often the poetic voice is equally clear while coming as an ostensibly objective appraisal. This is the case with Jing Ke, with the two Shus who "withdrew when their mission was accomplished"[21]—

誰云其人亡	Who says these men have perished?
久而道彌著	With time their way shines the brighter.

(*TYJ* 129)

alone" (*TYJ* 177). But the process is more subtle than seeking support for one's convictions, for it is not just that the objective mode provides more occasion for articulating one's sentiments, or that in the subjective imagination the legendary and fictional may cross over to the historical, which for its part may be freely refashioned. Felt as closely as the historical Qian Lou, Five Willows possesses the solid identity of a worthy: in the outcome of the lyrical dialectic, it is not the poet-historian who certifies Five Willows as a real figure but the latter who vindicates Tao's existential ideal. No single self can establish the larger structure of meaning underpinning all individual life, and it is the broad range of examplars that assures the poet of the universal validity of his quest. The process is a cyclical one in which human and transcendental symbolism merge into each other: as his vision is projected on his figures, it is also authenticated by the symbolic structure of "objective" testimony which they constitute from various spatio-temporal coordinates.

But it is in his visualization of Nature that Tao's symbolizing instinct works most spontaneously and comprehensively. After all, historical, fictional, and mythical symbols enter his writings as cultural paradigms; as such their personal and transcendental significations both interpenetrate and concur with each other. Not always so with Tao's natural symbols, for Nature constitutes not only his inner world but the setting of his life. This means that even natural images with cosmic resonances can take on diverse connotations as they relate to different aspects of his experience. Clouds, for instance, may suggest the self or the external agents bearing on it. Drifting lightly they embody lofty ease or rootless solitude:

雲無心以出岫 Clouds aimlessly move out from the peaks.

(*TYJ* 161)

孤雲獨無依 The solitary cloud alone finds no support.

(*TYJ* 123)

Hanging dense they become a source of obstruction:

靄靄停雲	Dense, dense, the hanging clouds;
. . . . . .	. . . .
平路伊阻	The level road is now obstructed.

(*TYJ* 11)

In the wind, too, the poet feels a life force both benign and inclement, or even an agent of sinister import:

平疇交遠風	The level fields meet the breeze from afar;
良苗亦懷新	The fine shoots, too, bear a new life.

(*TYJ* 77)

風雨縱橫至	Wind and rain come from every direction;
收斂不盈廛	The harvest does not fill household needs.

(*TYJ* 49)

飄飄西來風	Whirling, whirling, westerly comes the wind;
悠悠東去雲	Far, far, eastward go the clouds.

(*TYJ* 63)

The last excerpt is especially suggestive in that the poem was written to a friend who became adjutant to Liu Yu; the Confucian image of life-giving wind gently bending the grass, emblematic of a humane ruler's spiritual influence over the people (A 12/19, M 3A/2), has apparently turned into an ill wind driving the helpless clouds along. Indeed even birds, with which Tao most often identifies himself, occasionally strike him as covetous worldlings with whom he is out of touch:

朝霞開宿霧	The morning glow disperses the night's mist;
衆鳥相與飛	Flocks of birds join in flight.
遲遲出林翮	Slowly one flaps out of the woods,
未夕復來歸	And before dusk returns home again.

(*TYJ* 123)

The import of Nature in Tao's verse is thus more complex than is usually assumed. Indeed, insofar as the poet projects his experience on it, Nature cannot be all perfect; nor would it have carried the same epiphanic power had it been so perceived. As with his created and historical figures, however, the symbolic structure formed by Tao's natural objects is no mere subjectivism. When Qu Yuan first uses the orchid to stand for his virtue and later condemns it as an evil slanderer,[27] we may be sure his plants exist to express human values. Not so for Tao's Nature, which incarnates a self-existent realm of truth more illuminating than human paragons can be. For Laozi and Zhuangzi, it is the unitary Dao that generates the world's myriad phenomena (*L* 25, *Z* 6/29–32), and those who share the Daoist vision see Nature not only as reflecting a cosmic meaning but as the direct material embodiment of the transcendental principle. This is the "objective" basis for Tao's symbolic perception of Nature:

日入羣動息	As the sun sets all activities cease;
歸鳥趨林鳴	Homing birds hasten to the woods, chirping.

(*TYJ* 90)

木欣欣以向榮	Joyously the trees come to blossom;
泉涓涓而始流	Trickling, the springs begin to flow.

(*TYJ* 161)

Day and night, activity and rest, seasonal rejuvenation and the flow of vitality—such is the cyclical permanence and joyous spontaneity of Nature.

This immanent transcendence of Nature carries artistic implications. It means that natural objects take on guiding symbolic values (naturalistic and moral) in Tao's poetic landscape:

羈鳥戀舊林	The fettered bird yearns for the old woods;
池魚思故淵	The pond-fish longs for the former deep.

(*TYJ* 40)

望雲慚高鳥 臨水愧游魚	Gazing at the clouds, I feel mortified by the high-flying birds; Overlooking the waters, I feel shamed by the gliding fish.

(*TYJ* 71)

Manifesting natural freedom and bliss, the fish and the bird are affirming and admonishing animal symbols that find coordinates in the plant world:

芳菊開林耀	Fragrant chrysanthemums shine through the woods;
青松冠巖列	Green pines range atop the cliffs.
懷此貞秀姿	They carry such chaste and exquisite grace,
卓為霜下傑	Outstanding heroes in the frost.

(*TYJ* 61)

In Tao's works the symbolic capacity of a natural object largely depends on its attributes; some symbols are virtually universal (e.g., the bird), while others are so within their cultural framework (e.g., the pine and fish). In their silent endurance against severity, the chrysanthemum and the pine become "intrinsic symbols" of fortitude and serenity, fitting friends who welcome the poet on his return to Nature: "The three paths are overgrown, / But the pines and chrysanthemums still remain" (*TYJ* 161). It must be added that not all plants possess determinate symbolic meaning. Two examples are the peach and the willow: though Five Willows and Peach Blossom Spring represent Tao's personal and social ideals, the plants have no clear significance in these two works other than contributing to their names.[28] Nor does the willow suggest anything more specific than seasonal change and temporal movement in "The Day of the Zha Sacrifice" (*TYJ* 108) and "After an Ancient Poem" #1 (*TYJ* 109).[29] But both plants appear one more time in Tao's corpus—together in "Return" #1: "Elms and willows shade the rear eaves; / Peaches and plums range before the hall" (*TYJ* 40). Though again no exact symbolic import can be assigned to them (nor to the elms and plums which appear nowhere else in his works), they do form part of the setting of freedom and harmony. In this general sense, it remains meaningful that Tao's personal and social ideals are given plant names.

Not surprisingly, the peaceful, happy life of which the poet sings is one in rapport with Nature:

> When I saw the trees joined in shade and [heard] the season's birds changing their songs, I too would rejoice and be happy. (*TYJ* 188)[30]

衆鳥欣有託	The birds rejoice to have a roost;
吾亦愛吾廬	And I, too, love my hut.

(*TYJ* 133)

善萬物之得時	Admiring how everything finds its season,
感吾生之行休	I am moved that my life is coming to a repose.

(*TYJ* 161)

The seasonable progression of natural life is one in which the poet participates with a spontaneous delight, especially as he sees an analogy between himself and the birds—which of all natural creatures also seem nearest to him in the range of their emotional expression.[31] In fact, whenever Tao observes a natural scene, we may be sure he is feeling a larger meaning as well. Like the birds he has found a dependable abode, and come to rest after a period of activity.[32]

Indeed, it is in the bird in flight—not any static symbolism it offers—that Tao finds the closest dynamic truth illuminating his quest. The bird's ability to chart its course parallels the winging aspirations of the spirit, but the freedom and well-being of both bird and man remain vulnerable; the air may turn "chilly" and "harsh" (*TYJ* 67), and the natural rhythm of life may be disturbed: "When a wide snare is set the bird is frightened" (*TYJ* 147). Amid such disruptive forces, finding a roost or even a sense of bearing becomes a trial:

栖栖失羣鳥	Unsettled *(xixi)* is the bird lost from the flock,
日暮猶獨飛	Still flying alone in the dusk.

徘徊無定止 Back and forth, it finds no stable resting-place;
夜夜聲轉悲 From night to night, its voice turns more mournful.
厲響思清晨 With shrill cries it yearns for the dawn;
遠去何所依 But traversing far, on what may it rely?
因值孤生松 Then it meets with a solitary pine,
斂翮遙來歸 And folds its wings, having arrived from afar.
勁風無榮木 In the keen wind there is no flourishing tree,
此蔭獨不衰 Yet this foliage alone has not withered.
託身已得所 Now that it has a place to entrust itself,
千載不相違 Not for a thousand years will it leave.

("Drinking Wine" #4, *TYJ* 88–89)

Often one in a string of natural images in Tao's poetry (e.g., "Return" #1), here the bird is a sustained symbol of his spirit; running parallel to the coherent portrait of the bird's flight is a personal text evident from the start, with *xixi* recalling the same description of Confucius (*A* 14/32)[33] and showing the poet's disquiet to be rooted in his social calling. There is both continuity and distinction of mood between the poem's two halves, as they resonate with multiple internal echoes that amplify the bird's inner cadence: "alone" because "lost from the flock," "flying" because "unsettled," "still" struggling wearily at a time of day when all should return to their "stable resting-place," its voice turning more "shrill and mournful" in its lengthy and lonely journey yet stubbornly determined to "traverse far." Indeed, alienated from an incongruous flock and mournful over the frustrated aspirations he cannot quite relinquish, the poet, too, sometimes feels devoid of a clear sense of direction. Worn down through the wintry trial over the years, there are moments when he sees himself drifting "back and forth" along the labyrinth of being yet steering his chosen course: "The way ahead—how much further will it be? / I know not where my anchorage is" (*TYJ* 117). The poem's uplifting force lies in the fact that the bird never loses faith, but "yearns for the dawn night after night" until it finds a home where it can finally "fold its wings." In projecting his experience on Nature, Tao again draws support from it. Proving its "evergreen" life-force and its winterhardiness as the Master noted before (*A* 9/28), the unwithering pine becomes a crowning symbol of the natural spirit and its abiding firmness amid adversity, a comrade still solitary but internalized into a source of strength. The symbolic appeal of the two images lingers long after the reading experience is over—the one we empathize with and feel happy for, the other we admire and respect. Without writing directly about the poet, the poem has depicted his quest in a vivid, imagistic and touching way, and it is in the final couplet that the lyric voice emerges in full: the peripatetic bird that "entrusts itself" to a dependable abode also marks his spiritual odyssey.

Even more than his fictional-historical canon, Nature as the objective incarnation of Dao offers a world of luminous symbols lighting up the poet's way, a composite of natural and moral truths as already seen in "Stopping Wine." This reality is also evident in his "*Fu* on Calming the Passions,"[34] a more lyric kind of *fu* distinct from the descriptive Han variety and closer in sentiment to *shi* poetry.[35] Suffice it to note here that in Tao's *fu*, Nature serves to bring the speaker's passion for a beautiful woman back to the fold of Confucian propriety *(li)*, and to help him (in Daoist terms) transcend the bondage of emotions. Listening to the music of her zither, the speaker confesses "I would fain talk with her, knee to knee." But "fearing the error of trespassing propriety" (*TYJ* 154), his emotional tide remains bottled in until, stepping out to Nature and watching the carefree clouds passing silently by, he sees an epiphanic truth that liberates his heart:

迎清風以祛累	I welcome the clear breeze that blows away my burden,
寄弱志於歸波	And consign my weak resolve to the returning waves.
. . . .	. . . .
坦萬慮以存誠	I level all anxieties to preserve my sincerity,
憩遥情於八遐	And rest my far-reaching feelings at the Eight Limits.
	(*TYJ* 156)

The last couplet is aptly revealing, for "wandering free and easy" in a spirit of "sincerity" marks not only inner reconciliation in Confucian and Daoist terms but an integration of the two. It is unfair to dismiss the *fu* as a "tiny flaw" (*H* 1:9) in Tao's corpus in the manner of Xiao Tong, whose objection to the composition's lack of a moral shows a didactic bias. Nor, in light of the personal ideal evident in Tao's writings, would it suffice to read this *fu* purely by the conventions laid down by its precedents, for what appear to the observer as stock elements are not necessarily so used by the writer.[36] Though this *fu* is not among Tao's best works, the characteristic personal voice registered in the quoted lines, and the balanced potency of Nature that lifts the spirit to a higher plane, are what give the work a distinct touch of his brush.

It is useful to remember that Tao's natural images are more than objective correlatives to his sentiments. Often a more personal kind of natural symbolism, wherein images represent certain thoughts, feelings, and situations, is explicable in terms of stimulus-response inspiration:[37]

遵四時以歎逝 瞻萬物以思紛 悲落葉於勁秋 喜柔條於芳春	Following the four seasons, the writer sighs over the passage of time; Observing the myriad things, his thoughts well up in profusion. He laments the fallen leaves in stern autumn, And rejoices at the tender twigs in fragrant spring.[38]

> The vital force [of Nature] impels objects, and objects affect men. Thus men, with their nature and feelings moved, give form to them in dancing and singing. (*SP* 1)[39]

But such perceptions of Nature's effect on the lyric impulse do not fully explain symbolism with a transcendental dimension, in which images embody a self-existent structure of larger truths.

Meanwhile, the symbolism in Tao's poetry also raises the question of its occasional allegorical tendency. No doubt the debate over symbolism and allegory is a complicated one in Western literary criticism whose full ramifications are beyond the scope of the present analysis.[40] For my purpose here, and in order to maintain the discussion on the same level of comparison, I shall try to characterize the two modes in terms of some commonly agreed-upon attributes. Now Western criticism has long associated allegory with narrative (prose or poetry). While this may be a bias in that the allegorical mode operates visibly in Chinese lyric and descriptive verse,[41] it is useful to remember that critics make this association because they see continuity of extratextual reference and sustained purposive movement as the defining traits of allegory. Granted that not all allegories reflect a transparent "translation of abstract notions into a picture-language"[42] and that complex ones may be beset with interpretive uncertainties,[43] allegory shows a specific and carefully executed intent to convey ideas underlying surface materials. One may argue whether or not allegory also exposes and calls attention to its own arbitrariness in the reading process,[44] but the inherent authorial purpose certainly guides the direction in which interpretation takes place.[45] Where textual dynamics is concerned, allegory (however complex) is marked by a dual text that points to distinct levels of meaning, either transparently linked or bridgeable by established codes or private leads. In fact, since allegory sets out with a core of intended meaning that directs the formation of the literal text, the latter (whatever its degree of realistic credibility) remains subordinate to the former, whether in a simple paradigm like Bunyan's *Pilgrim's Progress* or a contemporary novel like Golding's *Lord of the Flies*. One might not entirely accept Frye's statement that allegory occurs "when a poet *explicitly* indicates the relationship of his image to examples and precepts"[46]—for a complex allegory may simultaneously hide what it reveals[47]—but it seems sure that a focused intent is discernible even if the external reference is not specified.

While also conveying other meanings via images and sometimes revealing a pattern of directed movement, the symbolic mode does not show the same convergent intentionality: the difference between symbolism and allegory on the authorial level is one not of presence or intensity but of *focus* of intent. In textual terms, if allegorical figures, functioning under a concentrated purposiveness, usually remain somewhat abstract and largely distinct from the ideas represented, symbolism tends toward narrowing the disjunction between them through embodying the subject in the figure.[48] "The symbolic does not simply point to a meaning, but rather allows that meaning to present itself," writes Hans-Georg Gadamer, "the symbolic preserves its meaning within itself."[49] Combining a suggestiveness with a concrete quality, a symbol does not so much stand for as it "partakes of the reality which it renders intelligible."[50] And since it bears a more implicit and diffuse relation to its referent, the associations provoked during reading are also more fluid and multiple, some bearing little relevance to the author's determinable intent, and best felt rather than explained. No doubt literary ideal types do not easily apply to complex works; even in Western literature with its sharp conceptual distinction between symbolism and allegory, critics warn that the line between the analytic categories may be nebulous in reality.[51] Such caution only underlines the care necessary in relating these terms to Chinese poetry, where the two modes may coexist in complementarity.[52]

A small number of Tao's poems are quite obviously allegorical. "The Homing Bird" is a case in point:

翼翼歸鳥　Fluttering, fluttering, the homing bird;
晨去于林　In the early morn it went out from the wood.
遠之八表　Far it reached beyond the Eight Directions;
近憩雲岑　Near it reposed among the cloudy peaks.
和風不洽　When the mild wind did not oblige,
翻翮求心　It turned its wings to seek its heart's wish.
顧儔相鳴　Looking at its fellows, it called to them,
景庇清陰　Its shadow hidden in the cool shade.

(*TYJ* 32–33)

Despite showing an outward similarity to "Drinking Wine" #4, discussed above, the poem here makes no pretence at being a realistic narrative. The second couplet summarizes experience rather than describes a journey, while the third enters the bird's inner world; Hightower says the bird "seldom persuade[s] the reader that [it is] even incidentally [part] of the natural scene" (*HT* 40). Used analogically to express the poet's feelings about his experiences, the allegorical image has little value before being translated back into the preexistent meaning motivating it.

Perhaps a more revealing example in the present context is "After Ancient Poems" #9, for symbolic and allegorical meanings are interwoven in it:

種桑長江邊
三年望當採
枝條始欲茂
忽值山河改
柯葉自摧折
根株浮滄海
春蠶既無食
寒衣欲誰待
本不植高原
今日復何悔

They planted mulberry trees by the Yangzi's bank,
In three years expecting to pluck their leaves.
But just when the twigs and foliage were about to turn
lush,
Suddenly the hills and rivers happened to change.
The branches and leaves snapped by themselves;
The roots and trunks floated on the blue sea.
Where spring silkworms have no food,
Whom can one look to for winter clothes?
Since first they did not plant on the high plain,
What is there to regret today?

(*TYJ* 114)

As noted earlier, this poem is no account of a failed sericultural attempt; the conventional symbol of the mulberry trees points to a response to the downfall of the Jin dynasty. If "The Homing Bird" is fairly transparent, here it is the signifier's coded meaning that gives a clue to an underlying political import (which would have been hard to surmise had Tao replaced the mulberries with, say, willows). In both poems we are looking not at natural objects and scenes with any serious claim to empirical reality, but through the surface narrative to a subtext which Tao is trying to communicate. On one level, this seems to satisfy Frye's criterion for allegory wherein "the events of a [text] obviously and continuously refer to another simultaneous structure of events or ideas."[53]

Beyond a visible intent, however, the images do not form a focused structure. For instance, what do the Yangzi bank and the high plain denote, other than one being a wrong and the other a right place to plant mulberries? Since Tao has long withdrawn from worldly affairs, who are the belatedly regretful planters?[54] Do the branches and leaves refer to the country's sociopolitical structure? And what do the silkworms stand for? Any attempt to tie these loose ends into a consistent allegorical reading makes up one interpretation, but the obliqueness of the images does not allow imposition of a single meaning. The fact that Ikkai Tomoyoshi perceives some personal concern in the poem, and Suzuki Torao sees Tao "writing in a mood of resignation about his ineptitude in worldly affairs" (*HT* 184), attests to the suggestiveness of the symbolic references. This is especially evident in the fourth couplet, which commentators have skipped in its resistance to identification in a "dynastic change" reading, but which seems to indicate, in its reference to a lack of food and clothing, a broadening of sympathy that extends the poem from a narrowly political to a general historical and humanistic context. The poem has outgrown its allegorical framework with a symbolic multivalence.

In fact, Tao's poetry can seldom be called allegorical whether in authorial intent, textual nature, or interpretive parameter. No more than a few poems in his corpus refer to specific political realities (e.g., "Shu jiu," *TYJ* 101–2), where an intended textual direction and reading are evident enough for them to be seen as allegorical. More importantly, though his poetry is informed by a structure of values blended from Confucian humanism, Daoist naturalism, and a love of Nature, he does not turn it into a mold that controls the movement of his compositions, as seen in the fact that even some of his key symbols with transcendental dimensions have variable or unspecific significance. The Dao that exudes from his writings is embodied in the literal text even as it is immanent in the phenomenal world, with no essential disjunction between the interfused levels of meaning and text. One might even say that for one who experiences Dao in empirical reality, the urge to write spiritual or moral allegory does not quite arise. Besides, Tao's poetry is basically one of lyric expression where images are aligned with feelings before ideas; the directness of his voice and the versatility of his natural symbols show that he is not engineering us through a verbal construct to some truth beyond,[55] but either expressing that truth as experienced in daily life or projecting his feelings on whatever touches his inner chord.

And yet Tao's direct expressiveness also points to a need for the term *symbolism* to be fine-tuned. For especially as understood in modern Western literary criticism, symbolism is no less conscious and sustained a process than allegory:[56] in both cases one is conveying something via another. It is useful to remember that, like allegory, modern symbolism is an attempt to reach beyond empirical reality to a realm of personal or transcendental truth.[57] The difference lies in the opposite ways in which imagery is linked to its referent: if the limiting allegorical text is one that refers to a subtext as transparently as possible, the limiting symbolist text is found in the at times impenetrable indirection of nineteenth-century French Symbolism, in which images are studiedly blurred to create a sensuous arcaneness that evokes an underlying mood or sublimity, while forcing the reader's attention on the immediate text so that he may perceive the subtlety. "Human" Symbolism becomes "an attempt by carefully studied means—a complicated association of ideas represented by a medley of metaphors—to communicate unique personal feelings,"[58] while transcendental Symbolism serves as a "transporting" agent conveying one to pure essences. Baudelaire writes of "correspondences" between "the spirit and the senses,"[59] of the poet as a "translator" of symbols;[60] and it was he and his followers who saw the poet as what Rimbaud calls a "poet-prophet-visionary,"[61] endowed with the capacity to perceive the truths of the Ideal world behind material forms. The way to portray "the flower absent from all bouquets," as Mallarmé puts it, is to "consign every outline" to "oblivion," so that out of this blurring of the tangible "there arises musically the delicate idea itself,"[62] uncorrupted by any vestige of the phenomenal world below. If anything, the obscurity of Symbolist poetry shows an even more deliberate effort to direct the reading process to the transporting experience of the symbol itself.

Insofar as textual meanings emerge via imagistic suggestion and then largely through intuitive and emotive associations, Tao's writings may be seen as symbolic. But if related to its modern sense of a systematic structuring of esoteric imagery,[63] so that the writing and reading of a Symbolist text at times seem like a trying rite of passage through a maze of opacity, then the term needs to be clarified before it can be applied to a poetry marked by simple language, lucid imagery, and direct lyricism. If in Symbolist poetry the blending of self, object, and truth comes from a careful obfuscation of boundaries, in Tao such fusion results from a natural identification with symbolic correlatives, based on the ontological equality of all in being imbued by the same Dao. If the Symbolist clothes language in a cryptic veil in order to unveil the enigma beyond, Tao simply expresses the truth of Dao which, though likewise ineffable, is immanent in material reality. Far from being the strenuous forging of a fluid polysemous language showing the power of art and artist to reveal the mysteries of being, his symbolism is essentially a lyric outgrowth of an inner vision. It may seem a little incautious to appeal to the basic Chinese poetic premise that "poetry expresses sentiments" *(shi yan zhi)*,[64] but it is a fact that literature had not grown as self-conscious in Tao's age as it did in later times; there existed no systematic theoretical work on literary composition, let alone concepts regarding the use and power of symbols. While a poet like Li Shangyin can prove rewarding for Symbolist poetics, in Tao's case what the reader may see as beautiful, pregnant symbols are often not so to the poet, but crystallizations of lived experience and felt truths. What is generally absent is the "carefully studied" effort to make a thing embody its referent: the mutable, multivalent, and at times imprecise symbolic import of some of his natural images reflects a largely unpremeditated response to or projection of personal experience on Nature, rather than painstaking labor aimed at special effects. Even in "After Ancient Poems" #9, the simple language and direct voice show that beyond the political necessity for oblique locution, the poem's indeterminacy is not part of an allegorical purpose that has adopted a thorough strategy of concealment, but the outcome of other associations made in the course of writing that exceed the poet's specific intent. With his sentiments and aspirations basically those of all idealistic *shi*, there is ultimately little that is impenetrable about his symbols, however complex they may be. Above all, there is no self-conscious elevation of the poet and his art in the manner of the Symbolists: no proclamation of himself as a semi-divine seer and of the imagination as the "queen of the faculties" "positively related to the infinite,"[65] nor any championing of rarefied emotional and aesthetic experience.

Goethe (1749–1832) believed "everything which the genius does as genius, eventuates unconsciously. The man of genius can also operate rationally, after careful consideration, from conviction, but all that only happens secondarily."[66] Without necessarily accepting the first part of this statement, what seems to mark a natural genius like Tao in the cooperation of artistic instinct and mental deliberation is the latter's secondary role in the creative process. Rather than brandishing its mercuriality and being declaratively aware of its own powers, his genial consciousness is in touch with a larger power via intuitive understanding, acting on an implicit wisdom far deeper than itself. Just as Tao's existential spirit rides along the transforming waves of Dao (*TYJ* 36, 162), so his poetic spirit follows Nature—the prime genial artist inexhaustible in her potentialities and forms—in crystallizing an art of flowing vitality, wherein any design remains secondary to a natural instinct that, without laboring over the connotations or ensuring the consistency of every symbol, envisions the world in a spontaneously symbolic way. This is generally true whether the lyric spirit follows a pivotal image conveying aspects of his experience ("Drinking Wine" #4 and #8), flows through a series of images unified by a central sentiment ("Return" #1 and "Miscellaneous Poems" #3), or moves from image to image as the spirit's mood and focus shift, due to either inner projection ("Singing of Poor Literati" #1) or response to scenes and objects ("Return" #5). Since examples from all three types have been discussed, I shall simply take "Singing of Poor Literati" #1 to illustrate the third lyric situation, a poem that exemplifies Tao's spontaneous symbolism particularly well:

萬族各有託	The myriad creatures all have their resort;
孤雲獨無依	The solitary cloud alone finds no support.

曖曖空中滅	Dimly it vanishes in the empty sky;
何時見餘暉	Do we ever see its afterglow?
朝霞開宿霧	The morning red disperses the night's mist;
衆鳥相與飛	Flocks of birds join in flight.
遲遲出林翮	Slowly one flaps out of the woods,
未夕復來歸	And before dusk returns home again.
量力守故轍	Gauging his capacity, he keeps to his old tracks;
豈不寒與飢	Does he not suffer cold and hunger?
知音苟不存	Even if no kindred spirit exists,
已矣何所悲	Let it be: what is there to be sad about?

(*TYJ* 123)

A sense of loneliness pervades the poem from the very beginning, where the contemplating poet sees in the cloud the same lack of supportive companionship afflicting his reclusion. Moreover, just as the cloud's solitude is aggravated by its sure fading into the void, Tao's gloominess over his unrealized vision is deepened by an awareness that not even an "afterglow" of his ideal will survive his death. But beyond a personal grief also lies a recognition of the shifting evanescence of existence, which gives the poem a more serene mood as he looks back on his path—and sees a different image. Lines 5–8 amount to a revision of the first couplet: it is a matter of choice that the hesitant bird does not fly in company (or conformity) with those rushing eagerly forward, and returns to its abode before it is too late. From this close parallel of the lone bird symbolizing his choice and rejection of worldly pursuits, the poet comes naturally to express a renewed insight into life; his lyric spirit shows a transition from the bird to the poor man of integrity in the ninth line that applies to both. Self-knowledge results in a choice that remains firm in adversity; and with the fortified understanding that life need not be sad even without a kindred spirit, he attains a certain peace of mind.

The poem develops through three images with no tight conceptual structuring of the symbolist kind: not only is there no fine web of images, but the clear transition between them may seem a shade untidy at first glance. Yet they are integrally unified in terms of the movement of the lyric spirit, not in stream-of-consciousness fashion (wherein the consciousness lends unity to its contents, however unrelated and randomly unfolded) but in that they form internal echoes. For one thing, the twin motifs of solitude and self-direction run through the images in keys tinged by the poet's changing mood. Besides, these motifs are amplified by his two-sided feelings about time, visible in other poems and joining the first two quatrains: a sadness over his ever-receding chance to realize his aspirations, and a thankfulness for having returned to his true home in time. Such feelings are in turn marked by the different diurnal moments depicted, so that the visual and emotional tones of the quatrains enhance each other. Meanwhile, registering a progress from personal grief to cosmic understanding that effects an inner transformation, the second couplet stands at once as the emotional counterpoint and psychospiritual basis for the second and third quatrains,[67] while the second in turn forms the symbolic "spring" for the directly expressive third, until the ending couplet virtually restates the initial feeling on an opposite note. The poem's internal links, resonances, and unity of effect thus come not from any studied artifice but from the lyric flow of a contemplative spirit as it relives the essence of his quest, draws in some of his cherished images, and reaffirms his existential faith. The ostensible untidiness of transition between the images attests to a natural progression of feeling and thought little detained by conceptual mediation: in other words, to an act of symbolization that is essentially instinctive.

Without discounting the mind's role in artistic creation especially in its later stages, the above analysis shows up a basic difference between the intricate design of modern Symbolism and the more spontaneous nature of Tao's symbolism, which, instead of manipulating images or draining them of an intensified sensuousness in order to evoke pure essences, represents less an artistic craft than the direct expression of a personal vision. If the Symbolist emblem is usually an oracular image enchanting in its cryptic charm, Tao's most fertile symbols consist of ordinary items in his rural life, lucidly immediate rather than obscure in that the transcendental is felt not beyond but amid material experience. If his poetry comes across with an unobtrusive symbolic force, it is not only because he speaks what he sees in Nature but because Nature embodies the substance that allows him to speak thus. One might even say that beyond the process of art, it is the innate pulses of Nature that give shape to Tao's lyricism, enabling it to flow naturally instead of coagulating around preconceived ideas.

Indeed, symbolic and visionary as it is, Tao's poetry remains firmly rooted in empirical reality—an attribute that takes on added significance when placed in historical context. Now it was during the Eastern Han that literati poets gradually picked up the five-character verse form used in folk ballads, replacing their largely narrative and dramatic mode with lyric expression. But while reaching its first peak in the Jian'an poets, with the rediscovered self manifested in a vibrant poetic personality, lyric verse showed little development in scope and depth over the next century and a half. One reason is that the Wei-Jin literati's spiritual flight often found expression in a fanciful pursuit of an immortal world. What with the spread of the immortality cult since pre-Qin times[68] and of religious Daoism during the Latter Han alongside social disorder, immortals had found a place in *yuefu* ballads[69] and become a popular fictional subject.[70] Meanwhile, in the plague of intrigues and usurpations that lasted from the end of the Han through the Western Jin, the lives of literati caught within the compass of factional strifes became utterly precarious, often ending in summary execution.[71] As we have seen, the Pure Conversation movement was in part a philosophical abstraction of the political Pure Criticism silenced by the persecution of dissidents. Compound such an ethos with the increasing turbulence of the times—peasant revolts, wars, floods, and famines—and the pervasive sense of dislocation easily drove the literary spirit to an immortal realm even as it propelled the mind to a metaphysical sanctuary.

Despite the anti-immortality note in the "Nineteen Ancient Poems," it is thus not surprising to find a "supernatural" streak of what has come to be called *youxian* (wandering immortals) verse in Cao Cao's poems, as one entitled "Mo shang sang" (Mulberry by the Path) will illustrate:

駕虹蜺　乘赤雲
登彼九疑歷玉門
濟天漢　至崑崙
見西王母謁東君
交赤松　及羨門
受要祕道愛精神
食芝英　飲醴泉
拄杖桂枝佩秋蘭
絶人事　遊渾元
苦疾風遊欻飄翩
景未移　行數千
壽如南山不忘愆

Straddling rainbows, riding red clouds,
I ascend Mount Jiuyi and pass the Jade Gate [of Heaven].
I cross the Milky Way, arriving at the Kunlun Mountains,
To pay my respects to the Queen Mother of the West and the Lord of the East.
Making friends with [the immortals] Chisong and Xianmen,
I was taught the vital, secret methods to cherish my spirit.
I take in the essence of the magic fungus and drink from the sweet spring,
Holding a cassia staff and wearing autumn orchids.
Cut off from human affairs, wandering in the undifferentiated oneness,
I roam as a gale, swiftly flying about.
The sun's shadow hasn't moved, yet I've travelled several thousand *li*;
My life-span is like the Southern Mountain, but I can't forget my mistakes.

(*XQH* 1:348)[72]

Here Cao Cao the sober-minded pragmatist has submitted himself to a temporary flight of fancy, in which the elements (rainbows and clouds) and dimensions (the Milky Way) of experience have risen to a celestial level. But the vivid empyrean descriptions point to where the flight begins: it is an awareness of decay that generates the need for "vital, secret methods to nurture [the] spirit," a sense of the earth's grinding oppressiveness that underlies the wish to be "cut off" from it and "swiftly wander in the undifferentiated oneness." While some *youxian* poems give straightforward descriptions of the immortal world and the human desire to join it,[73] this one seems to have arisen from a deeper expressive sentiment that employs the heavens as a metaphor for a loftier and freer world. As the final line shows, it is Cao's agony over his "mistakes" in handling "human affairs"—

errors which his brief life may not allow him to correct—that has motivated the poem.[74]

With the rising popularity of religious Daoism and alchemical practices among the social elite (as discussed in chapter 4), the *youxian* theme in poetry continued to grow in the course of the Jin, rising through writers like Xi Kang[75] to a climax in the famous "Youxian shi" of Guo Pu (276–324):

採藥遊名山	I roam among famous mountains gathering herbs,
將以救年頽	To arrest the decay of my old age.
呼吸玉滋液	With breathing control and jade liquid,
妙氣盈胸懷	A wondrous spirit suffuses my bosom.
登仙撫龍駟	Rising to be an immortal, I stroke my dragon-team,
迅駕乘奔雷	And with swift drive ride on the rolling thunder.
鱗裳逐電曜	My scaled garments gleam in the lightning;
雲蓋隨風迴	My cloud canopy swirls in the wind.
手頓羲和轡	My hands stop pulling the Xihe[76] reins;
足蹈閶闔開	My foot stamps for Heaven's gate to open.
東海猶蹄涔	The Eastern Sea looks like a hoofprint of water,
崑崙螻蟻堆	The Kunlun Mountains an ant-hill.
遐邈冥茫中	Far, far into the vast dimness
俯視令人哀	I gaze down—it makes me so sad.

(*XQH* 2:866)

Bearing resemblance to Cao's verse in basic sentiment and structure, Guo's poem shows a more acute sense of the pitiless passage of time. "Rising to be an immortal," the occult artist floats to an even higher supernal altitude (not arriving but looking down at Kunlun), describing his grand celestial trip in more elaborate detail before reverting to the *yonghuai* poet gazing back at an unforgettable earth. His attitude to Nature is not a realistic one: the natural details form part of a magical domain, while his journey, reminiscent of Qu Yuan's, is a flight of the imagination to a realm more attractive than the sordid world. Some of Guo's "Youxian shi," in fact, show a fine descriptive sensitivity to the beauty of Nature, while others are really discharges of his sense of frustration (*SP* 39), for like Qu and Cao, Guo turns his eyes back to the human world. All the same, his poetry contains a fantastic flavor typical of the literature of the time.[77]

For *youxian shi* is itself part of a wave of supernatural literature whose proliferation attests to the popularity of the idea of immortality. For instance, the Queen Mother of the West was turned from an ugly monster in *Shanhai jing* (Mountains and Seas Classic) into a beautiful immortal in *Han Wudi neizhuan* (Intimate Biography of Emperor Wu of the Han) and *Han Wu gushi* (Stories of Emperor Wu of the Han), while a collection of *Shenxian zhuan* (Biographies of Divine Immortals) was edited by Ge Hong to prove their reality. *Soushen ji* (Accounts in Search of the Supernatural) was intended to demonstrate the existence of spirits;[78] the same might be said of its sequel *Soushen houji,* in which several stories offer variations on a formula based on these elements: a man loses his way in some grove or grotto, stumbles upon an immortal realm (or at least arrives at its threshold), encounters immortals before reverting to the mundane world, and subsequently tries in vain to return again. The collection includes "Peach Blossom Spring" (with a few minor discrepancies), and was attributed to Tao probably for that reason.[79]

We may therefore return to a consideration of "Peach Blossom Spring," given its formal resemblance to the Six Dynasties *zhiguai* stories and its composition in an ethos known for its fascination with immortals. One story in *Soushen houji,* about a certain Liu Ziji whom Tao mentions at the end of his account, is especially pertinent to our discussion:

> Liu Linzhi of Nanyang, courtesy-name Ziji, was fond of roaming the mountains and rivers. While gathering herbs he once reached Hengshan, going deep into the mountains and forgetful of returning. He saw a brook, south of which lay two stone bins, one closed and one open. The brook was deep and wide, and he could not cross it. He wanted to turn back but had lost his way. Then he met a man cutting bows and asked him the way, and barely managed to get home. Someone said that the bins contained prescriptions for immortality, magic herbs and all manner of things. Linzhi wanted to seek them again but did not recognize the place any more.[80]

A juxtaposition with "Peach Blossom Spring" is instantly revealing, not only because the tales are similar in structure yet incongruous in spirit, but because the common mention of Liu Ziji brings their variant purposes into relief. Clearly in search of immortality in the *Soushen houji* story, Liu only seeks an ideal realm in this world in Tao's account (*TYJ* 166). While its inaccessibility and expressions like "fairy realm," "different roots," and "beyond the dust and noise" (*TYJ* 167–68) might invest "Peach Blossom Spring" with an aura of fantasy, the narrative is decidedly realistic, with references to dynasty and reign periods as well as political figures like the governor and his subordinate. So are the details about the agrarian community; Tao even writes "the clothes of the men and women were all like those of people outside" (*TYJ* 165). Though Tang poets like Wang Wei and Liu Yuxi (772–842) inject fairyland elements into their versions of Peach Blossom Spring,[81] Su Shi rightly notes that immortals do not kill chickens for food (*H* 2:341). Reflecting sentiments different from those motivating most Jin writers and compilers of supernatural stories, the tale expresses a social ideal rendered inaccessible only by man himself. No more exotic than a sublimation of quotidian reality, Peach Blossom Spring is a land of simple egalitarian happiness, utopian only in its immunity from sociopolitical exploitation and its perpetuation in accord with Nature's rhythm.

As lonely amid the literary trends as he was in the political ethos of the day, Tao has no more use for immortality in poetry than in life: "If one's understanding of things is lofty, / What need is there to climb Mount Hua or Song?" (*TYJ* 53).[82] Instead, he becomes the first great poet of the humble and ordinary, writing of his rural life with a touching immediacy that raises Chinese verse to a new level of expressiveness. While he devised no poetic program in the manner of Du Fu, Bai Juyi, or the Northern Song poets, his poetry can be seen as a development of the social realism initiated in *Shijing* (Book of Songs) and continued in the Han *yuefu* ballads. Any elevation of idealism present is grounded on a realism that stands out even more sharply against such exuberant writers as Zhuangzi, Qu Yuan, or Li Bai. Take Zhuangzi, who despite affirming the omnipresence of Dao often gives mystical depictions of the spiritual heights to be reached. We read about the spiritual man on Guye Mountain who "does not eat the five grains, inhales the wind, drinks the dew, rides the clouds and mist, straddles a flying dragon and roams beyond the four seas" (Z 1/29), the perfect man who "rides the clouds and mist, mounts the sun and moon and roams beyond the four seas untouched by life or death" (Z 2/72–73), who cannot be harmed by fire or water, heat or cold, birds or beasts (Z 2/71–72, 17/48–49). From the great roc and the long-lived caterpillar (Z 1/11) to the man who stands independent of time, space, and circumstances, Zhuangzi's world is one of "absurd and outlandish talk, silly and preposterous language, illogical and unbordered expressions" (Z 33/64), though every bit a true artistic reality created by his visionary imagination. It is precisely his "baseless" fabrication, unbridled exaggeration, and exuberant language that convey the true man's essence as a pure flow of spirit.

While sharing much of Zhuangzi's naturalistic vision and call for truthfulness and simplicity, Tao's idealism impresses us otherwise. For even at his most "fictional," there is nothing surreal or fantastic in his poetic world, none of Zhuangzi's mystical ambience, still less of what Liu Xie (465?–520?) calls "odd, extraordinary matters" or "incredible, strange tales" that characterize many poems in *Chuci* (*WD* 5/1:47). Exiled by his king for all his patriotism, Qu Yuan expresses his search for a way out through an imaginary journey that parallels his plight, bringing us through fireworks of mythical, historical, and natural phenomena ignited by the frictions of a committed life. We see whirlwinds gathering to meet him, clouds and rainbows bidding him welcome, until he is turned away at Heaven's gate to seek in vain for a "mate."[83] It is significant that while Zhuangzi's inward liberation and Qu Yuan's frustration with reality find expression in an imaginary world, Tao's spirit, often amid both sentiments, remains rooted in empirical reality. "I build my hut in the the realm of man" (*TYJ* 89), he writes, without escaping like Qu to some ethereal domain. Not only is there no exotic fabrication in his verse—no roc with cloudlike wings beating the whirlwind to rise ninety thousand *li* (Z 1/2–3), no "giants a thousand fathoms tall," "serpents with nine heads," or "red ants like elephants"[84]—but the kind of hyperboles often used by romantic idealists are absent. Li Bai's most common objects remain unrestricted by the laws of Nature: we read "thirty thousand feet of white hair," or hair "like black silk in the morning turned into snow at dusk" (*QTS* 5:1682, 1724)—images shaped by a poetic "heavenly horse" "traversing the sky with unrestrainable momentum."[85] The rustic objects and events of Tao's world, on the other hand, constitute a real picture of rural life. In effect, he fills in what Zhuangzi has left unfinished by showing how Dao resides in the ordinary,[86] as a homely Way that requires no flight beyond reality or emphasis on its heroic transcendence. Rooted in quotidian existence, the artistic truth of his poetry stirs a ready response from the reader, enabling him too to leave the "dusty net" awhile and share the poet's natural life.

The realistic basis of Tao's poetry and its difference from *youxian shi* are perhaps best exemplified by his "Return Home" *fu*, which like Cao Cao's and Guo Pu's poems also describes a journey, but one of an entirely dissimilar cast. Here, following the poet home upon his retirement, one is in touch not with the spectacle of the Ninth Heaven but with the music of the heart, as the graceful rhythm of the verse conveys his sense of inner liberation:

舟遥遥以輕颺	Rocking, rocking, the boat lightly tosses;
風飄飄而吹衣	Drifting, drifting, the wind brushes my robe.
問征夫以前路	I ask a traveler about the way ahead;
恨晨光之熹微	I regret the dawn light's faintness.
乃瞻衡宇	Then I see my humble house,
載欣載奔	Now rejoicing, now darting along;
僮僕歡迎	The servants welcome me,
稚子候門	The children are waiting at the gate.
三逕就荒	The three paths are overgrown,
松菊猶存	But pines and chrysanthemums still remain.
攜幼入室	Holding the children by the hand, I enter the house,
有酒盈罇	Where there is wine filled in a jug.
引壺觴以自酌	Taking up the jug and cup, I pour for myself;
眄庭柯以怡顏	A sideways glance at the courtyard trees lights up my face.

倚南窗以寄傲
審容膝之易安
園日涉以成趣
門雖設而常關
策扶老以流憩
時矯首而遐觀
雲無心以出岫
鳥倦飛而知還
景翳翳以將入
撫孤松而盤桓

I lean by the southern window in pride,
And ponder the easy contentment of lean
 sufficiency.
The garden I daily visit becomes a source of pleasure;
The gate, though standing, is always closed.
Staff in hand, I stroll or stop to rest,
At times raising my head and gazing afar.
Clouds aimlessly move out from the peaks;
Birds weary of flying know the way home.
The sunlight is dimming, about to sink;
Stroking a lone pine, I linger on.

(*TYJ* 160–61, ll. 9–32)

Unlike those in Cao's and Guo's poems, Tao's journey is not an imaginary spatial escape to some celestial clime for a brief sojourn, but an actual return to a home where he can anchor his life. Partly for this reason, while Cao's and Guo's empyrean tours remain fairly remote and largely on the narrative level despite their lyric sentiments, Tao's relation of his homeward journey vibrates with a deep artistic appeal that comes not from a direct expression of emotions but from their embodiment in the touching gestures recorded. Scene and feeling dance in unison: the boat lightly gliding along, the breeze caressing the poet's robe—all become natural resonances to a spirit released from the burden of a miry world. His joyous anxiety is not directly stated to us, but revealed in his inability to sit calmly in his cabin, as though we witnessed him standing and looking with great anticipation into the distance. We empathize with his restless excitement as he hurries along the road, impatiently "asking a traveler about the way" and "regretting" the faint light that reduces his vision (ll. 9–12). Then in a manner reminiscent of "Return" #1, we follow the tracking shot zooming in on the destination, every factual and emotive detail blending into an integral effect. We see him looking affectionately at his house, darting along in delight, embracing his sons and greeting his servants, moved by the pines and chrysanthemums as enduring as his nature, breezing indoors through the gate and path to his house where wine is waiting for him (ll. 13–20). The peace and delight of his rural life are likewise felt through details of lived experience. We see him enjoying the nectar of freedom and glancing fondly at the courtyard trees, pulsing with feeling as he leans against the window pondering his life, content within a closed gate that signifies not insulation or inhospitality but self-containedness. We follow him "staff in hand" strolling or resting in his garden, leisurely watching the clouds wandering by and the weary birds returning to their nests. Stroking the lone pine, pacing back and forth—the word "lone" adding to the narration's emotional depth with a hint of sadness rooted in his failed idealism—the poet becomes lost in contemplation in the setting sun (ll. 21–32).

I have gone at some length to paraphrase this part of Tao's *fu* in order to re-create a little of the reader's secondary visualization of the poet's experience, whose presentness lies both in its realistic credibility and in the vivid, mellifluous, imagistic depiction through which Tao's mood and spirit come alive. One is almost loath to stand back and reason, for our communion with the poet is as beyond anatomy as his is with Nature, and more remarkable in crossing the gap of time. To cite the traditional encomium of "interfusion of feeling and scene" *(qingjing jiaorong)* would be wanting here, for it is not just that inner and outer contours form an indissoluble whole. While the overriding note is a lyrical one, the lyric, dramatic, and narrative all enliven, extend, and enhance one another, giving a sublime union of effect that blends the best in music and painting into the poetic medium. In fact Ouyang Xiu (1007–72) went so far as to say "There is no [great non-*shi*] composition in the Jin but for the single exception of Tao Yuanming's 'Return Home' *fu*" (*H* 2:327). But as Ye Mengde (1077–1148) points out, the key to this art is truthfulness of sentiments based on experience (*H* 1:53): to borrow the fisherman's words in *Zhuangzi*, "Truthfulness means the ultimate of purity and sincerity; that which lacks purity and sincerity cannot move others" (*Z* 31/32–33). For such poetry cannot be fashioned *ex nihilo* by the greatest imaginative genius.

Never before in Chinese lyricism has earthy life reached such a poetic height. One recalls, for instance, how family life glides easily into Tao's verse in line with its centrality in the Confucian order:

弱子戲我側 My young son plays at my side,
學語未成音 Learning to speak, but cannot yet make the sounds.

(*TYJ* 60)

In this plain description, we see not only an infant's charming clumsiness but a loving parent sensitive to the burgeoning vitality of his son. In due course the same voice tells us how

通子垂九齡 Tongzi is about to turn nine,
但覓梨與栗 And seeks only pears and chestnuts.

(*TYJ* 106)

The fruits not only capture the child's caliber but enable us to vividly visualize a naughty child hopping around all day long. And instead of a stern father getting upset as the poem's title "Reproving My Sons" might suggest, we see a good-humored parent looking fondly at his naive child, perhaps shaking his head as he pours out wine, knowing that he cannot impose his wish on *ziran*—what is naturally so:

天運苟如此 If my Heaven-assigned lot be such,
且進杯中物 Just let me take what's in the cup!

(*TYJ* 106)

It is worth remarking, as Burton Watson has,[87] that *Shijing* rarely mentions children in its portraits of everyday life. Writing with an affectionate ease about his children and his hopes (*TYJ* 29), delights, and disappointments as a father, Tao goes beyond such sporadic prior efforts as Zuo Si's in taking up children as a subject of poetry.[88] The general social tendency toward intimacy in family life might have provided a certain atmospheric backdrop for Tao's parental lyricism,[89] but here again he has extended the scope and depth of Chinese poetry.

Discussing the "visualized scene" *(yijing)* in Chinese poetics, Wang Guowei (1877–1927) says:

> There is the created scene, and there is the descriptive scene. This is the basis of distinction between idealism and realism. Yet it is quite

> difficult to differentiate between them, for the scene a great poet creates always accords with the natural, and the scene he describes always approaches the ideal.[90]

This statement well characterizes Tao's poetry, in which inner and outer realities are brought together by personal sentiments. As we shall see (in chapter 8), its lyric and visionary dimensions will help explain why, while the refined natural descriptions by poets like Lu Ji, Zhang Xie (?–307)[91] and Xie Lingyun largely stay within the bounds of their specific import, Tao's rustic subjects carry a vitality and richness that overflow the limits of the concrete medium. Experienced in life and integrated into a symphonic unity, they exude a deep "relish beyond words and resonance beyond strings."[92]

In the outcome, this spontaneous symbolism and visionary realism manage to expand the ambit of Chinese poetry in an unprecedented way—all without necessarily willing it. With his voice equally infused into historical, fictional, and autobiographical writings, Tao extends the lyric mode "horizontally" by bringing within its scope the rich resources of the narrative mode. At the same time, he also extends it "vertically" through a symbolic vision that animates a cultural macrostructure of meaning. In fact, he is the first to successfully link natural symbolism to a cosmic frame of reference in poetry, and the first, conversely, to fully realize the potential that structure holds for lyric expression. The result is not only a rejuvenation of the lyric voice at a time when it seemed submerged by prevalent trends, but one that is inspiringly universal in its overtones.

6

Philosophical Poetry and "Abstruse-Language Verse"

This leads to the issue of the presence of philosophy in poetry. For about the time when *youxian shi* reached its apex of development, Neo-Daoist metaphysics, already coloring the verse of Xi Kang, Xi Xi (mid-third century), and others,[1] began to "spill over" broadly to Eastern Jin poetry (*WD* 45/2:331). Zhong Hong points to the leading writers of what has come to be known as "abstruse-language" verse *(xuanyan shi)*: "The poems of Sun Chuo [320–77], Xu Xun [?–365], Huan Wen [312–73] and Yu Liang [289–340] were all plain dicta like *Dao de lun* [by He Yan, d. 249]" (*SP* 1–2).

Given the paucity of extant specimens,[2] any attempt to sketch an outline of *xuanyuan shi* will be tentative. But its general drift may be seen from a poem by Sun Chuo written in reply to Xu Xun:

仰觀大造	I look up and view the vast creation;
俯覽時物	I look down and survey all matter existing in time.
機過患生	Once opportunities pass troubles arise;
吉凶相拂	Fortune and danger displace each other.
智以利昏	Wisdom is clouded by gain;
識由情屈	Understanding is cramped by feeling.

野有寒枯	In the wilds one meets with chill and drought;
朝有炎鬱	In the court one faces heat and depression.
失則震驚	Failing, one will be shaken with fear;
得必充詘	Successful, one is sure to be filled with joy.

(*XQH* 2:899)

Displaying a neat conceptual scheme, the poem opens with a macrocosmic view signaling its treatment of a universal topic, descends to a practical truth in the second couplet, offers a warning to the unenlightened in the third, and ends with specific counsel to the courtier. Reminiscent of *Laozi* in its epigrammatic style and mix of metaphysics with practical advice, the poem is devoid of emotive and imaginative resonance, reading like a wooden series of "wise words" couched in verse form. Similar pieces written by Sun to Wen Qiao, Yu Bing, and Xie An[3] indicate that *xuanyan shi* was a common literary exercise among the Eastern Jin elite, as an excerpt from Wang Xizhi's "Lanting shi" (Orchard Pavilion Poem) will show:

悠悠大象運	Slowly, slowly, the Great Form [Heaven] operates,
輪轉無停際	Round in cycles without a moment's cease.
陶化非吾因	Fostering and transformation happen not on my account;
去來非吾制	Coming and going are not within my control.
宗統竟安在	Where lies the fundamental order?
即順理自泰	Accord with things and your [inner] principles will be at peace.

(*XQH* 2:895)

Structurally there is the same macrocosmic appeal setting the tone of the poem as it expounds the self-sufficiency of Dao. The message is Zhuangzi's—"Do not let the mind impair Dao" (*Z* 6/9)—but one that remains artistically remote in the abstract.

Sure enough, criticism of *xuanyan* poetry came readily from the Southern Dynasties writers. It was decried by Liu Xie for being "mired in the abstruse ethos" (*WD* 6/1:45); by Zhong Hong for "stifling the inspired vitality of Jian'an poetry" (*SP* 2); by Tan Daoluan (fifth century) for "couching Daoist words in a rhymed form" and "shattering the [lyric] models of *Shijing* and 'Li sao'"(*SX* 4/85, n.1);[4] by Shen Yue for depriving verse of its "beautiful phrases" and formal elegance which his age so prized (*SS* 67/7:1778); and by Xiao Zixian (489–537) for "prospering the teaching of the Daoists."[5] Notwithstanding the validity of such criticism, the artistic flaw of *xuanyan shi* lies not in its intellectual content but its equation of rational with poetic discourse. After all, what "gave way" to landscape poetry was not the thought of Zhuangzi and Laozi, as Liu Xie claims (*WD* 6/1:67), but the "literary Zhuang-Lao" of *xuanyan shi*. If a rational exposition of Dao already betrays its nonconceptual essence, transplanting metaphysics to poetry is doubly pernicious in forfeiting the evocative richness and liquid beauty through which poetry achieves its effect. Given their like movement toward an existential truth ultimately ineffable, there is a real sense in which Chinese verse and philosophy are "sister arts" underlain by a common premise of expressive integrity, so that in later times Yan Yu's (fl. 1180–1235) *Canglang shihua* (Poetry Talks by [the Escapist of] Canglang River) discussed poetry in terms of Chan Buddhism. The challenge for philosophical verse is to illuminate without stifling the vitality of art.

Now Tao generally shares the Eastern Jin literati's affinity for Nature, both as physical setting and as embodiment of Dao. But while the feelings are blended with the poet's nature into his daily life, the two responses are more conceptually associated for the aesthetic-minded Pure Conversationists bent on capturing the spirit of things; to them Nature's splendid sights easily become the supreme manifestations of Dao through which the sublime communion Zhuangzi describes (Z 21/30) may be achieved. While Sun Chuo links a man's spirit (his *de)* to the landscape (*SX* 8/107), in his younger days Xie An "roamed hills and waters at ease, amusing himself with writing and analyzing principles" (*SX* 8/101, n.1). Yu Liang is described as "facing mountains and waters with *xuan*"—an empty, mystical mind that communicates with Dao (*SX* 14/24); and Zong Bing (375–443) says the Way is best understood through "mountains and waters [which] manifest Dao with their graceful forms."[6] That nature literature and painting made great strides during the Eastern Jin is an artistic outcome of a discovered spiritual vision.

Perhaps the Eastern Jin literati's dual attitude toward Nature is best reflected in the *Lanting* (Orchid Pavilion) collection of poems, written in 353 at an elite gathering for the customary late spring purification ritual:[7]

. . . .　. . . . .
仰望碧天際　I look up and see the limit of the blue sky;
俯磐綠水濱　I look down and survey the banks of the cerulean water.
寥朗無厓觀　Vast and tranquil is the boundless view;
寓目理自陳　In all that meets the eye, principle is self-evident.
大矣造化功　Great indeed are the workings of Creation;
萬殊莫不均　A myriad different phenomena, none unequal to another.

(Wang Xizhi, *XQH* 2:895)

茫茫大造　Vast, vast is the Great Creation;
萬化齊軌　The myriad transformations follow the same course.
. . . . . .　. . . . .
凡我仰希　All my support and hope
期山期水　Lie in these mountains and waters.

(Sun Tong, *XQH* 2:907)

馳心域表　I gallop my mind beyond the realm;
寥寥遠邁　Vast, vast as I stride far.
理感則一　Principle and feeling unite into one;
冥然玄會　Mystically the abstruse truth flashes on me.

(Yu You, *XQH* 2:908)

仰想虛舟說　I look up and ponder the discourse of the "empty boat";[8]
俯歎世上賓　I look down and sigh over the sojourners of the world.
朝榮雖云樂　Bloom in the morn may be considered joyous,
夕斃理自因　But decay at dusk follows as a matter of principle.

(Yu Yun, *XQH* 2:909)

散豁情志暢 塵纓忽已捐 仰詠挹餘芳 怡情味重淵	Idling in the open my feelings and aspirations find free rein; The bondage of the dusty world is swiftly cast away. I look up and sing, enjoying the overflowing fragrance; It delights my feelings to savor the abysmal depths.

(Wang Yunzhi, *XQH* 2:915)

According to Wang Xizhi's preface to the collection, Lanting was located amid "towering mountains and steep ranges, lush woods and tall bamboo, and a clear stream with swirling rapids" (*JS* 80/7:2099). One would expect the charming, spacious setting to inspire lofty roamings of the human spirit: as worldly ambition is dwarfed by height, disquiet soothed by genial company, and pugnacity dissolved by harmonious lushness, magnanimity of Zhuangzi's kind rises to a unison with the majestic openness beheld, and Nature offers cathartic relaxation and purifying fulfillment for the moment.[9] But while its delights are not unsung in fine description and occasional lyricism,[10] in the above poems natural details are virtually absent. Instead we find familiar theorizations in the manner of *xuanyan shi* stemming from a conscious effort to make Nature corroborate Dao. Sweeping "up and down" over the "vast, vast" landscape, the eye looks not at but *through* Nature to a "mystical" perception of the "self-evident principle" of Being. The vague references to "mountains and waters," "abysmal depths," or the workings of "Great Creation" do not reflect a deep emotive consonance with the concrete forms of Dao; even the expression of feeling in the last excerpt sounds rational in tone. Not only do the philosophical dominate the descriptive and lyric elements in a discordant mix, but the stronger the drive for spiritual elevation, the less likely the intuitive communion with Nature which alone can vitalize the principles explained. The distance from and metaphysicizing of Nature is a result of experiential confinement to its pleasurable aspects: Xie Xuan's "[choice of] a divinely charming spot in Nature in order to exhaust the meaning of lofty living,"[11] the lavish Xie An's likening of himself to the starved Bo Yi (*JS* 79/7:2072)—these display a typical blend of complacent ease and conscious identification of sublimity with Nature.

One of the marks of Tao's greatness lies in the fact that long before the Southern Dynasties critics voiced their objections to *xuanyan shi*, he had realized its untapped potential by wedding poetry to philosophy in a way that enhances the vitality of both. If the *xuanyan* poets' attitude to Nature is that of the refined spiritual-aesthetic connoisseur, Tao's affinity for Nature is unbiased by outward forms. While he may be prompted by mood to visit the wilds (*TYJ* 42) or by fine weather to "climb the heights and write new poems" (*TYJ* 57), he mostly experiences Nature in his farm work. It is this communion with Nature as the stuff of daily life, beyond the horizon of his elite contemporaries, that underlies the unity of the personal and the universal in his lyric voice.

Let us turn once more to "Return" #1 to illustrate the point:

少無適俗韻
性本愛丘山
誤落塵網中
一去十三年
羈鳥戀舊林
池魚思故淵
開荒南野際
守拙歸園田
方宅十餘畝
草屋八九間
榆柳蔭後簷
桃李羅堂前
曖曖遠人村
依依墟里烟
狗吠深巷中
雞鳴桑樹巔
戸庭無塵雜
虚室有餘閑
久在樊籠裏
復得返自然

Since youth I have not fitted the worldly tune;
From the first my nature loved mountains and hills.
By mistake I fell into the dusty net,
And was gone for thirteen years.
The fettered bird yearns for the old woods;
The pond-fish longs for the former deep.
Opening up some waste land by the southern wilds,
I abide by rusticity [*zhuo*], and have returned to my
farmland.
My homestead covers a few acres,
My thatched house several rooms.
Elms and willows shade the rear eaves;
Peaches and plums range before the hall.
Hazy, hazy, the distant villages;
Soft, soft, the smoke from hamlet lanes.
Dogs bark in hidden alleys;
Cocks crow atop mulberry trees.
Within my doors there is no dust or clutter;
In my empty rooms there is leisure to spare.
Long have I been in the confining cage;
Again I have managed to return to Nature.

(*TYJ* 40)

With truth and beauty internalized and accessible, there is no need to travel far to seek the spectacular for illumination. Where all things exude a mellow vitality in their natural place and rhythm, even the poem's form mirrors its content to give a unity of effect. Just as Tao's return involves a homeward motion from afar, so the poem moves from past to present and from general descriptions to concrete details as home draws near. As the poetic lens zooms in and out between tracking shots of neighboring villages and close-up views of his dwelling from in and out, the poet's rustic world takes on a dynamic visual presentness that enhances and vitalizes the truth of his life. At the same time, his move from the relinquished past to the present is structurally mirrored in a subtle series of inversions in which the first and last three couplets are correspondingly linked in transformational resonance: the confined bird and fish give way to the free dogs and cocks, prolonged exile to ample leisure at home, the dusty net to a house "empty" of dust, along with an expansion of inner space even as the physical dimensions of his life are reduced. Superimposed on these inversions are formal embodiments of unity and wholeness: the repetition of the negative (ll. 1, 17) represents a convergence of inclination and reality, while the progression from "poetic" images employed for lyric expression (bird, fish, net) to those forming natural parts of the farm scene also shows a "return" to unity in terms of imagery. One can also turn to the parallelisms of its inner (fourth through ninth) couplets, which are not so symmetrical as to check the lyric flow but close enough to convey a sense of smooth balance and self-sufficient wholeness. The parallel structure is especially significant in light of its infrequent occurrence in Tao's poetry and its absence in the other four poems of the group,[12] which, laced with anxiety and depression, also lack an atmosphere of brimming fullness. All these culminate in the concluding couplet as a quiet fulfillment of the initial yearning, for the worldly tune of the confining cage has turned into Nature's pristine music consummating his innate love of the earth. In this transformation from dissonance between self and the world to unity between self and Nature, the end is the beginning raised to a higher plane through the baptism of experience.

If the poem's initial nonparallel lines in any way imply an original freedom, the final reversion to the flowing form signals a recovery of this state on which the harmonious completeness embodied in the parallel couplets converges. A sense of "completeness in spatial extension"[13] and naturalness of temporal flow combine to give the easy persuasion with which the truth of natural existence comes home.

Shen Deqian (1673–1769) has said "poetry must not lack truth, but is prized only in having a philosophical relish"[14] rather than an odor of abstractions; in Tao's work one surely finds the "beauty of philosophical relish" *(liqu mei)* that became a standard in later Chinese poetics. The truth conveyed by "Return" #1, as embodied in the multivalent term *ziran*, is a return to Nature that is also a return to Dao and the inborn human nature, but as an artist Tao shows more than tells us the truth. While sharing the *xuanyan* poets' perception of Nature and bent for meditation, he does not let the intellect obstruct his feelings; "philosophy"—the Daoist idea of *zhuo* (l. 8)—is blended into art as he describes his life in concrete images and plain, fluid language, fusing them into a meaningful structure that re-creates his physical and spiritual return. The result is a poem profoundly philosophical without being visibly so, whose ambience of peaceful wholeness not only reflects the poet's state but infects the reader, as he is borne on the flow of Nature and poetry to feel the philosophical sense of his empathic and aesthetic experience. Where the personal and the universal merge into each other so seamlessly, the poetic laurel of *qingjing jiaorong* may be expanded to include *li*, an "interfusion of feeling, scene, and truth."

More openly philosophical poems depend on the aptness of their insights and the manner of their conveyance. Certain lines in *Chuci*, for instance, are at once lyric and meditative, resonant in their accurate expression of common truths and experiences which the reader can readily empathize with but not quite articulate:[15]

心不同兮媒勞	Courting is vain if hearts do not meet;
恩不甚兮輕絶	Love that is not deep is easily broken.

(*Jiu ge*: "Xiang jun" [Goddess of the Xiang])

悲莫悲兮生別離	No sorrow exceeds the parting of the living;
樂莫樂兮新相知	No joy surpasses having a new bosom friend.

(*Jiu ge*: "Shao si ming" [Lesser Master of Fate])

Though there are no images by which meaning is embodied or evoked, the language is terse, the lyric sense deep (diluted here out of context), and the truth accessible.

In a similar way, Tao's contemplative verse blends lyric immediacy with precision of tenor and vehicle. Often his generalizations (1 and 2) and restatements of old themes (3 and 4) come across with a memorable vibrance, as popular adages do in being essences of experience:

運生會歸盡	(1) The cycle of life must come to an end—
終古謂之然	From oldest times it has been stated so.
世間有松喬	Immortals Song and Qiao were once in the world,
於今定何間	But now where are they to be found?

(*TYJ* 55)

形迹憑化往	(2) My bodily form passes on with Change,
靈府長獨閑	But my spiritual core *(lingfu)* is always at ease.

(*TYJ* 82)

落地為兄弟	(3) All who are born to earth are brothers;
何必骨肉親	Must they be blood relations?

(*TYJ* 115)

朝與仁義生	(4) Having lived in humanity and righteousness in the morning,
夕死復何求	What more is there to ask if one dies in the evening?

(*TYJ* 125)

While *xuanyan shi* is wont to address metaphysical reality from a distance, Tao's verse mostly conveys the existential truths he feels. This closer proximity of subject matter to the poet's heart naturally makes for a personal voice—which is one mark distinguishing living experience from dry exposition in philosophical verse—and yet what makes *xuanyan shi* abstract is not just the relative remoteness of cosmic principles but the *xuanyan* poets' penchant to speak on the cosmological level. In the poem quoted earlier Sun Chuo tries to raise his practical advice into universal truths by stating it in an impersonal manner, and ends up devitalizing it while distancing himself. Tao, on the other hand, brings the universal down to the personal (1) and the cosmic to the existential (2) by writing what he feels. While the term *lingfu* (2) comes from a brief discourse in *Zhuangzi* on the spirit's independence from the change of things and workings of fate (Z 5/43–45), the lines (as in 1) are savored not as rational explanation but intimate conviction, conveyed through simple language and an unassertive voice. Couplets 3 and 4 come from the *Analects*: "All within the four seas are brothers" (*A* 12/5); "He who has heard the Way in the morning may die in the evening [content]" (*A* 4/8). But here the self-questioning form of the lines (as distinct from the original declarative statements) reflects heartfelt contemplation that makes them closer and more inspiring.

Excerpt 1 above quotes a poem's beginning couplets that move from a general truth in the first to intimate inquiry in the second. In contrast, there are other times when the effect of Tao's philosophical lines is closely linked to their position as crowning conclusions of experience. This is true of excerpt 4 above, a lyric ending to a poem praising the poor worthy Qian Lou, and also of the final lines in "Return" #4, a poignant response to a desolate site (see chapter 2): "Human life is like the changes of an illusion, / Ultimately returning to blank nothingness." Another example is given by "Drinking Wine" #14:

故人賞我趣　My friends appreciate my relish;
挈壺相與至　Wine-jars in hand, they arrive together.
班荊坐松下　Spreading out twigs, we sit under the pine;
數斟已復醉　After several cups we get tipsy again.
父老雜亂言　The old men break into disorderly babbling,
觴酌失行次　Pouring from the jar out of turn.

不覺知有我 Aware no more of my own self,
安知物爲貴 How would I know what things are valuable? 8
悠悠迷所留 Leisurely we remain rapt in where we are—
酒中有深味 There are deep flavors in the wine!

(*TYJ* 95)

Given in the first couplet and fleshed out in the next two, the poem's subject is social drinking, light-hearted rather than sternly metaphysical. The company's merriment is seen in their drunkenness and their discarding of social rites,[16] and the poem stays on this convivial level until the poet floats to a mystical illumination in the "limbo" of consciousness—self-forgetfulness and the dissolution of arbitrary values and differentiations that lead to a total sense of freedom. Taken in the abstract lines 7–8 sound like a versified statement from Zhuangzi, but here the illumination comes as a natural and unexpected culmination of the occasion, the wine having catalyzed the "fasting of the mind." It is important that Tao's feelings remain the poem's impelling force throughout, in fact intensifying toward the end when, sensing the fleetingness of the oblivious moment, he almost tries to prolong it by lingering in the "deep flavors" of the wine. Rising from vivid description vitalized by a sustained lyric presence, lines 7–8 elevate what might remain a local import, bearing out George Eliot's point that "a correct generalisation gives significance to the smallest details."[17]

A unison of form and meaning, the personal and the universal, thus marks Tao's philosophical verse from that of poets of his age. In particular, it will be instructive to turn briefly to his contemporary Xie Lingyun, who took nature poetry in another direction and stands as the founder if not originator of descriptive landscape verse *(shanshui shi)*.[18] Writing half a century after the heyday of *xuanyan shi,* Xie still reflects the Eastern Jin elite's rational-aesthetic attitude toward Nature. "Deng Yongjia Lüzhangshan" (Ascending Green Crag Mountain in Yongjia) will illustrate the point:

裹糧杖輕策 Packing provisions and taking a light staff,
懷遲上幽室 I wind my way up to the secluded place.

行源逕轉遠　As I go upstream the path leads further away;
距陸情未畢　When I step ashore my excitement is not yet spent.
潨激結寒姿　The ripples are congealed in cold beauty;
團欒潤霜質　The bamboos are sleeked with a frosty touch.
澗委水屢迷　As the gorge winds the water is often lost;
林迥巖逾密　As the wood deepens the cliffs get more clustered.
眷西謂初月　I peer westward, saying it's the new moon;
顧東疑落日　Then gaze eastward, wondering if it's the setting sun.
踐夕奄昏曙　I walk in the dark—so fast has dawn turned dusk;
蔽翳皆周悉　Hidden and secret spots are all familiar to me.
蠱上貴不事　Top of "Decay": best not to serve;
履二美貞吉　Second of "Treading":[19] good to be safe in rectitude.
幽人常坦步　A recluse always walks with calm steps;
高尚邈難匹　Noble is he, lofty beyond match.
頤阿竟何端　"Yes" and "no"[20]—which way is it really?
寂寞寄抱一　In solitude I find resort in embracing Unity.[21]
恬知既已交　Since serenity and wisdom have merged,
繕性自此出　The mending of my nature will from this ensue.[22]

(*XLJ* 56)

Victor Mair and Tsu-lin Mei note that Xie's landscape poems "resembled a series of beautifully crafted still-pictures strung together in linear progression."[23] Here, from preparation and ascent through observation to awareness of time passing, the trip is pictorially laid out in a neat order that alternates between land and water, heights and lowlands, far and close views, and opposite directions. We follow the first half of the poem not as a sequence of static scenes, but almost as a graph zigzagging between coordinates balanced on two sides of a poetic axis. Some of the evident qualities of Xie's verse—difficult vocabulary and the resultant jaggy lines, packed syntax, painstaking effort at parallelisms (notably the first ten lines)—are typical of the times, and will be further discussed later (in chapter 8). What is worth noting in this context is Xie's attempt to frame his landscape experience according to a predetermined structural scheme that would support the rationalizations he forges toward the end.

As Lin Wen-yüeh observes, there is a formulaic progression in Xie's landscape poems that comprises journey narration, scene description, personal response, and philosophical meditation.[24] This attribute Lin sees as testimony to Xie's superiority over poets like Bao Zhao (414?–66) and Xie Tiao (464–99), whose landscape poems do not display such formal neatness. But the same evidence also reflects Xie's greater determination to extract meaning out of experience, especially when accompanied by structural disunity and assertiveness of tone. Lines 5–10 show Xie's approach to poetic creation to be a largely mental one: the observation of the ripples and bamboo and their placement in a parallel pattern; the mind's reasoned accounting of visual effects due to shifting angles of perception; and the eyes' strenuous "peering" and "gazing" at Nature in contrast to Tao's spontaneous "seeing" of the Southern Mountains (*TYJ* 89). While in Tao's "Return" #1 meaning exudes from a balanced, liquid form mirroring his inner state, with Xie we see a form conceptually designed to generate such import. The immediate goal of consolation and pleasure[25] is fulfilled not through merging freely into Nature, but through gratifying the senses with her beauty—mostly sight and hearing (as in this poem) but also taste, smell, and touch—and meticulously capturing scene and sensation in ornate language. If Xie had been content with the sensuous fullness of his descriptive world, he might have let go his lyric self and achieved a better integration of the two.

Yet even more than the *xuanyan* poets, Xie is intent on having "the landscape manifest Dao with its graceful forms." Especially since he is a learned Buddhist who has gone through the "emptiness" of politics, his poems (like his excursions) are ultimately to be appreciated as cries for inner liberation, the motivated point of closure which the formal movement from sumptuous description to meditative conclusion is meant to reach. But the abrupt jump in the last eight lines to raw wisdom mined from the Neo-Daoist quarry reflects a change of gear from one mechanical process to another: persuading himself with hexagrams from *Yijing* and two expressions from *Laozi* that it is best to be a noble recluse, he compounds this quadruple allusion with another from *Zhuangzi*, his causal argument heightening a rationalizing tone: "*Since* serenity and wisdom have merged, /

The mending of my nature *will* from this ensue." The message is undermined by its assertiveness, while jamming the lyric voice and leaving the descriptive lines as a discrete block.[26] The urge for philosophical generalization has abstracted a "picture" of life into a "diagram."[27]

For all his fine skill, Xie's "discursive mode of description"[28] often prevents feeling, description, and meditation from coming together, so that structural incoherence remains a basic problem in his landscape poems. To mention one other example briefly: out of eighteen lines in "Fuchun zhu" (The Island off Fuchun River), Xie devotes the first eight to describing his river journey and his impressions along the way (with the usual alternation between land and water scenes), then shifts to a double dose of *Yijing* wisdom in a "deliberate attempt at calmness":[29]

洊至宜便習
兼山貴止託

"Coming recurrently":[30] one should be at ease amid repeated dangers;
"Double mountain":[31] it is important to rest in one's abode.

(*XLJ* 45)

This he further expounds with eight lines of intellectual self-comfort to assure himself of his progress toward spiritual freedom. The philosophizing block not only shows little organic link to its descriptive counterpart but obscures the latter's vividness.

Unlike *xuanyan shi,* Xie's philosophical landscape verse addresses situations in life rather than the cosmos. But if the former's macrocosmic sweep omits to flesh out the universal spirit, the fine verisimilitude of Xie's descriptive realism struggles to go beyond local import to unite with his reflections. Beyond their stylistic divergence, what Xie and the *xuanyan* poets share is an intellectual approach that attempts to make poetry the handmaid of philosophy. But where truth is experiential and assimilable only intuitively, the artistic and philosophical irony of rationalization lies in its self-discounting nature. If no static pattern is discernible in the form and structure of Tao's contemplative verse, it is because no formulaic course can be charted in his experience. While poems like "Return" #1 and "Drinking Wine" #5 sing of the truth of naturalness and simplicity, none reveals (in Buddhist terms) a conscious "craving" for epiphanic insight. Precisely because Xie is often praised as a descriptive poet, the contrastive examples offered by him, Tao, and the *xuanyan* poets point to certain parameters of Chinese philosophical verse. If its artistic basis lies in sentient experience rather than abstract speculation (given the broadly existential nature of Chinese philosophy), its persuasion depends on a unison between the heart, spirit, and mind, which is to say that any convincing appeal to universal truths hinges on the poet's level of illumination. For however skillful he may be, any deficiency in inner understanding and lived conviction is bound to show up as a spiritual and emotive aridity, leaving a rigid mental design and a strident exposition of ready-made ideas as the only substitutes possible. Lyric inspiration and imagistic pregnancy remain the keys to conveying the universal, which even if imparted explicitly can ripple a poem's meaning when voiced at an optimal point. Only when vitalized as living experience and heartfelt lyricism, embodied in evocative imagery, and couched in reverberating language, will philosophy take on artistic validity and lend depth to personal expression.

Blending the best in *xuanyan shi* into his verse to give a profound yet assimilable "relish," Tao's meditative lyricism realizes the potential of a marriage between philosophy and art. It would be no misnomer to consider him the unwitting founder of Chinese philosophical verse, for later poets were to follow the path he opened up:

白日依山盡　　The white sun fades by the mountains;
黃河入海流　　The Yellow River flows into the sea.
欲窮千里目　　If you want to exercise your far-sighting eyes,
更上一層樓　　Go up another story!

(*QTS* 8:2849)[32]

問余何意栖碧山　　You ask me why I lodge in the green hills;
笑而不答心自閒　　I smile without replying, my heart easy of itself.

桃花流水窅然去 別有天地非人間	Peach blossoms drifting on flowing waters leave in silence— There is another realm different from the world of men.

(*QTS* 5:1813)[33]

橫看成嶺側成峰 遠近高低各不同 不識廬山真面目 只緣身在此山中	A range seen from the front, a peak from the side; Far, near, high, low—every angle looks different. I know not the true countenance of Mount Lu, Only because I am in its midst.[34]
竹杖芒鞋輕勝馬 誰怕 一簑煙雨任平生	Bamboo staff, grass sandals, lighter than a saddle— Who cares? A straw cloak in mist and rain, unfettered all my life.[35]

The sparkling resonance of these lines requires no further elaboration. Suffice it to say that in a masterly hand any higher truth is an additional dimension integrated into a self-contained text, and that Keats could not have criticized a true philosophical poet for intruding upon art with a "palpable design."[36]

7

"Farmstead Poetry" and the Western Pastoral

Thus far, we have seen how Tao's poetry is marked by a polyhedral unity between the realistic and ideal, the spiritual and material, the finite and infinite, the personal and universal, and the artistic and philosophical. The same unity also makes his nature poetry the prototype of what has come to be known as "farmstead poetry"*(tianyuan shi)*: poetry that deals mainly with rural subjects observed or experienced, from country scenes and objects to the life and feelings of rustics or the poets themselves.[1] It is reflective of a universal human spirit that this focus on rural life and frequent praise of rustic simplicity over urban sophistication have prompted Sino-Western comparatists to call *tianyuan shi* "pastoral,"[2] perhaps in a loose "modern use" of the term to mean "any poem of rural people and setting."[3] The equivalence is not drawn without deeper reason, for both *tianyuan shi* and pastoral verse stem from a common yearning for happiness and innocence, and a shared perception that these ideal states can be realized in Nature. As taken by most critics, however, "pastoral" usually means "an elaborately conventional poem expressing an urban poet's nostalgic image of the peace and simplicity of the life of shepherds and other rural folk in an idealized natural setting"[4]—typically, it may be recalled, in the context of an imaginary golden age. This brings to attention the nature of the rural worlds in Tao's poetry and pastoral verse, along with the perspectives from and manners in which they are portrayed.[5] An outline of the essential attributes of pastoral verse is thus in order.

As noted in our previous discussion of Theocritus (in chapter 3), pastoral verse is from the outset an urban myth about rural matters. The "pastorals proper" of his *Idylls* feature shepherds basking in emotional leisure and material plenty, engaged in song contests and love pursuits where frustration becomes occasion and inspiration for more poetry. The disappointed pastor's hyperbolic protestation of love in Idyll 3 shows his "ache" and "restlessness" to be literary rather than real,[6] while the ugly Polyphemus's sentimental lyricism in Idyll 11 reaches comic proportions as he sings all day to the nymph Galatea, leaving "his flock . . . [to] come home to the cave unshepherded":

> But fine looks could not buy me the flock I graze,
> A thousand strong, nor the milk I draw and drink
> Nor the cheese which lasts through summer into autumn
> And loads the racks down even to winter's end.
> No other Cyclops plays the pipe as I can,
> Singing far into the night, my silver pippin. . . .
> Baytrees and slender cypresses grow [by my cave], ivy
> With its dark leaves and vines with sugary grapes.[7]

Economic abundance, enchanting music, and a lovely dwelling form the Cyclops's line of persuasion, but more remarkable is how the hideous becomes infected with an idyllic charm undiminished by his "sadness." Peter Marinelli notes "no one ever recorded that pastoral nostalgia propelled Theocritus into action to leave Alexandria and recover the simple delights of his boyhood";[8] the pastoral sentiment is a townsman's longing for rusticity that knows itself to be a fantasy.

That this is so is more amply borne out in Virgil's *Eclogues*, modelled on the *Idylls* and even further removed from rural realities. Not that all is perfect in Arcadia: we hear Meliboeus complaining "where strife has led / Rome's wretched citizens,"[9] and witness a sharp quarrel between Menalcas and Damoetas.[10] But everything is readily resolved within an easy atmosphere: the "ripe fruit / And mealy chestnuts and abundance of milk cheese" to which Tityrus treats Meliboeus neutralize the latter's misfortune, while the discord between Menalcas and Damoetas soon transforms into a harmonious amoebean song. With its equable climate and soft contours, Arcadia is essentially a disinfected mythical space where "keen pleasure grips forest and countryside, Pan also, and the shepherds, and the Dryad maids."[11] In fact, the pagan sentiment soon took on a Christian connotation through the convergence of meanings in the word *pastor*, shepherd and priest, and "through the influence of pastoral life visible in the Scriptures."[12] While Arcadian life reaches its most idyllic in the "Messianic eclogue" (#4) that ties the golden-age prophecy to the birth of a wondrous child, the Bible seems from the start to lend support to the pastoral vision, at least during man's prelapsarian days when the ready-made fertility of Eden was replete with animal and plant life awaiting his use: "And out of the ground the LORD God made to grow every tree that is pleasant to the sight and good for food."[13] The common ground between the pagan and Christian visions thus guarantees pastoral as a universal emblem of innocence and a plentiful setting for happiness—perennial desiderata shared by both traditions as man looks back with nostalgia and regret.

It is, of course, these desiderata which underlie the perpetual charm of the Arcadian landscape, for as a token of inner yearning it carries a capacity to defy empirical veracity yet remain close to the heart. Through the personal, moral, and allegorical concerns Spenser (1552?–99) explores in *The Shepherd's Calender*, for instance, the pastoral life depicted remains similar to that in Theocritus and Virgil, even though the tone and intent with which it is conveyed varies among his eclogues.[14] The pastoral life comes to a highlight in Marlowe's (1564–

93) famous "The Passionate Sheepheard to His Love," where the enamored swain sings of rural bliss much like Theocritus's Cyclops:

> Come live with mee, and be my love,
> And wee will all the pleasures prove,
> That Vallies, groves, hills and fieldes,
> Woods, or steepie mountaine yeeles.
>
> And wee will sit upon the Rocks,
> Seeing the Sheepheards feede their flocks,
> By shallow Rivers, to whose falls,
> Melodious byrds sings Madrigalls.
>
> And I will make thee beds of Roses,
> And a thousand fragrant poesies, . . .
> Fayre lined slippers for the cold:
> With buckles of the purest gold. . . .
>
> The Sheepheards Swaines shall daunce and sing,
> For thy delight each May-morning.[15]

The wooer's promise of expensive ornaments for his love, the reduction of time to spring mornings, the birds' singing of complicated songs and the ubiquitous "pleasures" which everything "yeeles" reflect a familiar suspension of reality and artificiality of imagery. Much the same high rhetoric, underlined by the classical mythical pantheon which Marlowe did not employ, is evident in Pope's (1688–1744) season-structured "Pastorals." Pope admits that "this sort of poetry derives almost its whole beauty from a natural ease of thought and smoothness of verse"[16]—so much so that even the sting of death is transformed into jubilation. Another convention laid down by Virgil in his fifth Eclogue, this trick of apotheosis, with "the mode of the dirge yielding to the mode of the panegyric,"[17] is one adopted (with Christian overtones) by Spenser in *The Shepherd's Calender*, Milton in "Lycidas" and Pope in "Pastorals."[18] Even the ultimate existential experience is translated into literary terms.

For conventional pastoral is based not on experience but on "a sentimental or aesthetic illusion" stemming from "a double longing after innocence and happiness."[19] Since "pastoral is an image of what they call the Golden age," the "illusion" one must use to sustain this image "consists in exposing the best side only of a shepherd's life, and in concealing its miseries."[20] What counts is not "Object" but "Idea"; pastoral verse "must not be confin'd to the bare Representation of real Truth" but "ought to rise as far as Ideal Truth."[21] This desire to shun reality intensifies when the impulse of wish-fulfillment is mixed with the town-poet's contempt for the peasant's coarseness and simplicity—the very things he idealizes[22]—so that despite laying claim to an imaginary ideal, pastoral verse has been slighted since first noted among the literary genres during the Renaissance.[23] If perfecting reality offers one reason for the artificiality of pastoral verse, the same is vindicated on the ground that the subject matter is poetically worthy only with due embellishment—and then largely as a testing ground for serious literary destiny. Pastoral verse becomes in part a kind of verbal training not accountable to reality: just as Virgil "graduated" from the *Eclogues* to the *Aeneid*, so Spenser, Milton, and Pope (who wrote his "Pastorals" before he was twenty) all took pastoral verse as a poetic apprenticeship or initiation from which to move to more heroic forms.

The result of such conceptions and attitudes is that realism is not part of the core pastoral heritage. This does not mean it is all decorative—only that those whose frame of reference is a social alternative have to face the problem of its reality. Even while affirming the regenerative power of the country and the values it fosters, Shakespeare and Jonson, with measured humor and irony, deflate not only pastoral's stock conventions but its possibility as a social option—both on the basis of realism. Not only do we see Amiens laud the banished Duke Senior for poeticizing the forest of Arden "into so quiet and so sweet a style," and the caricatured Silvius and Phoebe set against the real figures of Audrey and William, but rustic people and life are revealed in their imperfection. Touchstone's wooing of Audrey is pure farce, and their marriage is no index of social integration. In

Jonson's poem the fish's and fowls' eager volunteering as food shows that he is poking fun at the social vision he portrays. Clearly Shakespeare and Jonson recognize that the pastoral world cannot be transplanted to reality.

Pastoral thus continues largely as a fabricating mode borne out of a perennial psychological impulse, slighted yet used for various purposes by serious poets not content with its decorative terms, and who remain critical of its untruthful nature even though they recognize it is never meant to be realistic. While Marlowe draws his picture of overflowing love, music, and leisure, Ralegh (1552?-1618) fills in what Marlowe has denied by writing "The Nimphs Reply to the Sheepheard":

> Time drives the flockes from field to fold,
> When Rivers rage, and Rocks grow cold, . . .
> The flowers doe fade, and wanton fieldes,
> To wayward Winter reckoning yeeldes.[24]

While Shakespeare and Jonson mock their own nostalgia, Cervantes (1547–1615) makes game of his hero in *Don Quixote,* whose pastoral dream is as much an imitation of literary convention as his self-appointed mission to revive feudal chivalry.[25] Invoking his fancy again after the bankruptcy of his enterprise, Quixote yearns, in a gesture of double pretense, "to revive another pastoral Arcadia" after witnessing an aristocratic staging of the same:

> We will wander through the mountains, woods and meadows, singing here, lamenting there, drinking of the liquid crystals of the springs, or of the limpid streams, or the mighty rivers. The oaks shall give us of their sweetest fruit with generous hands; the trunks of the hard cork-trees shall offer us seats; the willows, shade; the roses, perfume; the broad meadows, carpets of a thousand blended colours.[26]

Coordinating its utility for man without "till and keep" such as is required even in Eden in order to maintain its harmony,[27] Quixote's nature bears out the fantastic and at times escapist vein of pastoral as it does his own.

More than any other difference, it is the divide of realism which marks Tao's farmstead poetry from pastoral verse. On one level pastoral presumes a contract between writer and reader: its unnatural portrait of life in nature is accepted as a deliberately artificial construction that is the basis of its exotic charm. And had it offered a pure aesthetic fancy, there would have been less ground for a comparison with Tao's poetry. But the inherent ambiguity of pastoral is that its world is no mere expedient mental territory but also a critical expression of social sentiment, and it is this serious undercurrent which nullifies its immunity from the measure of realism. What Shakespeare, Ralegh, and Cervantes indicate is that the invisibility of rural realities in pastoral represents a falsification of experience that remains an artistic flaw, for which no picturesque charm of the landscape or mellifluous grace of lyricism can be adequate recompense.[28] Here one returns to Tao's *tianyuan shi*, which, borne out of husbandry experience, shows a balanced appreciation of the freedom and vulnerability of rustic life, from the delights of work and material privation—

平疇交遠風　The level fields meet the breeze from afar;
良苗亦懷新　The fine shoots, too, bear a new life.

(*TYJ* 77)

風雨縱横至　Wind and rain come from every direction;
收斂不盈廛　The harvest does not fill household needs.

(*TYJ* 49)

—to domestic contentment and plaintive reflection—

好味止園葵　My favorite food stops with garden mallows;
大歡止稚子　My great delight stops with my young sons.

(*TYJ* 100)

人生似幻化　Human life is like the changes of an illusion,
終當歸空無　Ultimately returning to blank nothingness.

(*TYJ* 42)

—and even simple rural scenes:

種豆南山下	I planted beans below the southern hill;
草盛豆苗稀	The weeds flourish, but the bean shoots are few.

(*TYJ* 42)

日入室中闇	As the sun sets the house turns dark;
荆薪代明燭	Thorn firewood takes the place of bright candles.

(*TYJ* 43)

Complete with the inclemencies of rural life and a range of moods, Tao's verse features not aesthetic shepherds but real farm workers worried about their crops; the variegations of its spectrum correlate to those in his life and ideals.

One poem, which touches on the main themes of Tao's poetry, will further illustrate the point:

藹藹堂前林	Thick, thick the woods before the hall;
中夏貯清陰	In midsummer they store up cool shade.
凱風因時來	The south wind comes with the season;
回飈開我襟	Its swirling gusts flap open my gown.
息交遊閑業	Done with socializing, I enjoy relaxing pursuits;
臥起弄書琴	Rising from sleep, I fondle my books and lute.
園蔬有餘滋	The garden greens grow to a surplus;
舊穀猶儲今	Last year's grain is still unfinished today.
營己良有極	Providing for oneself has its limits;
過足非所欽	More than enough is not my desire.
舂秫作美酒	I pound sorghum to brew good wine,
酒熟吾自斟	And when the wine is ripe, I pour it out myself.
弱子戲我側	My young son plays at my side,
學語未成音	Learning to speak, but cannot yet make the sounds.
此事真復樂	These things are truly delightful,
聊用忘華簪	For a while helping me forget the ornate hairpin [of office].
遙遙望白雲	Far, far off, I watch the white clouds,
懷古一何深	How deep is my longing for the past!

("Matching Recorder Guo's Poem" #1, *TYJ* 60)

Set in a season of ripening, the poem begins with lively images of a cordial Nature, its lush foliage keeping the poet cool in midsummer and its fresh breeze "flapping open" his heart. Enjoying the added company of his lute, books, and "relaxing pursuits," he is spiritually and emotionally at ease in his rustic life of quietude and simplicity. Meanwhile, with his usual realism following experience rather than stock portraits of reclusion, he sings of the ample provisions that allow such eremitic joys, made more accessible by their modesty and by his appreciative attitude to his circumstances—which also include good wine and his young son. The reader would agree that "these things are truly delightful," for he is in touch not with assertions of happiness but with vivacious images, concrete conditions, and detailed activities attesting to the poet's rapport with Nature and existence. In fact, with both experienced at their most benign, line 16 would have been a convincing ending to the poem—had it not suddenly turned to the image of the white clouds. Linked to the poet's "deep longing," this final image is indefinite in import but hints at disquiet. Coming at the end of a poem joyous throughout, the clouds seem to symbolize in their floating form the freedom and transcendence of the spirit. But such a state remains tantalizingly remote, showing that for all his contentment, Tao knows he is far from attaining the perfect peace of mind that is the desideratum of his being. What is more, the image itself remains ambiguous, for it also suggests a veil of gloom (perhaps even rootlessness) cast over his heart much like the hanging clouds do in their namesake poem (*TYJ* 11). With a deeply embedded sense of mission never forgotten save "for a while," Tao cannot overcome his frustration at being denied the chance to carry out his duty to mankind. The domestic tranquility of the present seems to drift away as the white clouds convey his longing back to a purer and more fulfilling past. The plurality of theme, the complexity of mood, and the realism of content in this representative poem all distinguish Tao's poetry from pastoral verse.

But perhaps the contrast between the two is seen at its sharpest in "Peach Blossom Spring," for it shows that even at his most "Arcadian," Tao's rural landscape is never removed from a solid sense of reality, a sublimation rather than a distortion of experience. As scholars have long noted, the world of "Peach Blossom Spring" is very familiar;[29] it will suffice to recall some of the scenes in Tao's farming life mentioned before:

榆柳蔭後簷	Elms and willows shade the rear eaves;
桃李羅堂前	Peaches and plums range before the hall.
曖曖遠人村	Hazy, hazy, the distant villages;
依依墟里烟	Soft, soft, the smoke from hamlet lanes.
狗吠深巷中	Dogs bark in hidden alleys;
雞鳴桑樹巔	Cocks crow atop mulberry trees.

(*TYJ* 40)

晨興理荒穢	At dawn I rise to clear away the weeds,
帶月荷鋤歸	Bringing along the moon, I return shouldering my hoe.

(*TYJ* 42)

漉我新熟酒	I strain my newly ripened wine,
隻雞招近局	And to a single chicken treat my neighbors.

(*TYJ* 43)

農務各自歸	After farm work each returns to his home;
閑暇輒相思	In our leisure we always think of one another.

(*TYJ* 57)

That is why Tao's ideal landscape remains real: the utopian community is realistic in construction though idealistic in conception, purged of whatever fantastic elements the original tale might have had as a popular legend about immortals (*D* 1:200). If Zhuangzi gives us a sense of the spirit's infinite expansion to unite with Dao, what Tao imparts is a sense of the Way residing in the daily rhythms of existence. The classless society with its lack of exploitation is idealistic in the absence of historical evidence, yet strikes one as real not only because one may readily agree this is how reality should be (the same cannot be said of the all-easy pastoral world), but because all that is needed to realize this ordinary ideal is the peacefulness of human motive.

Besides, there is a difference in language between Tao's *tianyuan shi* and pastoral verse, whose parlance is as much convoluted rhetoric as its content. In Quixote's speech springs are "liquid crystals," meadows colorful "carpets," mother earth a "fertile and broad bosom," rivers "mighty," and abundance "glorious."[30] But if Quixote at least speaks as a man of education, the words put into the rustics' mouths have always demanded us to suspend our disbelief. Theocritus's "verbal gymnastics" involves a "vocabulary . . . often far-fetched" as "he constantly strains his language in search of novelty in idiom and construction"; even his supposedly rustic Doric is an "invented dialect" mixed eclectically with other dialects for literary purposes.[31] Virgil's Arcadians live even farther beyond their verbal and intellectual means,[32] and their cultivated effusions show Virgil consciously taking pastoral in literary terms. While most Renaissance critics declare "by the law of decorum . . . that [pastoral] style should be 'base and humble,'"[33] actual style remains formal and elaborate despite all guises, for "artificial" language was usually highly regarded by the Elizabethans.[34] Marlowe's creation of a world of musical harmony, for instance, shows an even more sophisticated presentation of rusticity than its classical models. The repeated long and short "I/i:" sounds in the first stanza set the mellifluous key; the singing birds signify Nature's echo of the poem's melody; and the light, swinging rhythm of the first line in the last stanza enacts the "delight each May-morning." It is significant that Ralegh's response makes a similar use of sound effects: the rhymes in long vowels /əʊ/ and /i:/ and the alliteration of /f/, /r/, and /w/ also add up to a meandering musicality, except that with the restored realism and the landscape's darkened tone, the song quality has an ironic, hollow ring about it, sustained only to prove its own falsity.

In contrast, Tao's farmstead poetry is marked by lucid language and a directly expressive voice, his farmscape free from mythical allusions and populated by ordinary creatures rather than gods. If hills, birds, fish, and one or two plants are more readily identifiable as images, the line between image and object is often hard to draw where his language expresses quotidian experience, for it points to both the poet's diction and the rustic's life. "Farmer's words"[35] like "hamlet lanes," "level fields," "dogs bark," "cocks crow," "fine shoots," "beans and millet," "frost and hail," "shouldering hoe," and "work keenly at farming" blend life and art into a simple beauty without heavy adornment:

相見無雜言	When we meet there is no idle chatter,
但道桑麻長	Only talk of how mulberry and hemp have grown.

(*TYJ* 41)

晨興理荒穢	At dawn I rise to clear away the weeds;
帶月荷鋤歸	Bringing along the moon, I return shouldering my hoe.

(*TYJ* 42)

Since Tao speaks personally and in a lucid style, there exists no problem of artistic language, be it the ambiguity of a precious presentation of simplicity or of shepherds speaking beyond their means. The former always threatens to be a contradiction; the latter is a question of realism amplified by the often dramatic form of pastoral verse, for it incurs the necessity of invoking verbal gems from uncouth lips.

It would be hard to locate earlier literati verse that takes rural life as its main subject.[36] Only in folk lyricism do we hear "the hungry man sing of his food and the weary man sing of his tasks,"[37] but even in *Shijing* there are but a few pieces dealing centrally with agricultural life in either a largely factual (e.g., #154) or celebratory manner (e.g., #210–12). Even after farming had come to be wedded to reclusion as literati shunning politics took to rustic life,[38] very little poetry of reclusion that actually mentions the farmstead was written in the millenium between *Shijing* and the sudden full-blown maturity of farmstead poetry in Tao. The only significant poem in the present context is the short "Wood-Hitting Game Song" (mid-first century at the latest):

日出而作	When the sun rises I get up;
日入而息	When the sun sets I rest.
鑿井而飲	I dig a well to drink;
耕田而食	I till the fields to eat.
帝力於我何有哉	The emperor's might—what is it to me![39]

(*XQH* 1:1)

The general descriptions and collective voice in *Shijing* have given way to an immediate individual lyric presence that serves as an important link to Tao—as do the authentic existence and natural freedom which the simple life and fields constitute.[40]

In writing about his daily life, then, Tao stands as the unwitting founder of what became another poetic genre three centuries later with the efforts of his High Tang emulators.[41] In due course *tianyuan shi* developed a more social outlook with broad sympathy for rustic suffering, but never again did it achieve the same immediacy of lyric effect. One reason is that the widening of perspective from the personal to the social necessitates a relative shift from the lyric to the descriptive. But another lies in the way experience affects the poetic voice—and not only in that imitative idealizations of farmstead life are bound to be a shade wanting beside the expression of a poet who lived that life. For if later poets can express the joys of reclusive country life in the first person, they generally have to stay within the third-person voice in describing rural hardship because they lack the personal experience to speak directly, and cannot put poetry into the rustics' mouths in the manner of the pastoral poets. On the other hand, though Tao does not set out to expose rural woes, the farming concerns and privations which he expresses directly have a lot in common with those of his fellow rustics, so that his personal lyricism may well take on a social dimension in reflecting what they could have said:

躬親未曾替	I have never deserted my work,
寒餒常糟糠	Yet in cold and hunger I often eat chaff.

(*TYJ* 119)

夏日抱長飢	On summer days I bear continuous hunger;
寒夜無被眠	Through winter nights I sleep without a cover.
造夕思雞鳴	Toward dusk I long for the cock to crow;
及晨願烏遷	At dawn I wish the sun would move away.

(*TYJ* 49–50)

If pastoral is ultimately too conventional a form for an author to discover himself in it, Tao's farmstead poetry is an integral part of his personal history and artistic individuality, marked not by a customary disjunction but a close expressive link between imagination and reality, artist and creation, tenor and vehicle. We do not expect to find the pastoral poet inhabiting the blissful land he depicts, but we know Tao leads the life of his verse because it is a graphic record rather than a cartographic projection. If we find the slices of life he draws close and touching, it is not because he somehow engineers us to preconceived effects, but because, as Coleridge reminds us, "the loveliness and the wonders of the world" often blurred by "the film of familiarity and selfish solicitude" become manifest "where there is a meditative and feeling mind to seek after them."[42] Without being conscious in a Wordsworthian manner of an "augmented and sustained" soul in himself and seeing it his "office upon earth" to break through habitual response and revive numbed feelings,[43] Tao manages without over-willing it "to give the charm and novelty to things of every day, and to excite a feeling analogous to the supernatural, by awakening the mind's attention from the lethargy of custom" that has blinded the common sight to the luster of ordinary experience.[44] Sensitive perception, deep feeling, and truthful spirit converge in a rare union that underlies an original gift of revealing what is lost to the bedimmed eye—the radiant beauty of simple life and the transcendental truth immanent in the natural world.

8

Crystallinity of Language and Style

Granted that all art has its technical side, it would be a contradiction in terms were a truth of simplicity and naturalness couched in a language muffled in its adornments, so that stylistic simplicity is also a thematic attribute in Tao's work. It is part of the poet's artistic instinct that his language and style are as unaffected as the life from which they flow, notable since here again he was above the confines of his age. For about the time when *xuanyan shi* had spent its force, there revived an opposite trend toward embellishment that was to dominate Chinese aesthetics until the early eighth century, a taste evident in the "florid exuberance" of Cao Zhi (*SP* 20) and pervasive among Western Jin poets like Zhang Hua (232–300), Pan Yue (247–300) and Lu Ji. It is as if the lyric void of *xuanyan* verse rekindled a need for a sense of fullness in descriptive luxuriance. Usually dubbed Taikang (280–89) style, such poetry is considered "weaker in vitality than Jian'an writing" (*WD* 6/1:67), as may be illustrated by Lu Ji's "Zeng Shangshulang Gu Yanxian" (Presented to Secretarial Court Gentleman Gu Yanxian):

朝游遊層城	At dawn I set off, traveling to the storied city;
夕息旋直廬	At dusk I rest, returning to the officers' lodge.
迅雷中宵激	Swift thunder peals in the middle of the darkness;
驚電光夜舒	Startling lightning streaks in the lit-up night.
玄雲拖朱閣	Black clouds drag across the vermilion towers;
振風薄綺疏	Flapping winds press against the lattice windows.
豐注溢修霤	Lavish downpours overflow from the long gutters;
黄潦浸階除	Yellow puddles steep the terrace stairs.
停陰結不解	The stagnant gloom clots and does not disperse;
通衢化爲渠	Wide thoroughfares are transformed into trenches.
沈稼湮梁潁	Sunken crops lie under water in Liang and Ying;
流民泝荆徐	Refugee peasants drift toward Jing and Xu.
眷言懷桑梓	With deep concern I think of my home—
無乃將爲魚	Aren't they all turning into fish!

(#2 of 2, *XQH* 1:680–81)

Ornate diction, meticulous description, and lavish parallelisms (five out of seven couplets are completely parallel) comprise the rhetorical devices that give the poem an effect of dense refinement. The graphic portrayal of Nature certainly differs from Guo Pu's fantastic imagination, but Lu's penchant for verbal elaboration plants the stormy spectacle (to which four couplets are devoted) squarely at the center of the poem, thus displacing somewhat the human tragedy and the commiserating lyric voice. In time to lead to the aesthetic formalism of "palace-style" poetry *(gongti shi)* during the Liang (502–57) and Chen (557–89) dynasties,[1] such a flowery style was in full bloom in Tao's time under the painstaking efforts of Xie Lingyun and his admirers.[2]

In order to place Tao's lucid style in better perspective, it will be useful to look at Xie's verse in some detail again, not only because he was the laureate poet of the Southern Dynasties but because he and Tao, coevals who apparently never met, were China's first major nature poets who turned the same broad theme into sharply contrastive effects. With his keen power of observation, Xie presents the beauty of natural forms in striking language:

白雲抱幽石　　White clouds embrace the dark rocks;
綠篠媚清漣　　Green dwarf-bamboos grace the clear ripples.

(*XLJ* 41)

石淺水潺湲　　The stones lie shallow as water purls over them;
日落山照曜　　As the sun goes down the mountains reflect its glare.

(*XLJ* 51)

曉霜楓葉丹　　In the dawn frost the maple leaves flush red;
夕曛嵐氣陰　　In the evening glow mountain mists turn dark.

(*XLJ* 54)

密林含餘清　　The dense forest carries a lingering freshness;
遠峰隱半規　　A distant peak hides half the disc of the sun.

(*XLJ* 82)

One can see how care is taken to capture almost every sensory aspect of the landscape—its views and objects, visual charms, and auditory effects—including an optical illusion created while viewing the scenery in motion:

洲島驟迴合　　Isles and aits abruptly swerve and join;
圻岸屢崩奔　　Shores and banks repeatedly crash and rush.

(*XLJ* 191)

Not only is Nature framed into an order of tidy beauty, but the observer accurately follows the sensory logic of the scenes before him:

澗委水屢迷　　As the gorge winds the water often goes astray;
林迥巖逾密　　As the wood deepens the cliffs get more clustered.

(*XLJ* 56)

崖傾光難留　　With the cliffs so sheer the light can hardly linger;
林深響易奔　　With the forest so deep sounds easily echo.

(*XLJ* 174)

連岩覺路塞	Linking crags make me feel my way is blocked;
密竹使徑迷	Thick bamboos cause the path to become lost.

(*XLJ* 178)

石横水分流	The rocks lying traverse, the water divides its flow;
林密蹊絶蹤	The wood being dense, the trail loses its course.

(*XLJ* 118)

It is obvious that such a style borrows heavily from the techniques of the Han descriptive *fu*, with its exhaustive verbiage meant to conjure up an overwhelming effect and well-suited for grand spectacles of all kinds.[3] Description in *Shijing* is brief and guided by the lyric impulse, occurring mostly because of the stimulus effect scenes and objects have on the sensibility *(xing)*, or of analogical or contrastive comparisons between a human situation and a natural correlative *(bi)*. While more elaborate descriptions are found in *Chuci*, they remain subordinate to the lyric purpose in the main pieces like "Li sao"; it is in poems like "Zhao hun" and "Da zhao," with their detailed depictions of the horrific wilderness meant to frighten the wandering soul home, that we see something of the method amplified in Han *fu*. The generic weakness of the epideictic *fu* is that its exuberant verbal fabric sometimes deteriorates into a catalog of names and details, blotting out in their enumerative excess any clear sense of a coherent panorama. Such delineation typically ends with a set moral message, to be sure, but often so inconsequential and haphazardly tacked that it provides little more than a flimsy excuse of piety for descriptive indulgence.

Notwithstanding its limitations, it is easy to see how the florid language of Han *fu* would appeal to the Six Dynasties poet. In the case of *shanshui shi*, moreover, the borrowing is also related to its subject matter. Despite the early efforts of such poets as Lu Ji and Zhang Xie, there existed before the Eastern Jin no *shi* heritage with the landscape as its main subject, so that techniques for a fine, realistic portrayal of Nature remained to be developed. No doubt thinking that Nature's vivid forms and sounds should be matched by a colorful language, Xie, like most writers of his time, turned to *fu* for the verbal resources and extended natural descriptions it offers.[4] Such cross-generic influence was reflected in a similar characterization of *fu* and the *shi* of this period: while Shen Yue remarked how "[Sima] Xiangru skillfully fabricated a language of formal verisimilitude *(xingsi)*" (*SS* 67/6:1778),[5] Liu Xie observed that

> In recent times literature has been prized for formal verisimilitude. Poets fathom their feelings amid the landscape, exploring the forms of grass and plants. . . . Hence the use of skilled phrasing for precise delineations like ink paste for imprinting seals, which without further shaping and trimming present the minutest details in exact form. (*WD* 46/2:345)[6]

Now the part of Shen's *Song shu* containing the above quotation was finished in 488,[7] and it is a moot point whether or not Liu Xie borrowed the term *xingsi* from him. But Liu certainly saw the link between Han *fu* and the *shi* of his time when he noted that since the early Liu-Song,

> Writers have adopted parallel couplets that extend to hundreds of words, and vied to achieve the wondrous by a single line. Their wish is always to present things via a thorough description of form, while their language exhausts all effort in pursuit of the novel. (*WD* 6/1:67)[8]

For the technique of *fu* is itself one of "thorough treatment of sounds and visual forms in order to exhaust literary effects" (*WD* 7/1:88), which includes arranging words in parallel lines like "columns of fish" (*WD* 46/2:341). While expressing sentiments or intent, *shi* was also striving to describe things *(ti wu)* in the manner of *fu* (*WD* 8/1:88, 46/2:345).[9]

It is clear Xie has transplanted the verbal pyrotechnics of Han *fu* to his poetry. A description of mountains invokes such lexical erudition as *yan'e* 巘崿 ("high") and *quqin* 嶇嶔 ("crisscross"), while pheasants' cries become *yao yao hui fang gou* 鷕鷕翬方雊 ("'Yao, yao' cried the hen-pheasants, and the cock-pheasants too were crying") (*XLJ* 54, 64, 161). Added to these epideictic words are other simple-looking ones that are in fact "incomprehensible without a teacher's instruction" (*WD* 39/2:236): the first two words in *xie zuo jing he gan*

解作竟何感 (*XLJ* 118) refer to Hexagram 40 "Xie" in *Yijing*, and the line can be literally rendered as "'Unleash' and 'arise': what does [Nature] pulse?" to give some sense of the compressed syntax due to obtrusive philosophical allusion. Even without such allusion the syntax may be packed: *lan dai huan cu jin* 攬帶緩促衿 ("I pull at my belt—slack is the once-fitting gown"; *XLJ* 54) probably takes its cue from a more smoothly expressive line in "Nineteen Ancient Poems"#1—*yi dai ri yi huan* 衣帶日已緩 ("The belt of my robe daily grows looser")—but with more information loaded and words excised to fit the five-character mold.[10] As He Yisun (fl. 1637) writes, "[Xie's verse] is densely packed and not spacious enough; though abounding with fine lines, it is too heavy and hurts the spirit."[11]

There are, in fact, moments when Xie's Nature "pulses":

雲日相輝映	Clouds and sun each reflects the other's radiance:
空水共澄鮮	Sky and water share a crystalline freshness.

(*XLJ* 84)

海鷗戲春岸	Seagulls play on the spring shore;
天雞弄和風	Pheasants sport in the mild breeze.

(*XLJ* 118)

Scenes vibrant with Nature's flowing vitality are not easy to come by, however, and Xie's fine delineations of natural forms usually consist of individual couplets. The general artistic effect is one of overwrought denseness, so that even Zhong Hong, for all his admiration of Xie's "ornate richness" (*SP* 2) in line with period taste, felt compelled to criticize his verse for being "rather encumbered by superfluous ornateness" (*SP* 29). As Qian Zhongshu incisively points out, "while Xie's poetry takes its material from the objects and phenomena of Nature, his style is unnatural; the artificialities of his words and phrases frequently show the chisel marks of a sculpturing that never quite manages to remove the patching traces of workmanship. He never reaches the stage where the most skillful seems not to cut and polish at all, where one who is capable of fine craftsmanship appears not to exert any effort."[12]

Perhaps even more visible is Xie's pervasive use of parallelisms:

山行窮登頓
水涉盡洄沿
岩峭嶺稠疊
洲縈渚連綿
白雲抱幽石
綠篠媚清漣

Trekking the hills, I exhaust their heights and depths;
Fording the waters, I comb their courses upstream and
down.
Crags stand sheer, ranges densely layered;
Islets curve about, sandbanks stretch on and on.
White clouds embrace the dark rocks;
Green dwarf-bamboos grace the clear ripples.

(*XLJ* 41)

舍舟眺迴渚
停策倚茂松
. . . .
俛視喬木杪
仰聆大壑灇

Leaving my boat, I look out at the distant sandbanks;
Halting my staff, I lean against a lush pine.
. . . .
Looking down, I view the tops of the tall trees;
Looking up, I listen to the torrents in the broad valleys.

(*XLJ* 118)

遡溪終水涉
登嶺始山行
. . . .
憩石挹飛泉
攀林搴落英

Moving upstream, I finish fording through the water;
Climbing the ranges, I begin hiking up the hills.
. . . .
Resting upon a rock I cup a cataract,
And climbing trees cull dying blossoms.

(*XLJ* 98)

Schematically arranged with mountains followed by waters, a view of the above by one below, a distant by a close-up view, such parallelisms leave everything neatly mapped out against one another.[13]

While it would be idle to suppose this is how one takes in the landscape, parallelism has by this time become a naturalized feature in *shi* poetry. In fact, Chinese verse has from the outset leaned toward the couplet as a prosodic unit, with rhymes generally occurring at the end of even-numbered lines and with each line being a grammatically complete sentence. Then with the establishment of five-character verse in the second century, a poem's lines became typically equal in length with an equal number of characters and syllables;[14] graphically enhanced by the square shape of the Chinese character, this feature is made possible by the mainly monosyllabic and the uninflected, isolating nature of the Chinese language, which foster acoustic, semantic, and syntactic coordination between a couplet's lines. At the same time, the occasional need to clarify grammatical relationships within the line makes a useful device of parallelism, whose construction is further facilitated by the normally fixed positions of caesuras. As Hans Frankel notes, "when two statements, equal in overall length, in prosodic structure, and in the size of their constituent parts, are placed side by side and coordinated, it is natural that they should closely match"[15] to give an architectural beauty to poetic construction. On a subtle level, it may even be that the Chinese poet's love for parallelism reflects a cultural instinct traceable to a bipolar cosmological vision wherein the world's myriad phenomena are endowed with balancing attributes:

> Creation, in investing things with form, always endows them with paired limbs; the transcendental principle functions in such a way that nothing stands alone. And when the mind generates literary expressions, organizes and ponders over a hundred considerations, the high and the low entail each other, naturally forming parallelism. (*WD* 35/2:189)[16]

That a sense of aesthetic beauty and philosophical truth can come from ordering the experiential world into a balance may be seen in the following couplets by Xie:

野曠沙岸淨	The wilds are vast, the sandy shores pure;
天高秋月明	The sky is lofty, the autumn moon bright.

(*XLJ* 98)

池塘生春草	The pond's banks are putting forth spring grass;
園柳變鳴禽	The garden willows have changed the singing birds.

(*XLJ* 64)

Conveying a sense of coordination and coextension without being mechanical, the parallelisms here reflect a sensitivity to the macroscosmic grandeur and microscosmic vitality of Nature.

Yet such isolated examples also highlight many others of Xie's formulaically assembled parallelisms, with variations on stock formations like "both/and," "look left/look right," "look east/look west," "looking up, I see/looking down, I listen":

側逕既窈窕
環洲亦玲瓏

The mountain by-paths are narrow and deep;
The ring-like islets, too, are luminous and crystalline.

(*XLJ* 118)

過澗既厲急
登棧亦陵緬

Wading across the torrent I tuck up my gown;
Scaling plank paths along the cliff, I also climb high.[17]

(*XLJ* 121)

極目睞左闊
迴顧眺右狹

Straining my eyes, I squint at the broad plains on the left;
Turning my gaze, I survey the narrow gorges on the right.

(*XLJ* 68)

眷西謂初月
顧東疑落日

I peer westward, saying it's the new moon;
Then gaze eastward, wondering if it's the setting sun.

(*XLJ* 56)

俛視喬木杪
仰聆大壑灇

Looking down, I view the tops of the tall trees;
Looking up, I listen to the torrents in the broad valleys.

(*XLJ* 118)

However carefully crafted, forced parallelisms are bound to produce a landscape too rigid to beat with a natural pulse. It is one thing to perceive creation metaphysically in terms of a self-balancing dynamic of parallel forces, and another to turn this into a versifying mannerism that orders everything into a symmetrical structure. Even more than sectional elements in an extended handscroll, corresponding components in a parallel couplet form internal coordinates which attach themselves to each other, so that individual parallelisms imparting a sense of fullness do not necessarily integrate into a totality. If Xie's poetry is deplored as being "broken and fragmented in style" (*H* 1:153), it is because its refined constituents do not often cohere into an organic whole.

The above discussion is certainly not meant to be a total castigation of Xie's art, or that of other Southern Dynasties poets who followed him in pursuing poetic formalism (embellished rhetoric has a place in court poetry, for instance). There are poems in which Xie's efforts have produced more inspired results,[18] and the historical importance of his pioneering work to the development of Tang nature poetry is indisputable. But if systematic portraits of natural forms mark both Xie's strength and his weakness, the latter is rendered more serious by the content of his verse, simply because no mechanical structure can adequately capture the flowing vitality of Nature or lead to the spiritual oneness, simplicity, and freedom he so passionately wants. It is to Tao's credit as a nature poet that the "patching traces" and "chisel marks" of word-sculpturing common in his age—obscure vocabulary, jagged syntax, obtrusive allusions (especially philosophical jargon), mechanical parallelisms—are absent in his writings. In fact he does not seem particularly interested in verbal wit, striving neither like Du Fu and Han Yu to startle his readers nor to make his poetry intelligible to old women as an anecdote tells of Bai Juyi. He who has internalized Nature feels no urge to photograph its forms by grinding at his verbal sawmill;[19] the scenes in Tao's verse mostly issue from his farm life. The grace of his natural style can thus be seen bilaterally: if it reflects the poet's being and becoming in an abode where he can "settle himself and anchor his life" *(anshen liming)*, it is also the formal attribute ordained by his inner ideal.[20]

One way to see Tao's poetry is thus as a convergence of natural inclination and the artistic logic entailed by his vision. From simple views to lucid expression, we find the same spirit enlivening and fusing the tenor and vehicle of his art. The use of reduplications *(diezi)* is a case in point:

曖曖遠人村	(1)	Hazy, hazy, the distant villages;
依依墟里烟		Soft, soft, the smoke from hamlet lanes.

(*TYJ* 40)

眇眇孤舟逝 綿綿歸思紆	(2) Far, far, the lonely boat goes; On, on, thoughts of return linger.
	(*TYJ* 71)
榮榮窗下蘭 密密堂前柳	(3) Blooming, blooming, the orchids under the window; Lush, lush, the willows in front of the hall.
	(*TYJ* 109)

The use of reduplicated words is of course not unique to Chinese poetry; they can, for instance, be employed to achieve lively effects in English:

> Oh! what's the matter? what's the matter?
> What is't that ails young Harry Gill?
> That evermore his teeth they chatter,
> Chatter, chatter, chatter still!
> . . . .
> At night, at morning, and at noon,
> 'Tis all the same with Harry Gill;
> Beneath the sun, beneath the moon,
> His teeth they chatter chatter still![21]

The repetition of "chatter" vivifies aurally and semantically the motion of the teeth. In general, though, word reduplication must be used with care lest it produce a clumsy effect, especially in polysyllabic languages.[22] Chinese seems to have a wider latitude here, for its largely monosyllabic nature easily lends musicality to a reduplicated pair that may take on a trance-like wonder (1), enhance a sense of vitality (3), or amplify poetic overtones in line with corresponding connotations (1–3): "hazy, hazy" feels more ethereal than "hazy"; "far, far" more distant than "far."

In his discussion of poetic language, Liu Xie comments

> Thus *zhuozhuo* embodies the freshness of peach blossoms; *yiyi* fully captures the form of willows; *gaogao* represents the countenance of the rising sun; *biaobiao* imitates the appearance of snow falling; *jiejie* transcribes the sound of orioles; *yaoyao* imitates the chirping of insects. . . . A thousand years may pass in deliberation, but is it easy to replace these words? (*WD* 46/2:341)[23]

This is in part a circular, tautological argument, insofar as the import of the reduplications is defined in the context of the *Shijing* lines where they first occur. Nevertheless, the choice of certain sounds to convey certain meanings implies that there are times when aural qualities are more naturally associated with some meanings rather than others.[24] It is no doubt to an intuitive feel for poetic music that Liu Xie appeals in endorsing the quoted examples. Take *yiyi,* or *·jəd·jəd* in ancient Chinese:[25] moving from a glottal stop to medial *-j-* and nuclear vowel ə in a frictionless continuous airstream before coming to a gentle halt in the ending *-d* (no plosive but a relatively soft stop), the effect of *·jəd* is one of a tender brisk touch. But it is not so much that the isolated sound suggests the willows' slim static form, as that in reduplication *·jəd·jəd* captures their gentle sway and its concomitant emotive overtones, making the word's senses of "tender, lingering" natural semantic correlatives to its sound qualities. That this is no arbitrary justification can be seen by linking *·jəd·jəd* to, say, a hippopotamus (which, incidentally, sounds fitting for an animal of its mass). It must be added that while the connotative range of some sounds may be traced through the contexts of their occurrence, not every reduplication can be explained with the same clarity in terms of auditory-semantic association. But what is remarkable about Tao's reduplications—and here one can only follow Liu Xie in invoking intuition for the unanalyzable—is that almost every pair seems to accord with its context in sound, color, spirit, and emotional overtones. While existing reduplications may have their meanings extended—*yiyi* is used in "Return" #1 for the slowly rising smoke which resembles softly swaying willows—new ones may be coined: *shuangshuang* graphically describes swallows coming to his hut "pair after pair" (*TYJ* 110).[26] Developing the resources of folk poetry handed down since *Shijing*, Tao's *diezi* constitute a vibrant means of conveying empirical and inner realities.

Meanwhile, Tao's language is marked by an infrequent use of exact and extended parallelisms, for he knows that overwrought rhetoric violates the essence of the Nature it presents. It may be useful to return briefly to a short poem by Xie Lingyun consisting entirely of parallelisms, entitled "Ye fa Shiguanting" (Setting out at Night from Stone Pass Pavilion):

隨山踰千里	I've been going along the hills for more than a thousand *li*,
浮溪將十夕	Drifting along the streams for almost ten nights.
鳥歸息舟楫	As the birds fly home I rest the oars;
星闌命行役	When the stars grow pale I give orders to set off.
亭亭曉月暎	High and clear the dawn moon shines;
泠泠朝露滴	Chill and pure the morning dew soaks.

(*XLJ* 50)

A traveler responding to Nature in the light of his situation is a context conducive to lyric expression (witness Tao's poems about his journeys). This is in part realized by a direct voice unobstructed by baffling diction, jammed syntax, obscure allusion, or forced message, but the rigid parallelisms compartmentalize the poem into three discrete narrative-descriptive couplets. Instead of leading up to a total effect, the poem evokes little beyond the surface meaning of the lines, and reads as though it has been truncated. Compare an excerpt from Tao's "Miscellaneous Poems" #2:

白日淪西河	The white sun sinks into the western river;
素月出東嶺	The pale moon rises from the eastern range.
遥遥萬里暉	Far, far, its beams of myriad miles,
蕩蕩空中景	Vast, vast, its radiance in the sky.

(*TYJ* 115)

The parallelisms not only form a coherent view (with the second couplet describing the moon in line 2), but enhance the scene's physical and emotive dimensions through the sense of spatial extension imparted by parallel coordinates. It may be recalled that the vista blends into an expression of the poet's sadness over his frustrated calling, and it is significant that while in "Return" #1 domestic scenes make up the parallelisms conveying the happiness of his modest life, here they give expansive imagery which, like far-reaching flights and heroic language (*TYJ* 113, 138), is invariably associated with his public sentiments. In other words, Tao's parallelisms merge smoothly into the flow of a language impelled by his lyric sensibility; it is lines like the above, vitally liquid rather than strained, which exemplify how the Chinese perception may "naturally form parallelism."[27] Besides, if Nature is more a balanced than a symmetrical unity, one might expect many of such natural parallelisms to be a shade less than exact. The inner couplets of "Return"#1, for instance, show precise and imprecise parallelisms mixed with each other, with both forming parts of a mellifluous flow. Reflective of a faith to follow Nature's rhythm in ways that escape formulas, these inexact parallelisms are like "gliding clouds and flowing water" *(xingyun liushui)*, to borrow Su Shi's terms:[28]

野外罕人事　In the country human affairs are few;
窮巷寡輪鞅　In the narrow lanes wheels and harnesses are rare.

(*TYJ* 42)

目倦川塗異　My eyes grow weary of the strange rivers and roads;
心念山澤居　My heart yearns to dwell amid hills and vales.

(*TYJ* 71)

氣變悟時易　As the air changes I realize the season is shifting;
不眠知夕永　Sleepless, I feel the night is so long.

(*TYJ* 115)

While far simpler and less neat or adorned than those of Xie, such lines are more effective in conveying Tao's experiences and the spirit of Nature.

The appeal of Tao's verse, however, depends far less on correspondences within couplets than on multiple links and echoes among lines in a poem, as amply seen in the poems discussed above. "Miscellaneous Poems" #5 offers another case in point:

憶我少壯時　I recall the time of my youth and prime,
無樂自欣豫　Lacking pleasures, but happy of myself.

猛志逸四海	With valiant aspirations reaching beyond the four seas,
騫翮思遠翥	I raised my wings, and thought of distant flight.
荏苒歲月頹	Gradually the years and months slipped by;
此心稍已去	This heart is partly gone.
值歡無復娛	When I meet with delights, I am no longer joyous;
每每多憂慮	Often I am laden with worried thoughts.
氣力漸衰損	My spirit and strength have slowly worn away;
轉覺日不如	I come to feel each day as a decline.
壑舟無須臾	The boat in the gully[29] pauses not for a moment,
引我不得住	Drawing me on and allowing no rest.
前塗當幾許	The way ahead—how much further will it be?
未知止泊處	I know not where my anchorage is.
古人惜寸陰	The ancients grudged every inch of time;
今此使人懼	Thinking of this makes me alarmed.

(*TYJ* 117)

Tracing Tao's changing inner state through the stages of his life, the poem is another piece of direct lyricism, marked by straight chronological movement through a simple temporal structure of past, present, and future, and materialized in lucid language and a transparent style. As always, it is this lean base which generates all the richness and resonance of the poem. In every sense and on every level it is characterized by descent: from youth to feebleness physically (ll. 1, 9, 10), sprightliness to joylessness emotionally (ll. 2, 7), "valiant aspirations" to waned ardor (ll. 3, 6) and soaring, expansive idealism to depressing, introverted anxiety spiritually (ll. 4, 8)—all underlined by the inexorable progression of time as the poet counts its passage first in years and months, then by the day and finally by every moment and "inch of time" (ll. 5, 10, 11, 15). The poem's complex of contrasts, interlinks, and reverberations converge on the poet as he stands before an uncertain future, giving his voice a poignant profundity as he feels "drawn on" by time and change without any sense of "anchorage" (ll. 12–14). But in a final twist echoing that in "Miscellaneous Poems" #1 (see chapter 2), the poem gains an added pregnancy by rising out of its melancholy in the ending couplet. In #1 he begins by lamenting the rootlessness of human life and concludes by urging himself "to strive hard while you have time"; here he remembers how the ancients—including his great-grandfather—strove to put "every inch of time" to good purpose.[30] Coming directly from Tao Kan's warning not to "relinquish oneself," the final "alarm" is a hortative ring that places the poet's spirit back on the alert.

Lean in imagery and temporal in movement, the above example shows Tao's crystalline language and style employing the narrative mode for lyric expression. But the same verbal flow is equally at home within a spatial structure in which rich imagery and vivid description work toward a total effect, as illustrated by "The Ninth Day of the Ninth Month, in the Year Jiyou":

靡靡秋已夕	Slowly, slowly, autumn is coming to an end;
淒淒風露交	Chilly, chilly, the wind and dew mingle.
蔓草不復榮	The creeping plants no longer put out blossoms;
園木空自凋	The garden trees are shedding their leaves.
清氣澄餘滓	The clear air is cleansed of its last impurities;
杳然天界高	Far and remote, the bounds of Heaven reach high.
哀蟬無留響	The sad cicadas leave no lingering sound;
叢雁鳴雲霄	Flocking geese cry in the sky.
萬化相尋繹	A myriad transformations follow one another;
人生豈不勞	Is human life not toilsome?
從古皆有沒	From oldest times all have had to die:
念之中心焦	Thinking of it makes my inner heart burn.
何以稱我情	How can I satisfy my feelings?
濁酒且自陶	With cloudy wine just let me gladden myself.
千載非所知	A thousand years are beyond my knowledge;
聊以永今朝	Just let me prolong this morning.

(*TYJ* 83)

Trailing a middle path between the remote, abstract cosmos in *xuanyan shi* and Xie's highly specific mini-portraits that often remain local details, Tao's depictions of Nature are marked by simple language, direct style, and imagery on a medial level between concreteness and generality to which the human spirit readily responds. This makes his landscape more immediate than Xie's even on a descriptive level, and more pregnant as well. Pervading the poem here is a stern, gloomy atmosphere of late autumn: the cold soughing *(qiqi)* wind, withering creepers, bare trees, the departure of cicadas, cries of homing geese, air feeling almost empty in its freshness, and a remote, unfathomable Heaven make up a resonant panoramic view. In form and movement there is no internal division throughout the description: as the initial reduplications capture the slow but inexorable passage of time, language and imagery flow from line to line and from earth to sky, giving a symbolically charged scene whose visual and auditory elements mark time at the most poignant moment of its spiral motion. With its "myriad transformations" encompassing all, line 9 is at once a link between the poem's two parts and a divider between the natural and human conditions, for time, as felt by the conscious human, is cyclic and renewable for Nature but linear and irretrievable for him. The still, silent observation in lines 1–8 gives way to feeling expression as the poet is reminded by scene and occasion of the prospect of mortality and the futility of human endeavor. Death cannot threaten and destroy as much without the human spirit investing his life with a larger purpose, and Tao knows it is his sense of duty which makes life "toilsome" and "his inner heart burn." Blending into and deepening his dispirited mood, the natural scene becomes the cosmic resonance of the poet's inner state as he broods over the meaning of existence.[31] Part of the poem's presentness of effect comes from the self-directed queries, reflecting an inner dialogue that underlines the poet's solitude; striking a truce with his idealistic self through the enjoyment of wine, he comes to a stoic acknowledgment of the terms of existence. Free from obscure vocabulary, packed syntax, mechanical parallelisms,[32] heavy allusions, and any rigid structure, this poem fully illustrates the artistic power of plain language and straightforward style. It is with good reason that Huang Tingjian (1045–1105), who emphasizes rigorous training in poetic craft as a means to effortless effusion,[33] looks up to Tao as a natural genius whose writings "integrate naturally without fussing about rules and tailoring" (*H* 1:39). Or that Chen Shidao (1053–1101), characterized by Huang as "shutting himself up in search of a phrase,"[34] sees Tao as one immune from the pains of literary craftsmanship: "Yuanming does not write poetry, but only expresses the subtleties of his heart" (*H* 1:42).

If the colors of Xie Lingyun's landscape are those imparted by his measured, pigmented strokes, the rich tones of Tao's poetry come from a lucid, crystalline language as it refracts into a chromatic spectrum. Rather than using the sophisticated resources of *fu* for *shi* poetry, Tao's simple expression taps the vitality of living speech, perhaps exemplifying Wordsworth's ideal of poetic diction as a "purified" distillate of the common people's language.[35] Interlaced with his graceful style are oral expressions gliding smoothly into poems of daily concern, form, and subject matter enhancing each other in unison:

孰是都不營	How can one not provide for [food and clothing]
而以求自安	And yet seek peace for oneself?

(*TYJ* 84)

未知從今去	Who knows whether after today
當復如此不	There'll be another time like this?

(*TYJ* 44–45)

於今甚可愛	Right now it's very lovely;
奈何當復衰	Alas that it must wither afterward!

(*TYJ* 68)

雖有五男兒	Although I have five sons,
總不好紙筆	None is fond of paper and brush.

(*TYJ* 106)

One feature especially notable in this conversational style is his use of the question-answer form:

當年詎有幾　These prime years—how long can they be?
縱心復何疑　Follow my heart: why should I doubt any more?

(*TYJ* 74)

田家豈不苦　Isn't a farmer's life a trying one?
弗獲辭此難　But one can't shun these hardships.

(*TYJ* 54)

善惡苟不應　If good and evil find no retribution,
何事空立言　Why vainly lay down such words?

(*TYJ* 87)

行止千萬端　A thousand myriad manners of action—
誰知非與是　Who knows what's right and wrong?

(*TYJ* 90)

Recognizing the unity between tenor and vehicle is crucial here, for often unnoticed is a significance of the interrogative deeper than that of stylistic vigor. Especially in his moments of solitude, the form becomes the only mode of communication and inner fortification wherein the poet renews his ideals in the process of articulation. Every time he poses or answers a question, he is holding an internal dialogue with himself, querying the moral efficacy of Heaven, voicing a feeling of injustice, or reaffirming his existential choice. If the "living presentness" of Tao's conversational style is rightly hailed as a refreshing break from contemporary taste,[36] it is important to remember that this vibrant immediacy reflects more the natural register of one writing without verbal excess, than the planned innovation of an aesthetic mind rebelling against its age to assert its individuality.

9

Neo-Daoist Aesthetics and the Art of Nature

Although critics since the Southern Dynasties have often gauged the Neo-Daoist literary legacy in terms of *xuanyan shi* and dismissed the latter for dessicating poetry with metaphysics, some of the distinctive features of Tao's art can in fact be linked to Neo-Daoism. Without attempting a full assessment of its impact on artistic innovations during the Six Dynasties, it will be revealing to see how it underlies the pithiness and simplicity of Tao's verse, and its ability to convey the essential spirit of experience *(chuanshen).*

First, pithiness is a basic norm of Neo-Daoist language whether in metaphysical exposition, pure conversation, or textual annotation. Ruan Xiu (c. 270–312) was described as "laconic and incisive" (*JS* 49/5:1366), Wang Meng (309–47) as "concise in language and insightful" (*JS* 93/8:2419), Yue Guang (252–304) as "always using succinct words to explain principles" (*JS* 43/4:1243), and Wang Cheng (c. 275–320) as "illuminating the tenor [of his discussions] without embellishing language" (*JS* 75/7:1960). An anecdote about Yue will illustrate the point:

> A questioner once asked Yue Guang about the proposition "Specific meanings do not reach."[1] Yue for his part did not analyze the statement, but struck the handle of his fly-whisk straight against the table, asking, "Does it reach or not?"
>
> The questioner replied, "It does."
>
> Yue then lifted the fly-whisk and said, "If it reaches, how can it be removed?"[2]
>
> At this point the questioner understood and became convinced. Yue's use of succinct language to communicate meanings *(zhida)* was always of this kind. (*SX* 4/16)[3]

In fact, terseness was often so highly prized that language and meaning were seen in inverse relation to each other: Ruan Zhan (fl. 307–12) was praised for being "deficient in words and overflowing with meaning" (*JS* 49/5:1363), Guan Lu (209–56) for "not discussing the *Yijing* because he understands it well."[4] While Sun Sheng (c. 302–73) sees "the Southerners' learning [as] crystalline, penetrating, pithy, and precise," Zhi Dun (314–66) likens it imagistically to "peering at the sun through a window" (*SX* 4/25). Although the terse answers of the Pure Conversationists are sometimes little more than stylized legerdemain, pithiness is a genuine Neo-Daoist norm for those who do not abuse it.

Tellingly enough, Yan Yanzhi remarks in his funeral elegy for Tao that "in writing he aimed at communicating meanings *(zhida)*" (*H* 1:1). Yan may be alluding to Confucius's point about how "it is enough for language to communicate *(cida)*" (*A* 15/41), but the term *zhida* links Tao's style directly to Neo-Daoist pithiness. Without tracing it to the same root, Zhong Hong describes Tao's style as "lucid and pure," "graceful and fitting in the tenor of his language *(cixing)*" (*H* 1:9), where "tenor" *(xing)* is defined as "meaning overflowing the limits of language" (*SP* 4). Indeed one can see it is Neo-Daoism which lent inspiration to Tao in his mode of expression, given his stylistic difference from Zhuangzi despite sharing much of the latter's vision, and the contrast between the evocativeness of his lean language and the limited resonance of contemporary floridity (as exemplified by Xie Lingyun's descriptions). Rather than meticulous reproductions of natural details, the objects and scenes in his poems are largely those interacting with his spirit at the moment of experience, so that simple as they are, they never look repetitive but constantly unfold fresh perspectives, as in the following spring descriptions:

鳥哢歡新節	Birds chirp in welcome of the new season;
泠風送餘善	The gentle wind brings brimming good.

(*TYJ* 76)

仲春遘時雨	Mid-spring is met by seasonal rains;
始雷發東隅	The first thunder rolls from the eastern quarter.
眾蟄各潛駭	The hibernating insects are all stirred from hiding;
草木從橫舒	This way and that the plants stretch.

(*TYJ* 110)

日暮天無雲	At sunset the sky is cloudless,
春風扇微和	The spring wind fans a mild warmth.
. . . .	. . . .
皎皎雲間月	Bright, bright, the moon amid the clouds;
灼灼葉中華	Sparkling, sparkling, the flowers among the leaves.

(*TYJ* 113)

At the same time, we have seen how his terseness is free from the abstraction of *xuanyan shi*, but rather coupled with imagistic vibrancy and lyric immediacy. This is true of his prose as of his poetry: the disposition, feelings, and life of the Gentleman of the Five Willows are vividly depicted in 171 characters, while the entire narrative of "Peach Blossom Spring" is presented in 321 characters, probably the shortest piece of Chinese prose to have achieved its level of literary immortality.

Like its pithiness, the simplicity of Tao's style is in line with Neo-Daoist standards. No doubt aware that it would be a self-contradiction for champions of *ziran* to make their point through a dense mesh of words, the Neo-Daoists use relatively plain language, often employing observable phenomena to flesh out abstract principles:

> Yin Hao [306–56] asked, "If Nature [as principle] is without conscious intent in its endowment, why is it just that good men are few and evil men numerous?"
>
> No one present had anything to say. Then Liu Tan replied, "It's like water poured over the ground, flowing and spreading this way and that, just of its own accord. It is almost impossible to make it square or round." For a time this answer was hailed with the highest admiration, regarded as an illustrious clarification. (*SX* 4/46)[5]

An argument about the tendency of human nature is thus made graphic with a simple illustration. Even *xuanyan shi* is generally free from verbal obscurities, as Zhu Ziqing observes:

> While *xuanyan shi* copies formulaically from *Laozi* and *Zhuangzi*, what it uses does seem to be "language relatively close to speech," . . . [which alone] will permit a more comprehensive exposition of meaning and entry into the metaphysical; parallel phrases are incapable of the same directness. That famous book *Shishuo xinyu* is a record of this type of language. . . . The reason why Tao's poetry surpasses *xuanyan shi* is that he frees himself from the formulas in *Laozi* and *Zhuangzi*, and instead infuses his daily life into his poetry. (*H* 1:298)[6]

Through the varying tunes of his lyricism, indeed, Tao's language and style remain lucid, his voice intimate and direct, his lines conveying a fullness of experience without convoluted rhetoric:

久在樊籠裏　　Long have I been in the confining cage;
復得返自然　　Again I have managed to return to Nature.

(*TYJ* 40)

山氣日夕佳　　The mountain air is fair at sunset;
飛鳥相與還　　Flying birds in company return.

(*TYJ* 89)

The homely nouns and verbs, with few adjectives attached, bear out Su Shi's perception of Tao's verse as "seemingly plain but really beautiful, lean but really full" (*H* 1:35).[7] So do his allusions,[8] which we have seen are not forcibly hammered into his poetry like many Southern Dynasties "compositions [that] verge on bookish copying"

(*SP* 7). Internalized in his sensibility as living experience and merging into the flow of his poetry, his allusions are often not visible as such in that their historical and artistic distance from the poet has vanished. Zhong Hong considers Tao's style free from "elaborate wording," and points to the "elegance and grace" of some of his expressions (*H* 1:9); what remained unrecognized at the time was that such "elegance and grace" lie time and again in his uncouth "farmer's words" (see chapter 7), which preserve with little adornment the original colors of the realities conveyed and the poetic spirit conveying them.

Which leads us to the next point: in its capacity to convey the essence of experience, Tao's poetry can also be linked to Neo-Daoist aesthetics, as manifested in the arts of characterology and portrait painting. "When we understand a person's *quintessential spirit (jingshen)* we may penetrate the principles [within him] and fathom his nature,"[9] Liu Shao wrote, sounding an emphasis that was amplified in the Eastern Jin. To be able to forget the form and capture the spirit is the key to this aesthetic, as seen in the praise Zhi Dun received for elucidating ideas without attention to images or textual explications: "This is like [the expert judge] Jiufang Gao gauging horses, glossing over their color and picking those with an outstanding spirit" (*SX* 26/24). But since spirit cannot be pinned down in definite terms, the best means to convey it (despite Zhi Dun's inattention to them) lies in images that inspire the imagination, as *Shishuo xinyu* widely attests. Pei Kai (237–91), for instance, characterized Xiahou Xuan (209–54) as "solemn and dignified, making one feel like entering the court or an ancestral temple"; Zhong Hui (225–64) as an "armory" of "spears and halberds"; and Shan Tao (205–83) as being "like climbing a mountain and looking down—profound and remote" (*SX* 8/8). Yue Guang was compared to a "water mirror" (*SX* 8/23), while Sima Yu (320–72) carried a radiant aura about him "like dawn clouds rising" (*SX* 14/35).

This "spiritual aesthetic" is also evident in the portrait painting of the times, with its focus on the eyes. In discussing the manifestations on which physiognomical study may be based, Liu Shao remarked "When the spirit shows on the face emotions exude from the eyes,"[10] while Jiang Ji (first half of third century) likewise argued for knowing a person through the eyes because they best embody the spirit.[11] If Gu Kaizhi (c. 345–406) took his task so seriously that he "would paint a portrait and sometimes not dot the pupils of the eyes for several years," it is because he identified the essence of the painting with that of the portrayed:

> "The beauty or ugliness of the four limbs is basically unrelated to the subtle parts [of a painting]. What conveys the spirit and portrays the likeness lies just in these dots." (*SX* 21/13)[12]

Noting "'The hand brushing over the five-stringed lute' is easy to paint but 'the eyes escorting the homing geese' is hard" (*SX* 21/14, *JS* 92/8:2405), Gu confirmed formal verisimilitude *(xingsi)* and spiritual verisimilitude *(shensi)* as different orders of art. "Those who are consummate in their art enter the spirit [of things],"[13] remarked Sun Chuo, further attesting that "entering the spirit" *(rushen)* had become the supreme aesthetic of the time.

In retrospect, what seems surprising is that the potential of this aesthetic, widely applied to characterology by the Western Jin, remained untapped by the *xuanyan* poets. If *xuanyan shi* may be seen as an attempt to capture spirit in the abstract, Tao's poetry represents a fructification of the Neo-Daoist aesthetic in its ability to convey the essence of experience through lively images and exact language:

平疇交遠風	The level fields meet the breeze from afar;
良苗亦懷新	The fine shoots, too, bear a new life.

(*TYJ* 77)

The simple scene is vibrant with interacting meanings that come from a mellow voice of conviction: the level fields suggest an open spirit, the breeze a fresh, spacious atmosphere, and the swaying shoots the budding vitality of a free life. But beyond an apt analogy between the natural and human conditions, the images uniting them also point to his daily work, so that the shoots are actual fruits of his labor, testimony to an authentic life and a deserving delight. Chen Zuoming is right in calling the lines a "portrayal of the spirit of things" (*H* 2:132)—and of the poet's spirit as well.

淒淒歲暮風	Chilly, chilly, the wind at year's end;
翳翳經日雪	Dimming, dimming, the snow that falls all day.
傾耳無希聲	Inclining my ears, I hear not the faintest sound;
在目皓已潔	But before my eyes, all is white and pure.

(*TYJ* 78)

With the quasi-onomatopoeic *qiqi* simulating the bitter wind and the reduplication *yiyi* setting the scene's visual tone, the interplay between sound and color continues as the poet, finding the snowfall inaudible, beholds the winter scene. While the snow's ethereal lightness and purity well emerge through a language capturing the interaction of the senses, the poem goes on to express the "desolation within [his] empty house," and how "time and again [he] sees past heroes" of virtue from ancient books. Tao does not labor the point, but in the context of passing time the bleak wind and gloomy day serve as a foil to the human spirit standing "firm in adversity." While solitude pervades the atmosphere as he listens in vain for some sound, the scene of purity comes across with the overtones of a revelation. As Chen Zuoming notes again, "The 'inclining ears' couplet captures the spirit of the wind and snow, and [Tao's] lofty sentiments stand out transcendently as if plainly seen" (*H* 2:134).

飢來驅我去	Hunger came and drove me out,
不知竟何之	But I did not know where to go.
行行至斯里	Walking on and on, I came to this lane;
叩門拙言辭	I knocked at a door, stumbling over *[zhuo]* my words.

(*TYJ* 48)

What is conveyed here is not just awkwardness but a sense of dislocation (l. 2) to which chronic poverty has "driven" the poet. Wandering "on and on"—the reduplication reflecting the painful, indefinite dragging—he seems not even fully aware of his destination, so that he could not but "stumble over his words" when thrust to the point of begging. His gestures and looks vividly captured by the character *zhuo*,[14] the psychological reality of the moment is revealed in a few words.

有風自南 There is a breeze from the south
翼彼新苗 *Winging* those new shoots.

(*TYJ* 13, emphasis mine)

眾蟄各潛駭 The hibernating insects are all stirred from hiding;
草木從橫舒 This way and that the plants *stretch*.

(*TYJ* 110, emphasis mine)

As with *zhuo* above, there are often times when a key word animates scenes and objects. Here *yi* ("winging") conveys the "flapping vitality" of the new shoots, while *shu* ("stretch") captures the reactivated life of the plants stretching their limbs after a period of dormancy, just as humans do after a sleep. Moreover, the words are placed at crucial positions: while *yi* links the couplet into a flowing unit, *shu* withholds the plants' motion to the last until their vitality comes bursting out. Such verbs dynamize the descriptions and no doubt gave later poets inspiration for these acclaimed lines:

紅杏枝頭春意鬧 From branches of the pink apricots the spring mood is *bursting*.[15]

雲破月來花弄影 Clouds break, the moon comes, and blossoms *sport* their shadows.[16]

春風又綠江南岸 Again the spring wind *greens* the southern shores.[17]

It will now be in order to return to two short poems, which bring together the aesthetic attributes discussed in this chapter:

悵恨獨策還 Sadly I return alone, leaning on my staff,
崎嶇歷榛曲 Up and down the thicketed winding path.
山澗清且淺 The mountain brook is clear and shallow;
可以濯吾足 It will serve to wash my feet. 4

漉我新熟酒 I strain my newly ripened wine,
隻雞招近局 And to a single chicken treat my neighbors.
日入室中闇 As the sun sets the house turns dark;
荊薪代明燭 Thorn firewood takes the place of bright candles.
歡來苦夕短 Happy we are, but regret that night is short;
已復至天旭 Already dawn has come again.

("Return" #5, *TYJ* 43)

種豆南山下 I planted beans below the southern hill;
草盛豆苗稀 The weeds flourish, but the bean shoots are few.
晨興理荒穢 At dawn I rise to clear away the weeds;
帶月荷鋤歸 Bringing along the moon, I return shouldering my hoe.
道狹草木長 The path is narrow, the plants and trees tall;
夕露沾我衣 The evening dew soaks my clothes.
衣沾不足惜 Having my clothes soaked is no cause for pity,
但使願無違 Only let my wishes not be betrayed.

("Return" #3, *TYJ* 42)

"Return" #5 is a straightforward, mostly narrative poem which gains depth and appeal with a symbolic lyricism beneath its surface. The first four lines offer the realistic scene of a farmer treading a winding path and washing his feet in a brook, but also evoke the inward "ups and downs" of a poet-hermit, who at sad, lonely moments can only "lean on" the "staff" of his resolve along a "thicketed winding path" with no clear prospect, yet whose vision improves dramatically as he reaches the "clear" water and savors the relative purity of eremitic life. Line 3 not so much describes the beauty of a limpid brook as registers Tao's lyric response to a symbolically meaningful item in the landscape. An allegorical song in "The Fisherman" advises washing one's official capstrings when the water (of the political tide) is clear and one's retired feet when it is muddy,[18] but Tao modifies the allusion in line 4 in enjoying the clear rustic brook that washes not only his feet but his sadness clean. A similar symbolic appeal is felt as he strains the dregs out of his wine and spirits. The lyric sense of the gathering is conveyed not directly but by plain narration, through gestures, words, and objects that make up a warm, affectionate atmosphere: his enthusiasm in straining the wine and inviting his neighbors, the sprightly effect added to lines 4–5 by the words *wu* and *wo* that underline his springy steps,[19] and the modesty of the arrangements that highlights his brimming hospitality. All these culminate in the humble image of the thorn-fire, which lights up his home and the hearts of all present, conferring on the simple wine and meal an almost manna-like quality. The inner movement from the solitude of his "winding path" to the purifying delight of Nature and domestic affection—extra resources which the poet can now "lean on"—is complete.

It is notable how this lyrical and symbolic depth comes from a short poem not only realistic but mundane in content; a few objects (winding path, mountain brook, ripened wine, single chicken, thorn-fire) and matters (returning on staff, washing feet, straining wine, inviting neighbors) of common rural experience are blended with the poet's sentiments into a cinematic sequence that exudes a deep sense of life. There is nothing dramatic formally either: the narration is chronological, the language plain and terse. Covering a fair spatial expanse outdoors and indoors, the poem offers no extended narration but a selection of resonant items that allow it to be structurally focused and well-knit. There is a certain elasticity about the pithy language, with just enough details to evoke a pregnant atmosphere and achieve a concrete immediacy of effect. If in Xie's verse the uneven parts often add up to a lesser whole, in Tao's poetry the final work exceeds the sum of its ordinary components.

While "Return" #5 relates Tao's sparetime activity, #3 records his daily labor in its simple vehicle and even shorter length. Structurally, each of the four couplets leads to the next in a cohesive sequence that forms a picture of farm work: the trouble of unproductive planting calls for the long daily routine, which ends in the homeward walk and the poet's reflection along the way. The transition from outward motion to inner response in the last two couplets is also formally smoothed by the thimble *(dingzhen)* device and a similar melodious repetition of the word *zhan*, so that the poem reads as a tightly knit but flowing whole. At the same time, the language is plain and the style direct, with every word meaningful and evocative and none exaggerated or ornamental. The first six lines read like factual statements, but beneath their narrative-descriptive surface is a rich lyric, psychological, and symbolic content: while the sparsity of the shoots brings out the poet's disappointment and determined response to remove the weeds (ll. 1–3), lines 4–6 follow him moving hoe on shoulder along the narrow path and brushing through the dewy plants under the moonlight, giving a sharp, concrete image vivid in visual, aural, and tactile terms. Moreover, the dynamic movement of both poet and poem is brought out by the phrase "bringing along the moon," for walking in the open space under the moon often creates the optical illusion that the moon is following one's motion; recording this illusion adds a sense of living presentness to the homeward walk. The expression of sentiments in the final lines is preluded by the symbol of the "narrow path" in the third couplet, which subtly captures the poet fading and pondering the weight of his choice as he drags along his weary body, made heavier by the wet clothes. The moon and evening dew are multivalent images, not only indicating the time of his return and the toil of his work but evoking the beauty of the rural scene, thus embodying both the taxing and charming aspects of his life. Man and Nature come together again in the clothes soaked first by sweat and then by dew, as his garment transmutes from a physical object into a symbol of commitment. The expression in the final couplet comes not just as a lyric culmination of the unspoken undertones of the preceding lines, but as something of an artistic hub where the images of the hoe, moon, dew, and clothes converge as witnesses to his self-promise, itself embodied by the symbol of the "narrow path." The multiple resonances among the images, the pithiness of language, and its ability to *chuanshen*, are a remarkable praxis of the Neo-Daoist aesthetic.

The above readings demonstrate once more how in tenor and vehicle Tao's verse is best seen as a union of truthful lyricism and a poetics of natural simplicity. The latter does not imply that his main concern is an aesthetic one. In the first place, the line between a poetry and poetics of naturalness must remain nebulous for a natural genius capable of spontaneous effusion under the hold of inspiration. Moreover, the kind of reflexive discourse on literature spreading since the time of Cao Pi (187–226)[20] has no appeal to Tao. While Frankel's remark that Tao's verse shows "a conscious and persistent effort . . . to break up the monotony of [excessive parallelism] . . . favored in the poetry of his time" is well taken,[21] it does not mean the poet was charged with an intention to launch a literary-moral program against his age in the way of a Bai Juyi or a Wordsworth. Any eschewal of ornate writing is instinctive before deliberate, in that it is an artificial, drawn-out process befitting neither Tao's life nor his ideal.[22] For one daily interacting with the spontaneous vitality of Nature, any implicit poetics or conscious stylistic choice probably comes from a feeling that a work of art should be like a work of Nature, and an understanding that too much chiselling in art would hurt its natural life.

This leads to a question left out in my earlier discussion of the spontaneity of Tao's creative impulse, as to what a "relative" and "cultivated" spontaneity implies in the artistic process. Wordsworth writes "all good poetry is the spontaneous overflow of powerful feelings," which are recollected and contemplated in tranquility until an emotion kindred to the original one takes shape in the mind, "in [which] mood successful composition . . . is carried on."[23] There is admittedly far less spontaneous than nonspontaneous poetry wherein the creative process is more deliberate than Wordsworth's claim, and wherein measured craft and verbal sculpturing may even take precedence over feelings and experience. But the relevant point here is that in spontaneous writing the mind's functioning is guided by the feeling spirit, and the aesthetic impulse remains subsidiary to the expressive one; the beauty of language forms no goal of pursuit independent of the experience conveyed. Poetic spontaneity thus occurs in two ways on the verbal level: while words may flow effortlessly from the muse and come unsurpassably close to capturing the essence of experience, there are often times when the inadequacy of language leaves one with a memory of the "overflow," which one tries to recapture through finding the right words. Paring away inappropriate language becomes a kind of craft aimed at achieving truthfulness; guided by the original feelings, mental contemplation and verbal cultivation become the paradoxical way to recover (perhaps at times even purify and elevate) the earlier spontaneity. The process involves an artistic distance developed subsequent to the original experience, a distance maintained mentally while also progressively closed as one reaches emotionally back to the experience. There is a significant difference between a spontaneous art seeking to express life truthfully, and an art that subjugates life to its own pursuits.

For all its stylistic simplicity and casualness, Tao's poetry is obviously no transcription of free utterances but a formalization of experience; sentient life is filtered through a spirit that crystallizes it into an artistic form. Since the relationship between experience and form is a variable, simplicity should not be easily equated with an absence of design or just assumed to be an impression resulting from labor. In light of the current critical penchant for sophistication, it is perhaps the latter supposition that especially needs to be remembered, not only because design may be discounted in moments of spontaneous composition but because this assumption, while valid for some, may distort the creative experience of others by reversing the priority of life over art. Thus when Tao praises Zhang Heng and Cai Yong for "curbing extravagant diction and aiming at simplicity," he clearly sees the latter as a state of "tranquility and rectitude"[24] to which simple language is an apt correlative (*TYJ* 153). A similar view on the instrumental nature of writing is reflected in what few statements he has made in this regard: to him, it is because the ancients found their principles "not fitting in with their times" that they

> dipped their brushes in deep feeling, and could not but often express themselves. For isn't it only literature that gives full expression to one's aspirations and sentiments? (*TYJ* 145)[25]

When Su Shi remarked "Tao Yuanming does not mean to write poetry; poetry is but for expressing his meanings,"[26] what he probably meant is that aesthetic consciousness is part of a total existential consciousness.

It is an artistic commonplace that poets do not always live up to their pronouncements. But for Tao there is perhaps no necessity to distinguish between poetry and poetics, not only because he never claims what he does not practise (true to a *junzi* [*A* 2/13]), but because both are rooted and converge in his life. If Xie Lingyun's verse often strikes one as the execution of a set poetics, Tao's poetry starts not from art but from Nature that makes possible the perfection of art:

弊廬何必廣	Must a poor hut needs be spacious?
取足蔽牀席	I have enough to cover bed and mat.

(*TYJ* 56)

The plain words "bed and mat" correspond to objects in a life content in bare frugality. Tao's scenes are ordinary, but they radiate a truth and beauty beyond the reach of his contemporaries:

日入室中闇	As the sun sets the house turns dark;
荆薪代明燭	Thorn firewood takes the place of bright candles.

(*TYJ* 43)

The otherwise unexciting object of the thorn branch comes across as a homely, endearing image illuminating the poem's lyric world, and yet there is no reason to doubt that what we see as image and role is a factually recorded item necessary in the evening darkness.

It has been noted before that a direct lyric voice does not always mean straightforward effusion; poems in which Tao draws support from historical and mythological figures abound in allusions, while his archaic four-character poems and *fu* pieces can be mannered in keeping with the expectations held of them.[27] But as we have seen all along, his lyric voice comes through even conventional forms and objective modes, not to mention poems writing of his daily experiences. In "The Rime of the Ancient Mariner" we may be certain Coleridge is using imagery for a specific purpose; the dead albatross is a well-defined symbol of the seaman's guilt because it has no realistic justification for hanging about his neck. But where an object like the thorn firewood exudes a natural imagistic power, one can no longer be sure whether it is a product of "art" or an intrinsic quality revealed to the heightened sensibility. If, as Wordsworth reiterates in his Preface to the *Lyrical Ballads*, too much art is unnecessary where there is enough truth and beauty in life accessible to the sensitive heart, then the function of art is to express this sentient experience.

Faced with a spontaneous art that conveys the essence of experience with a minimal intrusion of itself, criticism needs to modify its usual operation in order to capture the essence of that art: an art of *chuanshen* calls for a criticism of *chuanshen*. The notions of natural genius, grace, and spontaneity are uncongenial to any view of literature as a self-conscious, measured (sometimes even manipulative) craft of strategies ordering means to ends. But if these notions may still be conceptually granted as rare, mysterious facts of creation and then shelved on the periphery of critical theory, they become unsettling in practice and had best be turned into something more deliberate and analyzable, for the critic can only gape helplessly at a work of art that does not readily exhibit rules or other methods of craft which furnish criticism with surer ground. A highly conscious artist determined to control his art is more reassuring in leaving more visible marks of his effort; the spontaneous stroke of genius that "passeth all understanding" becomes bafflingly elusive and recalcitrant to explanation. But though independent of limiting precepts, it is never anarchical and free from law, natural or artistic; the inner cultivation infusing his genius guarantees the coherence of his spontaneity, which by its own example may even originate artistic laws it has unwittingly obeyed and by which subsequent works may be judged. On such rare occasions the dissecting desire must give way to intuitive empathy; "riding with" the invisible flow of the artist's spirit becomes the only way to achieve understanding before critical scalpels can be picked up again.

Transcending the confines of fantastic *youxian*, rationalistic *xuanyan*, and overwrought *shanshui* poetry, Tao brings Chinese lyricism to a new expressive height with a poetry of *shensi* that crystallizes the quintessence of the literary legacy he inherited. But the Southern Dynasties' taste being one in which "works based on feeling grew scarcer every day and those in pursuit of literariness more abundant" (*WD* 31/2:147–48), he had to wait three centuries for broad recognition (by the High Tang poets), and another three for full appreciation (by the Song writers). Meanwhile, the formal and thematic originality of his work lies so far beyond the horizon of contemporary taste and expectations that he was essentially ignored. All Yan Yanzhi said of Tao the artist is that "in writing he aimed at communicating meanings," while Shen Yue did not even bother about appraising Tao's writings in his biography in *Song shu*. Liu Xie never mentioned Tao in his monumental work;[28] Yang Xiuzhi (509–82) thought he "does not excel in verbal refinement" (*H* 1:10); and Zhong Hong placed Tao in the middle rank of his three-tier gradation of poets, having to defend his "plainness and directness" *(zhizhi)* by pointing out expressions of "elegance and grace" (*H* 1:9). Even the sympathetic Xiao Tong, who considered Tao's works "unique and superb in all genres" (*TYJ* 10), was confined by the taste of his age to include but nine of Tao's poems in *Wen xuan* (Selections of Refined Literature), compared with thirty-two by Xie Lingyun. It is perhaps doubly ironic that Tao's ability to convey the essential spirit of experience was perceived early without being understood. For Zhong Hong's remark recalls Dong Zhongshu's (c. 179–c. 104 B.C.) comment that "poetry articulates sentiments, and so is good insofar as it is plain," which Su Yu explains thus: "Poetry expresses sentiments, which cannot be false; thus it is described as plain." To Zhu Ziqing's explanation that "plainness means naturalness,"[29] one might simply add that *zhizhi* implies a fidelity to original essences, an art of Nature in which Nature speaks through the poet as much as he speaks through it. The Neo-Daoist aesthetic has come to fruition at an almost unnoticed spot.

10

Luminosity of the Unconscious: The Ineffable Truth

Perhaps the best clue to Tao's link to Neo-Daoist aesthetics lies in two of his most memorable lines: "In this there is a true meaning;/ I would explain it, but have forgotten the words" (*TYJ* 89). For "getting the meaning and forgetting the words" is a basic principle in Neo-Daoism and its chief mode of communication; it aims at transcending the limits of language (indeed all instrumental forms) to reach for ineffable essences. Already discussed in *Zhuangzi*—"The fish trap exists because of the fish; once you get the fish you forget the fish trap. . . . Words exist because of meaning; once you get the meaning you forget the words" (Z 26/48–49)—the issue finds a more poetically oriented articulation in the "Appended Remarks" to *Yijing*: "Writing does not fully represent language, and language does not fully express meaning; . . . thus the sages set up images in order to express meaning thoroughly."[1] Combining the two statements, Wang Bi arrives at his own formulation:

> Nothing excels images in fully expressing meaning, and nothing excels language in fully representing images. Since words arise from images,

> we may perceive images by plumbing the words. And since images arise from meaning, we may perceive meaning by plumbing the images. . . . Thus words are for manifesting images; once you get the images you forget the words. And images are for preserving meaning; once you get the meaning you forget the images.[2]

Neither an end nor to be discarded altogether, words and images are expedient means by which meaning may be attained. By this premise, *xuanyan shi* is an attempt to secure meaning without the imagistic medium, Xie Lingyun's verbal flamboyance an overattachment to the *upaya* itself, and Tao's work a praxis of the aesthetic in perception and methodology. One recalls the laconic Gentleman of the Five Willows's interest in meaning rather than words, in inner illumination rather than pedantic explication: "Though fond of reading, he did not seek thorough comprehension of details; but every time some meaning flashed upon him he would become so happy as to forget to eat" (*TYJ* 175). There is no doubt he commands Tao's total sympathy, for we have seen how the "meaning" exuding from the poet's writings is often just the spiritual state embodied by the model that gives him strength and faith in hardship. In fact, described by Yan Yanzhi as "freeing himself from the strife of the times and setting his purpose beyond worldly bounds" (*H* 1:1), Tao's outlook on life is precisely an existential application of "getting the meaning (inner truth) and forgetting the words (material pursuits)."

We are now in a position to examine "Drinking Wine" #5, a deceptively transparent poem that brings together the distinct qualities of Tao's verse:

結廬在人境　I build my hut in the realm of man,
而無車馬喧　And yet there is no clatter of carriage or horse.
問君何能爾　You ask me how this can be?
心遠地自偏　The heart detached, the place naturally remote.
採菊東籬下　Picking chrysanthemums beneath the eastern fence,
悠然見南山　Far away I see the southern mountains.
山氣日夕佳　The mountain air is fair at sunset;
飛鳥相與還　Flying birds in company return.
此中有真意　In this there is a true meaning;
欲辨已忘言　I would explain it, but have forgotten the words.

(*TYJ* 89)

Giving a simple datum of his existence, the first line also defines the poet against the literati of his age, for "hut" denotes not just a physical setting but an existential choice distinct from the practices we have seen: the self-justifying "court-reclusion" or "city-reclusion"; the "comfortable retreat" in which the "hermit" lived in material ease and mixed with high officials; or the notorious "fake-reclusion." Making no dramatization of lofty insulation, though, the phrase "in the realm of man" shows Tao firmly rooted in a cherished humanity, echoing what he confesses elsewhere: "It is just because of my family and old friends / That I have not the heart to consider living apart" (*TYJ* 57). The positive description in line 1 gains depth in line 2 through the foil of a "negative" delineation—the clatter of carriage and horse defined by its absence. Again the line is more pregnant than meets the eye, for the "clatter" applies not only to anglers of riches and honor who "all day drive their carriages along" (*TYJ* 99)—who do not call on him because he is an "outsider" with no favors to dispense—but to the Eastern Jin elite for whom reclusion does not mean settling down. This of course contrasts with the poet's situation: what is for them an ironic discrepancy between appearance and reality is for him a unity that gives peace in an accessible world without its hustle. The internal relationship of the first couplet is thus a complex one: it moves along in a dialectic of presence and absence to define his life, and yet the two elements are not antithetical to each other. This is embodied by the logical-grammatical connective *er* casually linking the lines, which is both "yet," suggesting incompatibility on a profane level of perception, and "and," intimating the truth experienced by himself.

But because this truth appears as a paradox, line 3 serves as a self-directed rhetorical question inviting both reflection and response; line 4 becomes an intertext to the first couplet by providing what is missing there—the spirit of the hut-dweller that is the key to a clatter-free abode. With another quiet *zi* presenting the natural logic of line 4, even the connectives show a progression, from the *er* that suggests a paradoxical truth to the *zi* that integrates the four lines and conveys a now self-evident truth. The philosophical remark carries easy persuasion not only because it has been prepared for by the first couplet and seems valid in the abstract, but because it is shared with us as an insight distilled from the poet's existential praxis. And with every statement thus far carrying a subtext (or "countertext") for his contemporaries (e.g., "If the heart is not detached the place will never be remote"), Tao has subtly marked his position in an unsympathetic world without denouncing it in the manner of Qu Yuan. What comes across is a direct and unfeignable voice of one communicating a heartfelt insight into the Way.

With line 5 the poem seems to restart on another plane. Hitherto Tao has, however gently, defined the self in contradistinction to the Other, as if the poem were again charting a spiritual dialectic in the course of which his faith is reaffirmed. This renewal also coincides with a shift of focus to Nature: did the inner process rendered by the four lines, then, take place within the temporal frame of the fifth while he is picking chrysanthemums? One cannot be sure, but the possibility is sufficient to link it with the preceding lines and integrate all five into a unit. This possibility is strengthened by the symbolic connotations of the flowers, though we know they are picked for health reasons as well. For even in "On the Ninth Day, in Retirement" where he writes "chrysanthemums can arrest declining years" (*TYJ* 39), the flowers function as a symbol of purity as the poem ends by affirming the reclusive choice. Indeed we have seen more than once how they are paired with pines as symbols of loftiness (*TYJ* 61, 161). The insight in line 4 thus finds testimony in Nature even as it is made more immediate through the quietly presented slice of life.

Then, without being poised for anything, the poet looks up and catches sight of the southern mountains afar. Another modest scene of simple beauty, line 6 crosses its local bounds and resonates with symbolic meaning through his works. For mountains have always been what he loves by nature (*TYJ* 40), and years ago he "strained his eyes to make out the southern mountains" (*TYJ* 73) while passing the area on official duty.[3] On this level, the third couplet becomes an imagistic embodiment of Tao's existential stance and the poem's elevation to a higher plane; any contrast with the world previously implied has given way to a sense of unity with the larger framework of Nature. This is brought out by the descriptive *youran*, which, taken to indicate the distance of the mountains by Lu Qinli (*TYJ* 89) and Tao's spiritual state by Suzuki Torao,[4] probably means both in that it points not only to objective scene and lyric sensibility but to their essential oneness. Already wandering serenely, the poet's spirit is lost in communion with the spectacle beheld, time and space dissolved in an enlightening luminosity of the unconscious. Su Shi rightly decries the proposed variant of *wang* (watch) for *jian* (see) in line 6 as one that would destroy the spontaneity of the communion (*H* 1:29): as Cowper says, the "mercurial" intellect must yield to a meditative "quiescen[ce]" and "indolent vacuity of thought" before cosmic understanding is possible.[5] Significant is the word "vacuity," for it brings one back to Zhuangzi's point about the need for the mind to fast until, emptied of all desires and preconceptions, it becomes freely receptive and impartially responsive. As Wordsworth writes, it is "with an eye made quiet by the power / Of harmony" that "we see into the life of things."[6]

We are, of course, yet to fathom the essence of what Tao "sees into," which is retrospectively given in the fourth couplet after his moment of illumination has passed. The poem's meaning has quietly risen from the existential to the cosmic, for this is the only couplet in which the self is "absent." The shift is achieved by the *dingzhen* device carrying the last word of the sixth to the beginning of the seventh line, which at once effects the smooth transition and marks the union of the two perspectives. It is significant that among the things in the scene beheld, Tao is struck by two sets of details, a microcosmic within a macrocosmic one: birds homing to the mountains in a fair sunset atmosphere. For it may be recalled that by analogy or contrast, the bird is often associated with the poet in his soaring aspirations, his sense of weariness and confinement, or his liberating reclusion (*TYJ* 117, 161, 40). One more example will suffice to reinforce the point:

日入羣動息	As the sun sets all activities cease;
歸鳥趨林鳴	Homing birds head for the woods, chirping.

嘯傲東軒下	I whistle freely below the eastern eaves,
聊復得此生	Having somehow regained my life again.

("Drinking Wine" #7, *TYJ* 90)

While in this excerpt the analogy between the birds' and Tao's state is drawn by sequential juxtaposition, in the present poem the association is made more subtly by the *dingzhen* device: between lines 6 and 8, the mountains have turned from an object of the poet's perception into the destination of the birds' journey, the direction of his eyes and their flight merging at the same point. The seventh line is the common macrocosmic framework embracing man and bird: a "fair" atmosphere at the close of day, a time when all activity and striving should stop for rest and return. What is more, between man and bird exists no static affinity: in the word *fei* Tao is witnessing the birds' motion that constitutes a parallel to his own path. On this symbolic level the homing birds, long appreciative friends *(zhiyin)* and the natural embodiment of his spirit, become the focus of the poem's imagistic structure in offering an epitome of both the truth of Dao and a personal quest that has brought him to where he is. The poem's symbolic drift thus turns back to the beginning, as if the fourth couplet supplied in its overtones the experiential background that precedes the choice in line 1. With the reading of every line entailing a "circular" re-reading of previous lines, the bidirectional poem is almost a closed circuit with no clear beginning or end.

Almost, but not quite, for we have said this couplet moves to a higher plane in being an imagistic embodiment of immanent Dao. A spontaneous "fasting" of the mind (l. 6) to a vacuous, quiescent, and luminous state (Z 4/28, 23/69–70) has dissolved the self into the universal reality, in what Hsü Fu-kuan would call an aesthetic experience: not the insulated Western aestheticism pursued independently of "nonaesthetic" standards,[7] but that which, seeing the highest beauty in the dynamic oneness and harmonious equality of Nature,[8] translates into spiritual experience in the poet's lyric vision. The subsumption of the human within the natural is marked by the formal absence of the "I"; the poem has risen to sublimity by uniting the existential and the cosmic in the same flash of imagistic illumination.

Coming round from the "absent-mindedness" of his epiphanic moment, the poet "reenters" the conscious world in line 9. Musing on his experience, he can only speak of "a true meaning" in "this," a vague word aptly rendering his sense that it lies beyond the means of language. This is paralleled by his inability to go beyond hinting at the *zhenyi* assimilated, even though it clearly affirms his existence, and *zhen* finds frequent expression as the principle of Nature, the essence of his social ideal, the standard by which the world is gauged, and the goal of his quest in life (*TYJ* 55, 24, 145, 75).[9] Why then the holding back? Here, it seems, all the strands of "true meaning" have merged in a total illumination, and it is this undifferentiated wholeness that entirely eludes intellectual ordering and linguistic fragmentation. A century earlier Lu Ji wrote that artistic truth "cannot be verbalized / Or captured precisely by adorned words," attributing the trouble in poetic articulation "less to the difficulty of knowing than to the difficulty of doing"[10]—in other words, to the limitation of human ability. Tao's understanding, on the other hand, is rooted directly in the Daoist perception of the Way as a unitary "uncarved block" before being broken up (*Z* 7/35, *L* 28), and of language as an inherently distorting medium finally to be "forgotten." "Words strain,/ . . . slip, slide, perish, / Decay with imprecision," so writes T. S. Eliot, "[and] after speech, reach/ Into the silence."[11] Just as Five Willows's insights often come from intuition rather than a mercurial intellect, Tao's mind seems to have "fasted" to a point of silent void where he feels "great explanations find no words" (*Z* 2/59), and poetry too must return to the ineffable (*L* 1). Not only does language lose its limited utility once the truth it conveys is grasped (*Z* 26/48–49), but the more strenuously this crude tool is wielded, the less it often ends up signifying. The point is not any formulaic claim that this poem is in its closing silence open to *infinite* interpretation. Rather, recognizing the misguidedness of any reductive attempt to specify truth, the poet gives up his lyricism as the only way to preserve the artistic and philosophical integrity of his poem and experience.[12] In the same way that Dao can ultimately only be affirmed as real and elusive (*L* 21, *Z* 6/29), the least limiting use of the finite verbal medium in face of ineffable truth lies in acknowledging its assimilable but indefinable presence, through a negative mode of expression that becomes at once a positive evocation of the absent. Just as the essence of Five Willows stands independently without the man's name, and a Chinese landscape painting depends for its constitution on empty space, so it is the intimating silence of the final disclaimer—its verbal emptiness and restraint from rationalization—that crowns the poem with a mystical charm. Felt in the form of nonbeing, the impact of the open ending sends the reader back to the poem in search of the unsaid.

But the symbiotic unity between art and philosophy is felt above all in the images embodying the cosmic principle (ll. 5–8). For while Tao's epiphany can be understood as an intuition of the oneness and harmony of all, here it comes from a poet who "out-Zhuangzis" Zhuangzi with an imagistic scene as commonplace as it is profound. The effectiveness of the images may be seen via a brief comparison with some samples of English "mystical" verse by Cowper, Tennyson, and Blake, all predicated on a perception of cosmic oneness in a world of multiplicity:

> Not a flow'r
> But shows some touch, in freckle, streak, or stain,
> Of [God's] unrivall'd pencil. He inspires
> Their balmy odours, and imparts their hues,
> And bathes their eyes with nectar, and includes
> In grains as countless as the sea-side sands,
> The forms with which he sprinkles all the earth.
>
> (Cowper)

> Little flower—but if I could understand
> What you are, root and all, and all in all,
> I should know what God and man is.
>
> (Tennyson)

> To see a World in a grain of sand,
> And a Heaven in a wild flower,
> Hold Infinity in the palm of your hand,
> And eternity in an hour.
>
> (Blake)[13]

Evident in all the excerpts is a pantheistic sentiment variously rendered through comparable imagery. While Cowper's religious poetry openly praises the Divine presence in all natural forms, a similar tone in Tennyson comes from a first-person voice (in contrast to Cowper's third) that gives a closer sense of heartfelt experience. It is in Blake that we find the most intense expression, with the second line summing up Tennyson's excerpt plus three other lines each evoking the divine macrocosm with a microcosmic image, superimposed on one another to make up a total effect.

Yet Blake still shares with Cowper and Tennyson a direct exposition of wisdom; after all, philosophical verse is a time-honored tradition in the West traceable to Aristotle's *Poetics*, where poetry is valued above history on the grounds that poetry, in its imaginative and comprehensive treatment of possible human experience, is more philosophical and concerned with "the universal."[14] Blake's images are united into a sequence in his vision, but sand, flower, hand, and hour are disparate and do not integrate by themselves. Tao's images, on the other hand, resonate with each other and form an intrinsically coherent whole that enhances their individualities: chrysanthemums, mountain, evening air, and homing birds blend into an aura of placid purity embodying the cosmic truth.

But since poetry is necessarily an ordering of experience, one may ask whether the man-Nature communion in the fourth couplet is really one in which Tao "loses" himself. In other words, does there remain any subject-object dualism detracting from the fullness of the experience, a gap between the spirit feeling the sublimity and the Way which is the ontological source of that communion? I would suggest not, for the dissolution of the self into the whole is reflected by the formal absence of the "I." While its individuality is lost in the unity, the spirit is not even aware of it, so that there can be no subject-object dualism which is predicated on a consciousness nonexistent at this instant. It is only when the poet reverts to the realm of consciousness that he comes to recall the timeless moment—and he does not claim it to be an epiphany. Wang Guowei surely means spiritual selflessness rather than physical absence when he speaks of "absence of the self" *(wu wo)* in the poem.[15] As it moves from *you wo* (presence of the self) to *wu wo* and back to *you wo* again, we also relive the material content of the poet's spiritual experience, which is not so much *qingjing jiaorong* as *shenwu jiaorong*, an "interfusion of spirit and world," or *wuwo liangwang*, a "mutual oblivion of world and self."

The inescapable paradox, of course, is that Tao must operate within the fragmenting medium he distrusts. Just as the fish trap may be used to catch fish (Z 26/48) and the pointing finger to orient us to the moon,[16] the poetic mode of language, in embodying instead of explaining, suggesting rather than defining, offers the best aid to comprehending what lies beyond conceptual-linguistic tentacles. As Zhuangzi demonstrates in his own way, the signifying potential of imaginative language may be fully developed to transcend its own limitations. But on this score the poet necessarily goes beyond the philosopher, for however profound his distrust of language, Zhuangzi *qua* philosopher must employ its resources for the sake of persuasion; and however incisively he deflates rational discourse, he himself must aim at some degree of logical coherence and systematic generalization. It is the poet, communicating via a verbal structure that often embodies its truth rather than directing it to a referential context,[17] who remains truest to the Dao of evocative inspiration.

In every sense an epitome of Tao's poetic achievement, this short poem subtly condenses his personal quest, the ultimate of his poetics, and the Way's immanent truth into a simple slice of life, moving simultaneously on the lyric, existential, aesthetic, and cosmic levels. Yet even as it seems to reveal such an amazingly tight organization and complex structure where every line resonates with every other, sustained by unobtrusive structural and formal markers, the poem retains all the qualities of natural liquidity and casual directness characteristic of Tao's best work. Without even the help of the parallelisms used in "Return" #1, its sense of completeness is brought to new heights by the interpenetrating coherence of its internal units on all planes, by the spontaneous stream of natural images[18] that seems but a pure flow of spirit. How such flawless art can be seamlessly fused into a natural lyricism is one of those rare artistic wonders that mark the limits of critical analysis: perhaps the movement of the poem is the rhythm of Nature and the course of the poet's life.

11

Art as Embodiment of Life: Naturalness and Truthfulness

In the final analysis, every salient feature of Tao's poetry is an index of the being it reveals. Marked by a unity between tenor and vehicle, between feeling, scene, insight, spirit, and objects, his art is above all one of *zhen* and *ziran,* where Nature, at once his home, the pointer to his nature and ideals, and the incarnation of Dao, is embodied in a compatible language that fuses lyric, artistic, existential, and cosmic meanings into a totality. Undramatic as the words "truthfulness" and "naturalness" seem, they indicate his actualization of the highest artistic potential of the Daoist vision. For if in classical Daoism *zhen* is the reality of Dao and *ziran* the natural principle by which everything proceeds, in Neo-Daoism they are also seen synonymously as cosmic and existential norms: as Guo Xiang puts it, "truthfulness is being naturally so *(ziran)* without the mediation of things" (*ZJ* 6/1:242). It is thus in keeping with his being that Tao's verse flows naturally like a depth of limpid water, plain, resonant, and profound. When traditional critics make remarks like "All sumptuousness shed, there emerges true purity" (*H* 1:121)[1] and "Not even a single word is not pure and truthful" (*H* 1:102),[2] it is clear they are commenting on both the man and his style.

Considered conceptually, however, this unison of man and style does not quite elucidate Tao's uniqueness as a poet: the same may be said of Xie Lingyun's elaborate ornateness, Du Fu's meticulous seriousness, or Xin Qiji's bold heroism. That artistic style is often rooted in the personality is a perception shared by critics of various times and places: one thinks of Longinus's (first–third centuries) "Sublimity is the note which rings from a great mind";[3] Edward Gibbon's (1737–94) "Style is the image of character";[4] Schopenhauer's (1788–1860) "Style is the physiognomy of the mind";[5] Liu Xie's "Each follows the bent of his heart, [and styles] differ like faces" (*WD* 27/2:97); Zhang Jie's (fl. 1135) "Poetry, prose, calligraphy, painting—all largely come from the heart [in a corresponding way]";[6] Ye Xie's (1627–1703) "Poetry is the voice of the heart, . . . thus one's poetry is often seen from the person [and vice versa]."[7] Whether each cast of mind always finds a correlative mode of expression is beside the point here, but the proposition is too broadly valid for any appraisal to be precise.

One clue to Tao's artistic genius, I think, lies in the dual attribute that even as livelihood issues lend substance to his lyricism, the language of such matters infuses his style as well. Undramatic as always, this deceptively simple fact marks a double achievement that points to the independence and originality of a truthful, natural spirit. I do not mean merely that Tao surpasses his age in ignoring the contemporary code of taste and reader expectations imposed on every writer, for what he ends up breaking are heavier fetters which traditional values have implicitly placed on Chinese poetry. As Octavio Paz notes, there is a system of approvals and prohibitions in every society ranging from the express to the implicit; unvoiced prohibitions are especially powerful in that they are taken for granted and thus unconsciously and automatically obeyed.[8] It is in the face of one such taboo that Tao wrote the poetry for which he is best known. For since the time of the *Shijing* folk songs, material concerns have seldom found entry into literati poetry, due in part to the Master's dictum that "a superior man sets his mind on the Way rather than a living" (*A* 15/32).[9] When he censured Fan Chi for asking about husbandry (*A* 13/4), what Confucius inadvertently did was to stigmatize livelihood as a vulgar matter which became a literary taboo as well. The lyricism of Tao's *tianyuan shi* becomes doubly resounding when heard against this prohibitive silence of what should not be said—a silence that expresses itself as intermittent criticism of him for adulterating poetry with inelegant language and unfitting material. When Zhong Hong defended the poet against the charge of "farmer's words," he was reflecting more than the slighting response of a period taste to such earthy poetry. Likewise, when Mao Xianshu (1620–88) protested against Tao's "vulgarisms" (*H* 1:184), or when Wang Fuzhi (1619–92) wrote

> In writing "Hunger came and drove me out," Master Tao unwittingly dropped into the pitfall. Du Fu, unwarily, beat up the lingering waves. . . . Once students of poetry become tainted with the habits of these writers, they are like defiled white silk that ultimately cannot regain its whiteness. Keep away from [such habits]! (*H* 1:178–79)[10]

they were voicing a deep-seated cultural bias all the more emphatically, since Tao's status has never been seriously challenged since Song times.

Yet it is precisely such objections that highlight the uniqueness of Tao's *tianyuan shi* in clearing a new path for poetry, never attempted in literati verse before and seldom written with the same sureness of touch afterward. For while he has made the daily moods and events of rural life worthy subjects and enriched poetic diction with his simple language, few of his emulators can write with the same authentic stroke that stems unfeignably from personal experience. Tao made no vehement declaration against the inherited code of poetic taboos, but what is sure is that he would have betrayed the reality of his life—hence his artistic conscience and identity—had he followed that code. Thematically and formally, what his poetry reflects is a total trust in *zhen* and *ziran* capable of transcending even long-standing cultural orientations. Measured against these and the general experiential horizon of the literati, Tao's poetic achievement takes on a larger cultural significance. If his lyricism is rightly hailed as truthful and natural, it is also because, in restoring the material basis of spiritual life as the "infrastructure" of poetry, it unwittingly redresses a cultural slant perpetuated in literati verse most of the time.

Not that Tao was set on being a poetic and cultural iconoclast; as we have seen all along, he was following the guide of his intuition and experience. Yet it is a telling index of both traditional values and the poet's genius that even when the modern critic Lu Xun called for appreciating him as a "total man" in terms of his tranquil and ardent sides (*H* 1:286), his focus still remained on Tao's inner spirit. But just as his ideals are not disjoined from praxis, the material and spiritual sides of the poet's life merge with the form-content unison of his verse into a polyhedral unity that reveals in a total sense how Tao's poetry is really the man. And if this is what marks the literary and cultural originality of his "total art," the paradox must remain that it comes at times almost as a literary by-product not unlike that of his spiritual mentor Zhuangzi, who also wrote some of the most fascinating literature in the Chinese tradition in the course of expressing a vision of life. Often hailed by the Song poets as a paragon of "natural beauty" (*H* passim), Tao is the unwitting prophet who laid down a supreme aesthetic through truthful expression.

It is useful to remember that a poetry of *zhen* and *ziran* does not mean artistic automatism, as some Song critics seem to imply when they say Tao "does not write poetry." Shi Decao's statement that he "turns whatever he sees into poetry . . . without the least action" (*H* 1:56) is no isolated remark, but reflective of a common perception that comes perilously close to making his art a mystical Midas touch. But as always, the key to the poet's art lies in his life: just as his quest winds its course from an original innocence through a complicated world to a higher simplicity that incorporates the wisdom of experience, so his poetry is distilled from a sure instinct through the artistic process to a higher naturalness and lucidity. If language necessarily mediates and distorts truth, Tao must have known that a less contrived language which does not make itself a goal of pursuit, and returns to simplicity much like Zhuangzi's notion of "forgetting" mental exertion, at least comes nearer to the spirit of Dao; his "bland," natural style is thus best seen as the confluence of a life vision, spontaneous instinct, and knowing choice. We have shown how Tao transcends the intellectual gymnastics of *xuanyan shi*, the escapist fantasy of *youxian shi*, and the flamboyant taste which infected poets of his age, but it is more crucial to recognize that this artistic choice is part of a total quest for an undeflected "true meaning" in life. It is perhaps pastoral verse which offers the best touchstone for Tao's approach to poetry: not as a self-sustaining structure of art, but a lyric expression of experience and vision. But still Shi's remark would only make sense if taken to mean *wu wei*, the absence of artificial effort other than what pertains to "natural art." To see the naturalness of Tao's poetry as pure spontaneous overflow is to overlook the artistic process and the nature of language; to take it as an impression or a deceptive ploy born of manipulation is to be confined within the process and medium while missing the underlying spirit. The prismatic simplicity of the person is at once the crystalline transparency of his poetry, and the direction of the artistic quest becomes a symbolic parallel to the direction of the existential quest.

Here, it seems, we are in a position to see the multiple significance of the poetry to the artist. Whether or not Tao consciously worked with an "existential poetics" one cannot be sure, but in expressing his sentiments often as a substitute for communication lacking in the world, in recording the path of his existence and speaking the truth of the Way, poetry becomes both witness to his being and inspiration to his ideals, standing in mutualistic accord with his life. The lyric and the aesthetic converge in a total endeavor itself authenticated by the truth of Nature, and poetry will always serve as an available reel of experience which he can turn back to relive the memorable moments of his life, moments of faith and illumination that will sustain him through a shattering reality. And while we marvel at the rare sublimity that comes from the fusion of a natural art and a truthful spirit, we realize the paradox that this sublimity is ultimately not meant as art: for those who see into the *zhen*, *ziran*, and *shan* of things, it is no more than a crystallization of the intrinsic verve of original forms.[11] Tao never made the statement himself, but the unity of art and life is no stale dictum for the quintessential artist of life.

Epilogue

A Destiny between Fate, Nature, and Heaven's Decree

At the beginning of his *fu* "Moved by Literati Not Fitting Their Time," Tao states that since of all creation man alone is endowed with spiritual capacity, he should always be true to his nature:

或擊壤以自歡	One may delight himself with the *jirang* game
或大濟於蒼生	Or bring great benefit to mankind.
靡潛躍之非分	Neither hiding nor leaping ill-fits his nature;
常傲然以稱情	For he always nobly suits his feelings.

(*TYJ* 147)

These two wishes, as we have seen, define the fundamental tension of his inner spirit. Fulfillment of his social mission followed by a return to Nature would have constituted an ideal life, but while the *shi* "hopes to improve his virtue to match the time, / The time, when it comes, proves unpropitious" (*TYJ* 147). Instructed as he is by the ancients that "the way of Heaven . . . ever aids goodness and supports humanity" (*TYJ* 148), the poet is at times shaken by his painful experience and the tragic destinies of worthies like Bo Yi and Yan Hui to question the moral efficacy of Heaven:

疑報德之若茲	I wonder if the requital of virtue should be thus;
懼斯言之虛陳	I fear such works are falsely laid down.
. . . .	. . . .
蒼旻遐緬	Azure Heaven is so remote,
. . . .	. . . .
疇測其理	Who can fathom its workings?

(*TYJ* 148)

Bitterly he laments "I learnt the Way when my hair was bound in tufts; now, white-headed, I have accomplished nothing" (*TYJ* 15). And at the nadir of his faith, he even verges on a pessimism that sees life as empty of meaning:

人生似幻化	Human life is like the changes of an illusion,
終當歸空無	Ultimately returning to blank nothingness.

(*TYJ* 42)

吾生夢幻間	Born into the illusion of a dream,
何事紲塵羈	Why should I tie myself to dusty bonds?

(*TYJ* 91)

Still, born into times that cannot be altered for all one's idealism, "Better be firm in adversity and follow one's bent / Than stoop and burden oneself" (*TYJ* 148). The poet's innate truthfulness is refined through a lifelong quest into a higher composure, and contemplating his death in the poems "In Imitation of Burial Songs," his voice is objective and calm:

有生必有死	Where there is life there must be death;
早終非命促	An early end is not at the urging of fate.
. . . .	. . . .
得失不復知	Attainment and loss are no longer known,
是非安能覺	Right and wrong, can they be felt?

(#1, *TYJ* 141)

The tinge of resignation in the question is soon dispersed by a light sense of humor with which he looks at his "corpse":

但恨在世時	I only regret that while alive,
飲酒不得足	I did not have enough wine to drink.

(#1, *TYJ* 141)

The pathos of death seems a little stronger in #2 with its portrait of a desolate scene, but the depiction forms part of a factual, subdued description of the circumstantial differences between life and death, which is conveyed in the same balanced tone without lapsing into a self-pitying plaint about separation. Likewise, while the first half of #3 describes a bleak natural scene that seems to deepen the pathos, the latter is soon put into perspective:

向來相送人	Those who earlier came to escort me
各自還其家	Now return, each to his own home.
親戚或餘悲	My relatives may feel some lingering grief;
他人亦已歌	Others have already begun singing.

(#3, *TYJ* 142)

The weeping of the first two poems gradually gives way to sounds of singing, for death is as much a passing event as life, which soon reverts to normal from its brief interruption. Just as Zhuangzi asks "How do I know that the love of life is not a delusion and that . . . death is not like . . . a homecoming?" (Z 2/78–79), Tao speaks of death as a return to his "old abode" *(jiuzhai)* or "original abode" *(benzhai)*.[1] If Wordsworth reconciles himself to dear Lucy's death in seeing her "Rolled round in earth's diurnal course, / With rocks, and stones, and trees,"[2] Tao knows with the same inner serenity that he is returning to the universal cradle embracing and equalizing all:

死去何所道	Dead and gone, what is to be said?
託體同山阿	The body, entrusted to the hillside, has become one with it.

(*TYJ* 142)

With a clarity of vision reminiscent of the concluding insight in "Body, Shadow, and Spirit," the poet sees his "death" as a reunion of individual with cosmic being.

Meanwhile, echoing Sima Qian's eulogy of Confucius, he bequeaths his unfulfilled ideal to his sons in what is meant to be a testament:

> In the *Songs* it is said: "The lofty mountains I look up to, / The bright road I walk." Though incapable of this myself, I revere the ideal with all my heart.[3] Take heed [of the Way]! What more can I say? (*TYJ* 188–89)[4]

It is telling that Confucius's vision constitutes the content of the poet's "will," for it reveals not only the *shi*'s idealism to the last but a final meaning Tao's writings hold for him, one that, relating not to himself but to posterity, connects his personal identity as a poet to his larger identity as a trustee of the cultural heritage. Just as Confucius saw himself as a guardian of culture transmitting *(shu)* the Way (*A* 9/5, 7/1), and putatively compiled the *Spring and Autumn Annals* after the failure of his social mission in order to make his way "known to later ages" (*SJ* 47/6:1943), the poet hopes the link he has secured with past worthies can be extended into the future:

> As the year draws to its close, sadly I express the cares of my heart. If I do not transmit *(shu)* them now, how can later generations hear about them? (*TYJ* 106)[5]

In the ironic outcome, it is partly the altruist's failure that makes for the poet's immortality, as later generations came to be inspired by the moving expression of the life and ideals of one forced to the fringe of his time and his world. The need to "illuminate the Way" remains even as one lives obscurely in hopeless times (*X* 22/43–44), and writing as a transmission of truth becomes a substitute fulfillment of public duty, shown graphically in the words he bequeaths to his sons. On this level of concern, Tao is not just yearning for a kindred spirit to understand the tunes of his heart, but using literature as a means of preserving culture. If he does not have Wordsworth's proud confidence to pray that his verse "With star-like virtue in its place may shine, / Shedding benignant influence on all future generations,"[6] he certainly hopes to carry on the spirit of Dao through the sentiments conveyed in his writings: the eulogies of historical and fictional worthies, the recording of illuminations amid Nature, the delineation of the utopian society—all become signposts to archetypal ideals at a time when they seemed completely lost.

It is in part this undying sense of vocation, moving "precisely because he is not all tranquility and mildness," as Lu Xun puts it (*H* 1:286), that sustains the poet to the end. "Life and death are a matter of decree, riches and honor lie with Heaven," he instructs his sons (*TYJ* 187), quoting Confucius again (*A* 12/5). Just as classical Confucian texts teach the *shi* to "cultivate himself according to the Way" and leave fate to take its course, "do what is proper to his position, . . . live in ease of mind and await his destiny" (*Mn* 1,14; *M* 7A/1), Tao knows he must leave aside the inscrutable part of Heaven's dictates *(ming)* while striving to fulfill its moral decree *(tian ming):*

奉上天之成命	To revere the established decrees of Heaven above
師聖人之遺書	And model oneself on the bequeathed writings of the sages.

(*TYJ* 147)

But while affinity to mankind and Nature may both be natural, Tao is compelled by history to a painful termination of his social effort. In the outcome, the "rightful destiny *(fen)*" that he fulfills (*TYJ* 98) pertains only to the Daoist side of his disposition, and it is in Nature that he manages to "find delight in Heaven's decree" (*TYJ* 162). This delight, to be sure, is a distillate of dense complexities and an equilibrium of tensional sentiments, just as the prismatic lucidity of his art is one that refracts into contrastive hues. Still, as he looks back on his life in his elegiac piece to himself, the poet ultimately finds no regret for the "solitary course" he has taken in fidelity to his heart:

勤靡餘勞	My toil was free from excessive weariness;
心有常閑	My heart was filled with constant ease.

樂天委分
以至百年
. . . . . .
捽兀窮廬
酣飲賦詩
識運知命
疇能罔眷
余今斯化
可以無恨

Content with Heaven and accepting my lot,
I have lived out my hundred years.
. . . .
Remaining unyielding in my poor hut,
I drank to my heart's content and wrote poems.
I recognized fate and knew my destiny,
Though who can be without concern?
As I now undergo this transformation,
I can find no cause for regret.

(*TYJ* 197)

Indeed, anguished as he is at the solitary turnings in his quest, the poet sustains himself with the inner torch of wisdom that lights up his way. Given the frustration of his social idealism which no personal contentment can quite mollify, the seesawing tension between grief and delight, disquietude and peace of mind, solitude and independence is ultimately irresolvable:

徘徊無定止
夜夜聲轉悲

Back and forth, [the bird] finds no stable
resting-place,
From night to night, its voice turns more mournful.

(*TYJ* 88)

嘯傲東軒下
聊復得此生

I whistle freely below the eastern eaves,
Having somehow regained my life again.

(*TYJ* 90)

欲言無予和
揮杯勸孤影

I wish to talk, but there is none to answer;
So I raise my cup and urge my lonely shadow.

(*TYJ* 115)

知音苟不存
已矣何所悲

Even if no kindred spirit exists,
Let it be. What is there to be sad about?

(*TYJ* 123)

But in a living acceptance of the Way lies the fundamental capacity for self-transcendence. If Qu Yuan remains fettered because he cannot surrender his spirit to a larger frame of being,[7] Tao attains bliss and enlightenment during the lyric moments when he loses himself in Nature. "In a moment's glance I embrace the universe," he writes (*TYJ* 133), and the line rings of Mencius as of Zhuangzi (*M* 7A/13, *Z* 2/77), his Confucian and Daoist sentiments coming to a unison. If the self cannot fulfill its destiny in "perfect[ing] the empire," it can at least "return to purify [it]self" (*M* 7A/9, 5A/7; *TYJ* 147, 145) in a mode of existence to which it can faithfully belong. True piety is acting on what one knows, and understanding is lost if not translated into action. Riding through his lifelong trial with an abiding truthfulness, the poet knows that the choice of an authentic existence is never heroically made with a single leap of faith. The quest winds its course through an unending spiral, passing and returning to the same existential signposts at different levels of beckoning. In action predicated on self-knowledge, in honest living amid an illuminating Nature and an epiphanic vision that unites him with the Way, Tao attains the shifting repose he longs for. A shifting repose, indeed, for it needs to be revitalized every day of his life, every moment afresh and anew.

Notes

Notes for Introduction

1 For a summary of the historical controversy over the still unsettled issue of Tao's dates, see *D* 2:189–92. I have adopted the traditional dates in the absence of compelling evidence to overturn them.

2 Throughout this study I shall be using "sentiments" in a broader sense than that understood in eighteenth-century Western aesthetics to refer to "an attitude, thought or judgement permeated or prompted by feeling: a complex of emotion and idea" *(Webster's Third International Dictionary).*

Notes for Chapter 1: The Spirit of the Age

1 The "bonds" are those between ruler and subject, father and son, husband and wife, while the "rules" cover one's relationships with one's paternal uncles, brothers, relatives of the same surname, maternal uncles, teachers and elders, and friends. See Ban Gu (32–92), comp., *Baihu tongyi*, "Sangang liuji," in *Zhongguo zhexueshi ziliao xuanji—LiangHan zhi bu*, 2:452–53.

2 For a detailed analysis of the issue, see Yü, "Individualism and the Neo-Taoist Movement in Wei-Chin China," 121–43.

3 Strictly speaking, the term "Neo-Daoism" is not quite indicative of the intellectual movement in Wei–Jin China; thinkers like Wang Bi, He Yan,

and Guo Xiang are basically syncretic, being Daoist in their metaphysics and Confucian in their social and political philosophy. Nevertheless, "Neo-Daoism" remains a convenient term to describe the general trend of an intellectual movement centered around the texts of *Laozi* and *Zhuangzi*. Manifested mainly as "abstruse learning" *(xuanxue)* and "pure conversation" *(qingtan)*, the movement is a multi-faceted one characterized by a transcendental air, finding expression in metaphysics, art and aesthetics, life-style, and religion.

4 Liu Shao, *Renwu zhi*, 13 (ch. 4). For an English translation of Liu's work, see J. K. Shryock, *The Study of Human Abilities, The* Jen Wu Chih *of Liu Shao* (New Haven: American Oriental Society, 1937).

5 The term is used for convenience here; for a discussion of the notorious problem of authorship of *Laozi*, see Lau, trans., *Tao Te Ching*, 147–62.

6 Again the name refers less to the person than to the spirit revealed in the text that bears his name, especially its first seven "inner" chapters.

7 Ch'en, "Tao Yuanming zhi sixiang yu qingtan zhi guanxi," 1:383.

8 Commentary on *L* 1, 25, 19; in Wang Bi, *Wang Bi ji* [jiaoshi], 1:1, 77, 65. Cf. Rump and Chan, trans., *Commentary on the "Lao Tzu" by Wang Pi*, 1, 88, 78.

9 See also Mather, "The Controversy over Conformity and Naturalness during the Six Dynasties," esp. 164–65.

10 Ch'en, "Tao Yuanming zhi sixiang," 1:383.

11 See Yü, "Individualism and the Neo-Taoist Movement in Wei–Chin China," 141–43.

12 Hsiao, *History of Chinese Political Thought*, 1: 612; emphasis mine.

13 For Wang Bi, see Chen Shou, *Sanguo zhi, Wei shu* 28/3:795, commentary quoting from He Shao's *Wang Bi biezhuan*; also quoted in SX 4/6, n.2. For Guo Xiang, see *SX* 4/17. For a summary of the life circumstances of He Yan, Wang Bi, Xiang Xiu, and Guo Xiang, and the spirit of compromise permeating their commentaries, see Demiéville, 830–37.

14 See for instance Hsiao, 1: 616–18 for Xi Kang's and Guo Xiang's views on maintaining the political order as a minimal one that governs through *wu wei*.

15 阮宣子有令聞，太尉王夷甫見而問曰：「老莊與聖教同異？」對曰：「將無同？」太尉善其言，辟之為掾，世謂「三語掾。」
In *Jin shu* this incident is attributed to Ruan Zhan and Wang Rong (*JS* 49/5:1363), but the point remains the same. All translations are mine unless otherwise stated; translations of official titles follow Hucker, *Dictionary of Official Titles*. Cf. Mather, trans., *Shih-shuo hsin-yü: A New Account of Tales of the World*, 101.

16 Ch'en, "Tao Yuanming zhi sixiang," 1:390–95.

17 Ibid., 1:390.

18 See ch. 6 for a discussion of the Jin literati's identification of Nature with Dao.

19 See Z 6/1–20, 8/1–22.

20 See Gao Heng, ed., *Zhouyi dazhuan*, 205, 308. Cf. Wilhelm, trans., *The I Ching, or Book of Changes*, 78, 132.

21 *Chuci*, "Yufu," in Hawkes, trans., *Songs of the South*, 206–7.

22 Chen Shou, *Sanguo zhi*, *Wei shu* 21/3:606; also *SX* 18/2.

23 Watson, *Chinese Lyricism*, 75. Among those who wrote poems entitled "Zhaoyin" are Zhang Hua, Lu Ji, Zuo Si, Zhang Zai, Lüqiu Chong, and Wang Kangju; see *XQH* 1:622, 689–92, 734–35, 740, 750, 2:953. The list does not include poets who wrote on a similar theme or mixed it with others in poems that are not entitled "Zhaoyin"; see for instance Pan Ni's "Yimin yin" and Guo Pu's "Youxian shi," *XQH* 1:769–70, 2:865–67.

24 Ge Hong, *Baopuzi*, "Wai pian 1: Jia dun," in his *Baopuzi nei wai pian*, 3:404; see also Wang Yi-t'ung, *Wuchao mendi*, 1:237–38.

25 "Sigui yin: xu," *XQH* 1:643.

26 See also *JS* 79/7:2073, 2087; Sima Guang, *Zizhi tongjian*, 100/4:3177; 101/4:3183; *SX* 2/70, 6/28 n.1; 25/26–27.

27 A reference to *Shijing* #186, in which the host's effort to keep a guest from leaving subsequently became an allusion to a ruler's effort to retain his worthy officials.

28 See biographies of Fan Qiao, Ren Xu, Meng Lou, Guo Fan, Xin Mi, Liu Linzhi, and Gong Xuanzhi in *JS* 94/8:2432–33, 2438–39, 2442–48, 2459.

29 Murakami, "In-itsu," 461–79.

30 See *JS* 49/5:1368 and *SX* 18/6 for Ruan Yu; *JS* 80/7:2101 for Wang Xizhi; *JS* 79/7:2072–73 and *SX* 7/21 for Xie An.

31 As a question in Yang Xiong's (53 B.C.–A.D. 18) *Fa yan* attests: "Some people asked: Wasn't Liuxia Hui a *chaoyin*?" See "Yuan Qian," in *Fayan* [yishu], ed. Wang Rongbao, 2 vols. (Taipei: Yiwen yinshuguan, n.d.), 2:712.

32 Allusion to *A* 7/11.

33 See also biography of Yu Ai in *JS* 50/5:1395–96.

34 See biographies of Yu Ai, ibid., Xie Kun, Humu Fuzhi, Bi Zhuo, Wang Ni, Yang Man, and Guang Yi in *JS* 49/5:1377–85, esp. 1385.

35 See also *SX* 26/9, 16, 22; 27/12. Sun's self-justification was: "For those who comprehend the mystical and know the far-reaching, public life and seclusion end up being the same" (*SX* 4/91, n.1).

36 *JS* 94/8:2440–41; quotation taken from the biography of another hermit Suo Xi, *JS* 94/8:2449.

37 *JS* 94/8:2430, 2440, 2444–46, 2448; biographies of Zhu Chong, Guo Wen, Qiao Xiu, Zhai Tang, Zhai Zhuang, Guo Fan, and Liu Linzhi.

38 *JS* 94/8:2430, biography of Zhu Chong.

39 *JS* 94/8:2426–27, 2437–38; biographies of Sun Deng, Dong Jing, and Lu Bao.

Notes for Chapter 2: The Dilemma of Engagement or Reclusion

1 Literally "break the soil," a game like throwing darts, symbolic of the peaceful times of the legendary age. In contrast to the following line, it implies withdrawal as an alternative to public service.

2 *Yijing*, Hexagram 1 "Qian," an alternative expression for retirement and service. See Goa Heng, ed., *Zhouyi dazhuan*, 56–58; cf. Wilhelm, trans., *I Ching*, 7–9.

3 Throughout this book the titles of Tao's writings are given in English only. The Chinese titles are sometimes very long, and in any case can be easily located in any single-volume collection of Tao's works. The

Chinese titles of works by other authors mentioned in the book are given at first appearance.

4 Wang Zhongluo, *Wei Jin Nanbeichao shi,* 1:325–28, 333–39.

5 Ibid., 1:280–85, 358. Fu was emperor of the Former Qin kingdom (r. 357–85). The Battle of Fei River is regarded by some as having been less critical than historically represented; see Rogers, trans., *Chronicle of Fu Chien,* 64–69. However, neither this issue nor the subsequent loss of the recovered territories (as on previous occasions) would have annulled the battle's inspiring impact on the poet.

6 古之真人，不逆寡，不雄成，不謨士。…不知説生，不知惡死；…受而喜之，忘而復之。…與物有，而莫知其極。…利澤施乎萬世，不為愛人。…與乎其觚而不堅也，張乎其虛而不華也；…與乎止我德也。

Cf. *Z* 1/21, 2/52–53, 92; 33/65–67.

7 Allusion to *Liji* 32, "Biao ji," in Wang Meng'ou, trans., *Liji* [jinzhu jinyi], 2:704.

8 自真風告逝，大偽斯興，閭閻懈廉退之節，市朝驅易進之心。懷正志道之士，或潛玉於當年；潔己清操之人，或沒世以徒勤。

9 Liu Yi's statement as quoted in his biography in *JS* 45/4:1274. For an account of the development of the *shizu* system that became predominant after Wei times, see Wang Zhongluo, *Wei Jin Nanbeichao shi,* 1:142–56, 209–14, 319–25, 328–31. See also Wang Yi-t'ung, *Wuchao mendi,* vol. 1, ch. 1, 3, 4, 5, esp. paragraphs on the Jin.

10 See Lin Wen-yüeh, "The Decline and Revival of *Feng-ku* (Wind and Bone)," 130–66, esp. 135–45.

11 The Duke of Zhou is quoted by Sima Qian as saying, "At any meal I may spit out my food several times and rise from the table to receive men of standing, but still I worry about passing up the empire's worthy men" (*SJ* 33/5:1518).

12 *L* 70: "The sage wears coarse clothes and carries jade within him."

13 As Confucius describes his often hungry disciple Yan Hui (*A* 11/19).

14 The dwelling of the recluse. Master Ban is Ban Gu.

15 See *D* 1:82–83, 1:80–1/2:67–68 and 1:87/2:76–77 for a discussion of the issues involved, although Davis's reasoning does not settle them conclusively.

16 Okamura, *Tō Enmei,* 124–26.

17 These ran from the open insurgencies of Wang Dun (322–24) and Su Jun (327–29), through the smouldering dynastic ambitions of Huan Wen (347–73), whom Tao's maternal grandfather, Meng Jia, once served as aide, to the collective rebellion of Wang Gong, Yin Zhongkan, and Huan Xuan (398–99). See Wang Zhongluo, *Wei Jin Nanbeichao shi,* 1:331–39, 359–60.

18 Ibid., 1:365–67; Sima Guang, *Zizhi tongjian,* 8: 3723–24, 3732–40.

19 Wang Zhongluo, *Wei Jin Nanbeichao shi,* 1:130–31, 161–71, 212–14, 344–52.

20 Ibid., 1:361–65. See also Werner Eichhorn, "Description of the Rebellion of Sun En and Earlier Taoist Rebellions," *Mitteilungen des Instituts für Orientforschung* 2.2(1954):325–52; "Nachträgliche Bemerkungen zum Aufstande des Sun En," ibid., 2.3(1954):463–76; Hisayuki, "Local Cults around Mount Lu at the Time of Sun En's Rebellion."

21 Owen, "The Self's Perfect Mirror," 85, 81, 78.

22 Cf. Yu-kung Kao's distinction between "physical eye" and "mind's eye" pertaining to description in this poem; see his "The Aesthetics of Regulated Verse," 371.

23 This is everywhere evident in "Li sao"; see for instance ll. 89–96, in Hawkes, trans., *Songs of the South,* 70. The name of Qu Yuan is also used in this study for convenience, since there are problems regarding both the historical figure and the authenticity of the poems attributed to him. Ibid., 28–38, 51–61.

24 Bauer, "The Hidden Hero," 181.

25 See ibid., 162–63, for a discussion of the question of eremitism as raised in the *Analects.*

26 Not that the occupation is beneath the dignity of a *shi,* but that he should devote his limited energies to "the fundamentals" (*A* 1/2).

27 Perhaps also from an anecdote in *Zhuangzi* where a transformed Yan Hui preferred husbandry to serving (Z 28/52).

28 There is an antecedent to Tao's poem by Yang Yun (d. 54 B.C.): "I farmed that southern hill, / But the weeds could not be kept back. / I planted an acre with beans, / But they fell off, leaving bare stems"; see *XQH* 1:112–13, *HS* 66/9:2889–98. While Yang's verse (occurring in a letter) clearly refers to his experience at the court, there is no strong reason to read Tao's poem politically; Yang's circumstances as a disgraced high official turned landlord and grain speculator have little in common with those of Tao, who partly assimilated the former's language for his own purpose.

29 Owen, "The Self's Perfect Mirror," 88, 80, 78, 85.

30 *A* 15/1: "The Master said, 'The superior man stands firm in adversity; the petty man in adversity goes to excess.'" See also *TYJ* 78, 96, 148.

31 This refers to the self-serving opportunism practised by many Jin literati in the name of some high-sounding principle; see Wang Xizhi's statement on pp. 18–19.

32 It may be noted that in the Chinese ideal, the wish for "immortality" represents not a personal pursuit but a commitment to moral exemplification and cultural continuity. As laid down in order of priority in *Zuozhuan*, the three ways to immortality are the establishment of virtue, meritorious deeds, and teachings (Duke Xiang, 24th year [549 B.C.]); in Yang Bojun, ed., *Chunqiu Zuozhuan* [zhu], 3:1088.

33 These include Confucius's favorite pupil Yan Hui (*TYJ* 93, 148, 182) and Qian Lou (*TYJ* 125, 175), who remained indifferent to offers of high office; both lived contentedly in poverty. See also *TYJ* 123–28 for other eulogized poor scholars.

34 Commentary, ch. 2; in Zhu Xi, ed., *Sishu* [zhangju jizhu], 5.

35 "I wandered lonely as a cloud," ll. 21–22, in Wordsworth, *Poetical Works*, 149.

36 Witness Confucius's own anxiety as a frustrated social visionary, though he is no hermit (*SJ* 47/6:1942–4).

37 Such as those registered in "Return Home" *fu*, "Returning to Live on the Farmstead" #1, and "Drinking Wine" #5.

38 The Chinese *jiu*, translated as "wine" for convenience, is usually not grape wine but an alcoholic drink made from one of a number of fruits

or grains; see references to it in *Food in Chinese Culture,* ed. Kwang-chih Chang (New Haven: Yale Univ. Press, 1977).

39 Mote sees withdrawal to be "intrinsically valuable" for the Daoist, while Vervoorn contends that "eremitism, properly understood, was [for Zhuangzi] the highest ideal to which a man can aspire"; see Mote, "Confucian Eremitism in the Yüan Period," 256; Vervoorn, *Men of the Cliffs and Caves,* 280. However, eremitism involves a moral dilemma between public service and personal integrity that is no issue for the pure Daoist, because to insist on reclusion is to return to the realm of humanistic distinctions and fall short of a total independence from circumstantial confines.

40 First noted by Shen Yue in his biography of Tao in *Song shu,* in *H* 1:5. In his eagerness to prove Tao's loyalty, however, Shen wrongly claimed that Tao dated all his writings and put Jin reign titles on them up to the Yixi period (405–18). There are in fact only fourteen pieces dated according to the cyclical-sign system, and only one with a Jin reign title. See Zhu Ziqing, "Tao Yuanming nianpu zhong zhi wenti," s. 3, in *H* 1:307–12; *D* 2:188–89; Li Wenchu, *Tao Yuanming lunlüe,* 22–25.

41 See #1 and #6, *TYJ* 109, 112.

42 *H* 1:4–5, 8, 104, 133, 218.

43 *H* 1:269; Yeh, "Cong 'Haohua luojin jian zhenchun' lun Tao Yuanming zhi 'renzhen' yu 'guqiong,'" in her *Jialing lunshi conggao,* 42–43.

44 See also *TYJ* 14, 24, 99, 147, 179, 188. The "Three Dynasties" are Xia, Shang, and Zhou.

45 Yeh, *Lunshi conggao,* 43.

46 Fukunaga, "Tō Enmei no 'shin' ni tsuite," 50–51. He states that *zhen* appears 3 times in *Laozi* and 67 times in *Zhuangzi.*

47 Mou Zongsan, *Zhongguo zhexue shijiu jiang,* 20–27.

48 In strict Daoist terms, however, the truth of Dao is objectively immanent in all being, and there is no ground for making any distinction between the "intensional" and the "extensional," which is itself symptomatic of man's differentiating urge and misguided reliance on conceptual reason.

49 See Horie, *Tō Enmei,* 238.

50 See Fukunaga, "Tō Enmei," 61–69.

51 *Zuozhuan*, Duke Yin, 3rd year (720 B.C.): "The ruler's righteousness, the minister's conduct, the father's kindness, the son's filial piety, the elder brother's love, the younger brother's respect—these are what is meant by the six natural duties." In Yang Bojun, ed., *Chunqiu Zuozhuan*, 1:32.

52 *L* 39: "Heaven obtained the one and became clear."

53 In Xi Kang, *Xi Kang ji* [jiaozhu], 235.

54 Cf. Kao, "Lyric Vision in Chinese Narrative," 230.

55 See *TYJ* 115–19, #1, 2, 3, 5, 6, 7.

56 *Di* being the stalk or base of a leaf, flower, or fruit, this line is much more imagistic than is rendered here; the Chinese original evokes images of a rootless plant and a stalkless leaf/flower.

57 A bird into which the drowned daughter of the legendary Emperor Yan was transformed, which constantly carries twigs and stones in her mouth to fill up the sea where she was drowned.

58 Who had his head cut off in his struggle with the Heavenly Emperor, but continued to brandish his shield and battle axe.

59 Wang Changling, "Cong jun xing," *QTS* 4:1444.

60 Li Bai, "Guan shan yue," *QTS* 5:1689.

61 See *JS* 94/8:2460–64; *SS* 93/8:2286–91; Li Yanshou, *Nan shi*, 75/6:1856–59; in *H* 1:3–6, 11–14.

Notes for Chapter 3: Peach Blossom Spring and Visions of Utopia

1 It may be interesting to note that in one of the anecdotes about recluses in the *Analects*, "the old man carrying a basket on a staff" kills a chicken and invites Zilu to a meal (*A* 18/7). Tao himself, as we have seen, also killed a chicken to treat his neighbors (*TYJ* 43).

2 芳華鮮美，落英繽紛。…林盡水源，便得一山。山有小口，…初極狹，…豁然開朗。土地平曠，屋舍儼然。有良田、美池、桑竹之屬。阡陌交通，雞犬相聞。…黃髮垂髫，並怡然自樂。見漁人，乃大驚。…便要還家，為設酒殺雞作食。…自云先世避秦時亂，…問今是何世，乃不知有漢，無論魏晉。

3 See for instance the stories in Gan Bao, *Soushen ji,* 123–25. For English translations of selected *zhiguai* stories, see Karl S. Y. Kao, ed., *Classical Chinese Tales of the Supernatural and the Fantastic* (Bloomington: Indiana Univ. Press, 1985).

4 In Tao's writings I have found 6 references to Shun, 5 to the Yellow Emperor, 4 to Yao, 2 each to Fuxi and Shennong, only 1 to Yu, and none to Tang, Kings Wen and Wu, or the Duke of Zhou.

5 大道之行也，天下為公。選賢與能，講信修睦，故人不獨親其親，不獨子其子；使老有所終，壯有所用，幼有所長。矜寡孤獨廢疾者，皆有所養。…〔貨〕不必藏於己，…〔力〕不必為己。是故謀閉而不興，盜竊亂賊而不作，故外戶而不閉，是謂大同。

Liji 9, "Li yun," in Wang Meng'ou, trans., *Liji,* 1:290.

6 Yü, "Neo-Taoist Movement," 122. See also Yü's "Mingjiao weiji yu Wei Jin shifeng de zhuanbian," in his *Shi yu Zhongguo wenhua,* 404–8.

7 蓋無君而庶物定，無臣而萬事理，…君立而虐興，臣設而賊生。

Ruan Ji, *Ruan Ji ji* [jiaozhu], 170.

8 曩古之世，無君無臣。穿井而飲，耕田而食。日出而作，日入而息。泛然不系，恢爾自得。不競不營，無榮無辱。

Quoted in Ge Hong, *Baopuzi*, "Wai pian 48: Jie Bao," in his *Baopuzi nei wai pian*, 4:774. *Baopuzi* is in fact the only source for Bao, whose treatise is quoted in order to be refuted. A complete English translation of the treatise may be found in Balazs, *Chinese Civilization and Bureaucracy,* 243–46.

9 Graham notes that most scholars in China believe *Liezi* was written as late as A.D. 300, an opinion which he shares. See Graham, trans., *Book of Lieh-tzu*, xiii, 1, 12.

10 Yang Bojun, ed., *Liezi* [jishi], 41, 164.

11 Ch'en, "Taohuayuanji pangzheng," also in his *Wenshi lunji,* 1:183–93.

12 自桓玄以來，驅蹙殘敗，…逃亡去就，不避幽深。

13 Tian Chou's biography can be found in Chen Shou, *Sanguozhi, Wei shu* 11/2:340–45. For an English summary, see *HT* 172.

14 Wender, trans., *Hesiod and Theognis* , 62, ll. 112–17.

15 Innes, trans., *The "Metamorphoses" of Ovid*, 31–32 (Book I).

16 Whether or not this is meant literally is a moot point: while it may be a metaphor for all the plenitude and harmony described, the strongly mythical dimension in Ovid, with gods originally living in affinity with men, means that an unchanging "season" is not out of place. The issue, however, does not vitiate the argument here.

17 Wells, trans., *The Idylls of Theocritus*, 86.

18 Lee, trans., *Virgil: The Eclogues*, 57.

19 Richard Puttenham (1520?–1601?), *The Arte of English Poesie* (1589), bk. 1, ch. 18, in Barrell and Bull, eds., *English Pastoral Verse*, 21.

20 It is possible to see in the golden radiance of pastoral an expedient ideological tool serving the interests of those (including poet and patrons) who determine the political, economic, and cultural formations of society, by neutralizing the harshness of rural life and reducing complex inequalities to simple idyllic terms. Such interpretation along class lines, though, does not account for the total social relevance of the pastoral vision.

21 In Eclogue 1 a dialogue is held between Meliboeus, a shepherd dispossessed of his fields in the course of a civil war, and Tityrus (generally regarded as the poet's persona), who has preserved his land.

22 In Barrell and Bull, eds., *English Pastoral Verse*, 151–53.

23 This is admittedly the view of the periodicity of the golden age discernible in Virgil, rather than the Christian view which promises no such general recurrence; but whether taken in Christian terms or otherwise, the golden age remains an inspiring metaphor for all types of idealistic sensibility.

24 See Cervantes, *Don Quixote*, 902.

25 Both philosophies are broadly "humanistic" or "existential" in their focus on the realization of an authentic life.

Notes for Chapter 4: Mortality and the Meaning of Life

1 貴賤賢愚，莫不營營以惜生，斯甚惑焉。故極陳形影之苦，言神辨自然以釋之。

2 Given the epigrammatic terseness and ambiguity of *Laozi*, there are bound to be passages (e.g., *L* 10, 16, 50, 59) that could be construed as being concerned with immortality. For a discussion of some of them, see Welch, *Taoism: The Parting of the Way*, 65–76.

3 Wang Bi, *Wang Bi ji*, 1:29, 23; cf. Rump and Chan, trans., *Commentary on the "Lao Tzu" by Wang Pi*, 40, 29.

4 See *L* 16; Z 1/21–22; Wang Bi, *Wang Bi ji*, 37; *ZJ* 1/1:19–20, nn.10–13.

5 若夫仙人，以藥物養身，以術數延命，使內疾不生，外患不入。雖久視不死，而舊身不改。苟有其道，無以為難也。

Baopuzi, "Neipian 2: Lun xian," in Ge Hong, *Baopuzi neipian* [jiaoshi], 14. Replete with anecdotes and examples meant to attest the attainability of immortality, the book itself may be seen as part of the wave of immortality literature of the time.

6 苟得其要，則八極以外，如在指掌，百代之遠，有若同時。…上能竦身於雲霄，下能潛泳於川海。…掩耳而聞千里，閉目而見將來。

Ge Hong, *Baopuzi*, "Neipian 3: Dui su," ibid., 47, 49, 52.

7 Yü, "Life and Immortality in the Mind of Han China," 91–95, 105–8.

8 *Baopuzi* "Neipian 2: Lun xian," in Ge Hong, *Baopuzi neipian*, 20.

9 Ge Hong, *Shenxian zhuan*, *juan* 2, in Fukui, *Shinsen den*, 110–11.

10 Ch'en, "Tianshi dao yu binhai diyu zhi guanxi," esp. 155–74.

11 See Strickmann, "On the Alchemy of T'ao Hung-ching," 167–69; Welch, *Taoism*, 113–23.

12 Preface to the *Orchid Pavilion Collection*, in *JS* 80/7:2099.

13 See *JS* 94/8:2448 for Liu Linzhi, 2451 for Zhang Zhong, and 2457 for Dai Kui.

14 See Ch'en, "*Weishu* Sima Rui zhuan Jiangdong minzu tiao shizheng ji tuilun," 229–33.

15 Chisongzi and Wangzi Qiao, typical (religious) Daoist immortals.

16 See also *TYJ* 69, 116. These excerpts, as well as the prefatory statement and general drift of "Body, Shadow, and Spirit," do not square with Hightower's observation that both the body and the shadow at least grant the existence of ways to physical immortality; see *HT* 44.

17 See *X* 19/46,120; *Liji* 4, "Tangong xia," in Wang Meng'ou, trans., *Liji,* 1:125. Cf. Fung, *History of Chinese Philosophy,* 1:344–6, 349–50. It may be noted that Confucius himself refused to discuss matters beyond death (*A*11/11).

18 This is #13; a similar outlook is present in #3 and #15. See *XQH* 1:329–30, 332–33.

19 While some of the original teachings of Yang Zhu and Liezi have been incorporated into the *Liezi* we have today, there is no question that the text is apocryphal. The "Yang Zhu Chapter" is a particularly interesting one in that it portrays an inconsistent Yang Zhu: as an amoral egoist much like what is learned from *Mencius* (7A/26, 3B/9), *Lüshi chunqiu* (ch. 17, s. 6), and *Huainanzi* (ch. 13); as a hedonist but not egoist (also in *Huainanzi,* ibid.); as an advocate of self-preservation but not of sensual indulgence in material desires; and as one indifferent to death. See Chan, trans. and comp., *Source Book in Chinese Philosophy,* 309–10; Yang Bojun, ed., *Liezi,* 230–31, 238, 220; Graham, trans., *Book of Lieh-tzu* , 148–49.

20 Yang Bojun, ed., *Liezi,* 234, 220, 226, 238.

21 Ibid., Preface, 5.

22 As the counterpoint to the persona—the socially accepted mask and exposed part of the personality—the shadow is the rejected set of desires, emotions, and attitudes, usually repressed and unacknowledged.

23 Yang Bojun, ed., *Liezi,* 219–20.

24 Mather, "Controversy over Conformity and Naturalness," 179.

25 Ibid.

26 Ch'en Yin-k'o has expressed the same view, albeit without elaboration; see his "Tao Yuanming zhi sixiang," *H* 1:358.

27 Ibid., *H* 1:350–55. Ch'en also argues that Tao "revered *Tianshi dao*" because his family had always followed it (*H* 1:358). But surely Tao is not bound by family tradition to follow *Tianshi dao;* besides, we have seen how he is at odds with certain elements in it. In any case, Daoist and Confucian ideals are far more relevant than the religious sect in understanding the poet's inner constitution.

28 Lu Qinli, on the other hand, reads the poem as a polemic first against contemporary Buddhism with its emphasis on karmic retribution and the soul's immortality, and secondarily against the religious Daoist notion of physical immortality; see "'Xingyingshenshi' yu DongJin zhi Fo Dao sixiang," in his *Han Wei Liuchao wenxue lunji*, 218–46. But while Tao must have been aware of the debate surrounding the Buddhist ideas, there is no compelling ground for a Buddhist reading. In general, Buddhism seems to be of little relevance for understanding Tao's work, despite his reported friendship with Huiguan (334–416) and the marked development of Buddhism during the Eastern Jin.

29 Yoshikawa, *Chūgoku shishi*, 1:277, 283. See also *HT* 45 and *D* 1:36.

30 Mather, "Controversy over Conformity and Naturalness," 178.

31 As when Heaven bereaves Confucius of his short-lived favorite pupil Yan Hui (*A* 11/9, 6/3).

32 T. S. Eliot, "Little Gidding," V, in his *Collected Poems*, 222.

33 不仕無義。…欲潔其身，而亂大倫。君子之仕也，行其義也。道之不行，已知之矣。

34 彼遊方之外者也，而丘遊方之內者也。外內不相及。…反覆終始，不知端倪。芒然彷徨乎塵垢之外，逍遥乎無為之業。

Notes for Chapter 5: Spontaneous Symbolism and Visionary Realism

1 未嘗有喜慍之容。好酣飲，逾多不亂。至於任懷得意，融然遠寄，傍若無人。

2 閑靜少言，不慕名利。好讀書，不求甚解；每有會意，便欣然忘食。性嗜酒，家貧不能常得。親舊知其如此，或置酒而招之。…既醉而退，曾不吝情去留。環堵蕭然，不蔽風日。短褐穿結，簞瓢屢空。晏如也。常著文章自娛，頗示己志。忘懷得失，以此自終。

3 Yoshikawa, *Chūgoku shishi*, 1:284.

4 Owen, "The Self's Perfect Mirror," 78–88.

5 Thus Du Fu (712–70) writes "By my eccentric nature I am addicted to well-wrought expressions, / If my words do not startle others I shall not

rest in death"; "Jiang shang zhi shui ru hai shi liao duan shu," *QTS* 7:2443.

6 Owen, "The Self's Perfect Mirror," 81, 85, 79; even the "Return" poems, whose #1 and #2 Owen quotes, truthfully lay bare this complexity of mood.

7 Qian, *Guanzhui bian*, 4:1228.

8 Owen, "The Self's Perfect Mirror," 75.

9 In *Zhuangzi* "true man" (*zhenren*), "perfect man" (*zhiren*), "spiritual man" (*shenren*), and "sage" (*shengren*) are interchangeable terms for the same ideal of complete spiritual transcendence.

10 Mather, "Individualist Expressions of the Outsiders during the Six Dynasties," 208.

11 Owen, "The Self's Perfect Mirror," 85. For another brief critique of Owen's sceptical treatment of Tao's poetry, see Zhang Longxi, *Tao and the Logos*, 114–17.

12 In the preface to the "Drinking Wine" poems, there is a claim of casualness and spontaneity that has generated some critical responses: Owen views it as a disingenuous gesture aimed at manipulating the reader ("The Self's Perfect Mirror," 80), while Hightower sees a need for the poet to distance himself in order to stay out of political trouble; see his "T'ao Ch'ien's 'Drinking Wine' Poems," 42. Davis objects to Hightower's speculation but gives no alternative explanation, presumably because he agrees with traditional commentators that "originally there was 'no order' [in the poems, though] the final arrangement was skilfully executed" (*D* 1:105–6).

13 Coleridge, *Biographia Literaria*, ch. 15, 2:19–20.

14 A subgenre dating back at least to Ban Gu.

15 *Liji* 41, "Ru xing," in Wang Meng'ou, trans., *Liji*, 2:781.

16 Both Hightower (*HT* 225–28) and Davis (*D* 1:149–51) have given an English summary of Sima Qian's biography of Jing Ke and translations of Ruan Yu's and Zuo Si's poems on Jing as background to their translations of Tao's poem.

17 A musician-friend of Jing Ke's.

18 Similarly sardonic comments on the court politics of the day can be found in his other "Yongshi shi," notably #2, 7, 8, *XQH* 1:733–34.

19 See "Peach Blossom Spring," *TYJ* 166, 167; "Drinking Wine" #20, *TYJ* 99.

20 As pointed out by Tang Han, the Song Yi detail is taken from *Huainanzi* (*TYJ* 132). In this connection, *Yan Danzi* or *Yan Taizi Dan* also comes to mind as a possible source for Tao's poem. But since this text may be later than Tao, I have not compared the two. See Y. W. Ma's entry on *Yen Tan-tzu* in Nienhauser et al., eds., *Indiana Companion to Traditional Chinese Literature*, 930–31; Ma sees the text as a Six Dynasties piece of fiction, having reviewed opinions placing it anywhere between pre-Han and the Southern Qi.

21 These refer to Shu Guang and his nephew Shou, respectively Grand Tutor and Junior Tutor to the Heir Apparent of the Han Emperor Xuan (r. 73–48 B.C.). For abridged translations of Shu Guang's biography, see *D* 1:142–44; *HT* 216–17. The line alludes to *L* 9: "To retire when the task is done is the Way of Heaven."

22 黔婁有言：「不戚戚於貧賤，不汲汲於富貴。」極其言茲若人之儔乎？酣觴賦詩，以樂其忘。無懷氏之民歟？葛天氏之民歟？

23 This is especially notable in the *yuefu* tradition. See for instance "Mo shang sang," "Guer xing," "Jiao Zhongqing qi" (or "Kongque dongnan fei"), Xin Yannian's (Eastern Han) "Yulin lang," and Chen Lin's (d. 217) "Yin ma changcheng ku xing," *XQH* 1:259–60, 270–71, 283–86, 198, 367. The storyline may, of course, be abrupt and incomplete in shorter narrative ballads.

24 Thus Five Willows, the *shi* of the east, and Tian Chou are situationally closer to the poet than Jing Ke and the two Shus. For a discussion of the parallel between Tao and Tian Chou, see *TYJ* 232–33.

25 Kang-i Sun Chang, *Evolution of Chinese Tz'u Poetry*, 19.

26 This is not to ignore the occasionally obscure expression to which Tao was compelled in a poem like "Shu jiu." But there the poet does not speak through an "objective" mode.

27 "Li sao," ll. 9–12, 313–16, in Hawkes, trans., *Songs of the South*, 68, 77. A similar example is furnished by the pepper, ll. 25–28, 317–20, ibid., 69, 77.

28 This is partly because the traditional associations of the plants do not apply in Tao's poetry. Take the willow, which since the time of *Shijing* #167 has been linked to parting; see Frankel, *The Flowering Plum and the Palace Lady*, 95–103, esp. 95–96. As for the peach, it has been connected with sensuous female beauty since *Shijing* #6 (with erotic implications by extension in later usage), and with immortality since *Han Wu gushi*, a Six Dynasties piece of fiction of uncertain date. Were Tao aware of this latter association of the peach (and we cannot be sure), his use of the tree to name his utopia would underline its inaccessible remoteness, if not its status as an immortal realm.

29 See *HT* 170–71 for a discussion of the general indeterminability of the latter poem.

30 見樹木交蔭，時鳥變聲，亦復歡然有喜。

31 Like the poet, the bird may sing joyfully or sadly. The vegetative world and the fish are silent, while the cock and the dog do not have mournful voices in Tao's poetry.

32 Cf. Wu Qi's comment on "Drinking Wine" #7, *H* 2:177.

33 As noted by Yeh, "Cong bijiao xiandai de guandian kan jishou Zhongguo jiushi," in her *Jialing lunshi conggao*, 246.

34 For a more detailed discussion of this *fu*, see Kang-i Sun Chang, *Six Dynasties Poetry*, 43–46.

35 See ch. 8 for an expanded statement on the Han *fu*. The lyric *fu* has been existent at least since Wang Can's (177–217) "*Fu* on Climbing the Tower," but one can see Jia Yi's (200–168 B.C.) "*Fu* on the Owl" as a progenitor.

36 See *D* 1:189–91; Davis thinks that the author's individuality cannot be detected in this "incongruous" piece of writing. For a discussion on the possible precursors of Tao's *fu* and a translation of extant fragments of seven earlier pieces on the same theme, see Hightower, "The *Fu* of T'ao Ch'ien," 45–72.

37 Such as many *Shijing* songs exemplify. Certainly human symbolism is not always explicable in terms of stimulus and response, for the mood may exist before interaction with an external object. This was recognized in ancient Chinese poetics in the distinction between *bi* (metaphorical comparison) and *xing* (stimulus), reflecting the

psychoemotional process wherein feeling is poured into or aroused by scenes and objects.

38 Lu Ji (261–303), "Wen fu," in Guo Shaoyu, ed., *Zhongguo lidai wenlun xuan,* 1:170.

39 氣之動物，物之感人。故搖蕩性情，形諸舞詠。

40 For a summary of the general tendency since the Romantic period to place symbolism above allegory, see Krieger, "'A Waking Dream': The Symbolic Alternative to Allegory," 4. For a latter-day defense of allegory, see de Man, "The Rhetoric of Temporality," in his *Blindness and Insight,* 187–228.

41 As Kang-i Sun Chang shows in her *"Yüeh-fu pu-t'i,"* 353–85. One early example of allegory in nonnarrative Chinese poetry is "Ju song" in *Jiu zhang*.

42 As Coleridge states it in *The Statesman's Manual*. See *The Portable Coleridge*, 388.

43 A number of scholars have variously pointed this out in Bloomfield, ed., *Allegory, Myth, and Symbol*. For instance, Samuel R. Levin notes that while allegorical interpretation is bound to arise out of (indeed, is demanded by) language that shows a clear incompatibility between nouns and predicates, the legitimacy of any specific allegorical reading is far from certain ("Allegorical Language," 23–38, esp. 31–36). And J. Hillis Miller argues that allegory tends "to keep secret in the act of making public" ("The Two Allegories," 357).

44 This is de Man's position, as well as his ground for championing allegory over symbolism as the supreme figural mode.

45 Arguing that "in allegory, the author's intent is imperative," Kang-i Sun Chang quotes Northrop Frye's observation that "allegory is a structural element in narrative: it . . . is not added by critical interpretation alone" ("Allegory," in Preminger et al., eds., *Princeton Encyclopedia,* 12); Maureen Quilligan's explanation that "in dealing with allegorical narrative, a reading cannot escape the text's historical *intentionality*" (*Milton's Spenser: The Politics of Reading* [Ithaca: Cornell Univ. Press, 1983], 26); and Qian Zhongshu's distinction between allegorical writing as an apple with a kernel, and nonallegorical writing as an onion without a heart (*Yeshi ji* [Hong Kong: Guangjiao jing chubanshe, 1984], 121). See Chang's *"Yüeh-fu pu-t'i,"* 370.

46 Frye, "Allegory," in Preminger et al., eds., *Princeton Encyclopedia*, 12.

47 Modified but essentially different in position from J. Hillis Miller's categorical statement that "What the allegory reveals at the same time it hides," in his "The Two Allegories," Bloomfield, ed., *Allegory, Myth, and Symbol*, 358.

48 Even Miller grants that "what seems specific to allegory is a larger degree of manifest incompatibility between the tenor and the vehicle than we tend to expect in a symbol, where the 'material' base and the 'spiritual' meaning are thrown together . . . with some implication of overlapping, consubstantiality, or participation"; ibid., 357.

49 Gadamer, "The Relevance of the Beautiful," in *The Relevance of the Beautiful and Other Essays*, 34, 37.

50 Coleridge, *The Statesman's Manual*, in *The Portable Coleridge*, 388.

51 See for instance Holman and Harmon, *Handbook to Literature*, 11; Earl Miner, ed., *Literary Uses of Typology: From the Late Middle Ages to the Present* (Princeton: Princeton Univ. Press, 1977), 386 (Afterword).

52 As Kang-i Sun Chang demonstrates in her *"Yüeh-fu pu-t'i."*

53 Frye, "Allegory," in Preminger et al., eds., *Princeton Encyclopedia*, 12. It is worth reiterating that while the reference to another level of meaning may be transparent, the referent itself may not be so.

54 Both Hightower (*HT* 184) and Davis (*D* 1:124) read the poem in the first person; the poet is the supposed regretful planter. For the reason stated above, I have replaced "I" with an indeterminate "they," which is meant to be number-free.

55 The issue of intent does come in later when we consider Tao's visualization of poetry as fulfilling a cultural responsibility to posterity, but this intent is realized through lyric expression, and so is not noticeable as a determining factor behind it.

56 Even though no author is in complete control of his language; psychoanalytic and mythological criticisms, in particular, see works as revealing unconscious meanings.

57 See Chadwick, *Symbolism*, 1–7; Alfred G. Engstrom, "Symbolism," in Preminger et al., eds., *Princeton Encyclopedia*, 836–39. Transcendental symbolism may be visualized in Platonic or Christian terms.

58 Wilson, *Axel's Castle*, 21–22.

59 "Correspondences," in Peschel, trans., *Four French Symbolist Poets*, 95.

60 "Victor Hugo," ibid., 16.

61 Letter to Paul Demeny dated 15 May 1871; ibid., 22.

62 See Engstrom, "Symbolism," in Preminger et al., eds., *Princeton Encyclopedia*, 838, for a translation of this well-known passage.

63 See Engstrom, "Symbolism," and Norman Friedman, "Symbol," ibid., 836–39, 833–36.

64 Attributed to the sage-king Shun in *Shangshu* 1, "Yao dian," in Guo Shaoyu, ed., *Zhongguo lidai wenlun xuan*, 1:1. Luo Genze suggests that *zhi* may pertain to the "sagely Way" or "personal feelings"; see his *Zhongguo wenxue piping shi*, 1:42. Here "sentiments" (as broadly defined in the Introduction, n.2) is used to translate *zhi*, even though the Chinese character has no English equivalent, since it encompasses both "emotion and idea," intent in the empirical world and aspiration toward the ideal.

65 Baudelaire, quoted in Peschel, trans., *Four French Symbolist Poets*, 15.

66 Letter to Schiller, 6 April 1801; quoted in Abrams, *Mirror and the Lamp*, 211.

67 Cf. Yeh, "Cong bijiao xiandai de guandian kan jishou Zhongguo jiushi," in *Lunshi conggao*, 251.

68 See Yü, "Life and Immortality," 91–95, 110–15. Emperors like Qin Shihuang (r. 221–10 B.C.) and Han Wudi (r. 140–87 B.C.) helped to popularize the cult with their own obsession; see "Treatise on the Fengshan" in *Shiji*, *SJ* 28/4:1369–70, 1384–404.

69 See for instance "Changge xing," "Shanzai xing," and "Longxi xing," *XQH* 1:262, 266–68.

70 In fact, stories about immortals *(xian)* were on the rise during the Former Han; Ban Gu remarked in the "Bibliographic Treatise" of his *Han shu* that "writings of a deceiving and strange nature have become more legion." See *HS* 30/6:1780.

71 Wang Zhongluo, *Wei Jin Nanbeichao shi*, 2:738–41.

72 For more examples in Cao Cao, see his "Qichu chang" and "Qiuhu xing," *XQH* 1:345, 350.

73 See Cao's "Qichu chang," *XQH* 1:345. For earlier examples, see the Han *yuefu* ballads "Shang ling" and "Dongtao xing" (*XQH* 1:158, 264); "Bu chu Xiamen xing," in Guo Maoqian, ed., *Yuefu shiji,* 1:545.

74 That Cao's perception of the immortal world is more poetic than religious is evident in some of his other poems where he denies the existence of immortals; see "Jing lie," "Shanzai xing," and "Bu chu Xiamen xing," *XQH* 1:346, 353–54.

75 To avoid digression, I shall not labor to document the development of *youxian shi* during the third century. Xi Kang, though, is a key figure who deserves mention: he was known for taking drugs and herbs (Chen Shou, *Sanguozhi* 21/3:605), and his *youxian* sentiments are reflected in poems like "Youxian shi," "Shu zhi shi" #1, and "Wuyan shi" #3, *XQH* 1:488–89. A similar yearning is audible in the poems of Ruan Ji, who, however, mixes a general longing for the charm of the immortal world with a scepticism about its existence; see his "Yonghuai shi," *XQH* 1:501, 503–4, 510. One further problem about the entire issue pertains to the extent to which the poems are informed by earlier pieces since the time of "Yuan you" in *Chuci,* though it would be safe to say that as a trend the development of *youxian shi* was more closely related to the contemporary ethos than to literary tradition *per se.* See also Lin Wen-yüeh, "Cong youxian shi dao shanshui shi," in idem, *Shanshui yu gudian,* 2–6.

76 The mythical charioteer of the sun.

77 See Liu Dajie, *Zhongguo wenxue,* 1:237–38, 244–47.

78 Gan Bao, in Hu, ed., *Tiaoxi yuyin,* 1; see also *D* 1:198–200.

79 The ascription to Tao of this text, which contains stories dating ten or more years after his death, has long been challenged. See Yu Jiaxi, *Siku tiyao bianzheng,* included in Wang Shaoying, ed., *Soushen houji,* 147; *D* 1:198. Ch'en Yin-k'o, however, leans toward the view that at least some of the stories might have been written by Tao, and shares the general consensus that the text dates from the Six Dynasties period. See his "Taohuanyuanji pangzheng," *H* 1:343.

80 南陽劉驎之，字子驥，好遊山水。嘗採藥至衡山，深入忘返。見有一澗水，水南有二石囷，一閉一開。水深廣，不得渡。欲還，失道。遇伐弓人，問徑，僅得還家。或說囷中皆仙方靈藥及諸雜物。驎之欲更尋索，不復知處矣。

Wang Shaoying, ed., *Soushen houji*, 6; see also *JS* 94/8:2448. It is uncertain whether or not this story existed when Tao mentioned Liu in "Peach Blossom Spring." The only mention of Liu sure to be earlier than Tao is in Deng Can's (?–c. 384) *Jinji*, where Liu is portrayed as a virtuous recluse rather than one interested in immortality.

81 See *QTS* 4:1257–58, 11:3995; *H* 2:339–40.

82 Mountains associated with recluses and those seeking to become *xian*.

83 See "Li sao," ll. 203–64, in Hawkes, trans., *Songs of the South*, 73–75.

84 *Chuci*, "Zhao hun," in Hawkes, trans., *Songs of the South*, 224–25.

85 Zhao Yi, *Oubei shihua*, 1/1a.

86 Zhuangzi has a penchant for using extreme examples to make his point: while affirming Dao's presence even in shit and piss (Z 22/45), he does not show Dao in the context of daily living as convincingly as Tao does.

87 Watson, *Chinese Lyricism*, 53.

88 Zuo has a long "Poem on my Lovely Daughters" ("Jiaonü shi," *XQH* 1:735–36), a lively but slightly distanced portrait in which the father is not as personally involved as in Tao's poem. It may also be noted that parent-child emotions generally feature less in Western than in Chinese poetry, no doubt because the family does not occupy an equal place in the individual's life (see Schwartz, *World of Thought*, 99–102).

89 Yü, "Neo-Taoist Movement," 129.

90 有造境，有寫境，此理想與寫實二派之所由分。然二者頗難分別。因大詩人所造之境，必合乎自然，所寫之境，亦必鄰於理想故也。

Wang Guowei, *Renjian cihua*, 1/2.

91 For a discussion of Zhang Xie's descriptive nature poetry, see Kang-i Sun Chang, *Six Dynasties Poetry*, 54–57; idem, "Description of Landscape in Early Six Dynasties Poetry," 112–14.

92 Wang Guowei, *Renjian cihua*, 22/42.

Notes for Chapter 6: Philosophical Poetry and "Abstruse-Language Verse"

1 See "Dai Qiuhu ge shi" #5, "Da erh Guo shi" #3, and "Shu zhi shi" #2 for Xi Kang; "Da Xi Kang shi" #2 and #3 for Xi Xi. In *XQH* 1:480, 487, 489, 550. Philosophizing poems—in Confucian moral and sociopolitical terms—were in existence before *xuanyan shi*: see for instance Cao Cao's "Du Guanshan" and "Dui jiu," *XQH* 1:346–48; Fu Xian's (239–94) "Xiaojing shi," "Lunyu shi," "Maoshi shi," "Zhouyi shi," "Zhouguan shi," and Zuozhuan shi," *XQH* 1:603–5.

2 The writings of Yu and Huan are no longer extant, while the one remaining poem by Xu is irrelevant to our purpose.

3 Corroboration is also found in Jiang Yan's (444–505) imitation piece, meant to capture the essential flavor of a Sun Chuo poem; see *XQH* 2:1576.

4 In Tan Daoluan, *Xu Jin yangqiu.*

5 Xiao Zixian, *NanQi shu*, 52/3:908 (Remarks on the Biographies of Men of Letters); in Guo Shaoyu, ed., *Zhongguo lidai wenlun xuan*, 1:265.

6 Zong Bing, "Hua shanshui xu," in *Zhongguo meixueshi ziliao xuanbian*, 1:177–78. See Bush, "Tsung Ping's Essay on Painting Landscape and the 'Landscape Buddhism' of Mount Lu," 144–46.

7 Among those present were Wang Xizhi, Xie An, and Xie Wan, as well as Sun Chuo and Xu Xun. A total of thirty-seven poems were written.

8 An image for unburdened, purposeless freedom; allusion to Z 32/11.

9 As Wang Xizhi wrote in the preface: "Looking up to behold the vastness of the universe, and looking down to survey the richness of the various phenomena, we let our eyes roam and our hearts ramble about, finding enough to fully gratify our senses of sight and hearing" (*JS* 80/7:2099). Ironically, the preface is more lyrically resonant than the poems. Was Wang aware that his feelings had not found expression in the two poems he wrote for the occasion?

10 See poems by Yuan Qiaozhi, Wang Xuanzhi, Wang Huizhi, and Wang Binzhi, *XQH* 2:911, 914.

11 This is Xie Lingyun's remark on his grandfather in *Shanju fu*, *XLJ* 320.

12 The second one opens with two parallel couplets, but parallelism does not constitute a key attribute of the poem as a whole.

13 Expression borrowed from Kao, "The Aesthetics of Regulated Verse," 372.

14 Shen Deqian, ed., *Qing shi biecai,* 3 ("Fanli" [Guide to Usage]).

15 Cf. Wordsworth, *The Excursion:*

> Oh! many are the Poets that are sown
> By Nature; men endowed with the highest gifts,
> The vision and the faculty divine;
> Yet wanting the accomplishment of verse, . . .

ll. 77–80; in *Poetical Works,* 592.

16 The free drinking and talking are temperate by Neo-Daoist standards, and more reflective of a genuine liberation of spirit than the conscious self-indulgence of the "Eight Free Spirits."

17 George Eliot, "The Progress of the Intellect," in idem, *Essays of George Eliot,* 31.

18 See Frodsham, "Origins of Chinese Nature Poetry."

19 References in this couplet are to Hexagrams 18 and 10 in *Yijing*. See Gao Heng, ed., *Zhouyi dazhuan,* 205, 142; cf. Wilhelm, trans., *I Ching,* 78, 46.

20 Allusion to *L* 20.

21 Allusion to *L* 10, *L* 22.

22 These two lines allude to Z 16/1–2.

23 Mair and Mei, "The Sanskrit Origins of Recent Style Prosody," 393. Discussing his verse as representing a stage in the development of recent-style poetry, Mair and Mei see Xie as "a master of the antithetical couplet."

24 Lin Wen-yüeh, "Zhongguo shanshui shi de tezhi," in idem, *Shanshui yu gudian,* 49–50.

25 Xie's contact with Nature was in fact largely precipitated by exile ensuing from factional strife, a forced retreat with little sense of being a joyous liberation: "A traveller's heart is ever sad; / Grief succeeds grief in relay" (*XLJ* 68). See Xie's biography in *SS* 67/6:1753–54.

26 Cf. Yeh's analysis in "Cong Yuan Yishan *Lunshi jueju* tan Xie Lingyun yu Liu Zongyuan de shi yu ren," in her *Zhongguo gudian shige pinglun ji,* 37–41.

27 As the same George Eliot espousing a "correct generalisation" is aware; see Gordon S. Haight, ed., *The George Eliot Letters*, 7 vols. (New Haven: Yale Univ. Press, 1954–56), 4:300.

28 Mair and Mei, "Sanskrit Origins," 398.

29 The remark is by Fang Dongshu (1772–1851); *H* 1:225.

30 Hexagram 29, Image. In Gao Heng, ed., *Zhouyi dazhuan*, 274; cf. Wilhelm, trans., *I Ching*, 116.

31 Hexagram 52, Judgment and Image. In Gao Heng, ed., *Zhouyi dazhuan*, 427–28; cf. Wilhelm, trans., *I Ching*, 201–2.

32 Wang Zhihuan, "Deng Guanquelou."

33 Li Bai, "Shanzhong wenda."

34 Su Shi, "Ti Xilin bi," in his *Su Shi shiji*, 4:1219.

35 Su Shi, *ci* poem to the tune "Dingfengbo," in Tang Guizhang, ed., *Quan Song ci*, 1:288.

36 Letter to John J. Reynolds, 3 February 1818; in Keats, *Letters*, 96.

Notes for Chapter 7: "Farmstead Poetry" and the Western Pastoral

1 The term is usually not clearly defined by critics and historians of classical Chinese literature, but taken as understood from compositions by poets like Tao, Wang Wei, Chu Guangxi (707–c. 760), and Fan Chengda (1126–93).

2 Both literary critics and intellectual historians have done so. See for instance Marie Chan, "T'ao Ch'ien," in Nienhauser et al., eds., *Indiana Companion*, 768; Michael S. Duke and C. S. Chang, "Lu Yu," ibid., 610; "Index," ibid., 1047, which likewise gives "pastoral poetry" as the translation for *tianyuan shi*. See also Joseph J. Lee, biographical entry on "Ch'u Kuang-hsi," in *Sunflower Splendor: Three Thousand Years of Chinese Poetry*, eds. Wu-chi Liu and Irving Y. Lo (Garden City, NY: Anchor Press, 1975), 552; Tu Wei-ming, "Profound Learning, Personal Knowledge, and Poetic Vision," 23; Lin Mao-sung, *A Comparative Study*, 33. The latter explicitly claims *tianyuan shi* to be the Chinese generic equivalent of pastoral verse.

3 See "Pastoral" in Holman and Harmon, *Handbook to Literature,* 361.

4 Abrams, *A Glossary of Literary Terms,* "Pastoral," 127. For succinct discussions on the subject, see ibid., 127–29; Holman and Harmon, *Handbook to Literature,* 361–62; J. E. Congleton, "Pastoral," in Preminger et al., eds., *Princeton Encyclopedia,* 603–6.

5 For a more detailed discussion of *tianyuan shi* and its differences from pastoral verse, see Kwong, "The Rural World of Chinese 'Farmstead Poetry.'"

6 Wells, *Idylls of Theocritus,* 66–68.

7 Ibid., 91–92.

8 Marinelli, *Pastoral,* 39.

9 Eclogue 1; Lee, trans., *Virgil: The Eclogues,* 35.

10 Eclogue 3; ibid., 47–53.

11 Eclogue 5; ibid., 65.

12 Marinelli, *Pastoral,* 10. On one level, of course, the pastoral presence in the Scriptures simply points to a fact of life in the ancient Mediterranean. The Samaritan text of the Pentateuch dates from the fifth century B.C., while the Greek version of the Old Testament, the *Septuagint,* dates from the third century B.C.

13 *Genesis* 2.9, in May and Metzger, eds., *New Oxford Annotated Bible,* 3.

14 Thus while pastoral life is light-heartedly described in "March" and rejected for an active dedicated life in "May," its material content is not at issue.

15 In Barrell and Bull, eds., *English Pastoral Verse,* 77.

16 Pope, *Poetry and Prose of Alexander Pope,* 8. See for instance "Summer," ll. 59–76, ibid., 13–14.

17 Poggioli, *Oaten Flute: Essays on the Pastoral and the Pastoral Idea,* 76.

18 In the November Æglogue Dido "is enstalled nowe in heauens hight"; in Milton's poem Lycidas is "mounted high"—words virtually duplicated by Pope in "Winter," where Daphne also "mounts on high."

19 Poggioli, *Oaten Flute,* 1–2. See also Laurence Lerner, *The Use of Nostalgia: Studies in Pastoral Poetry* (New York: Schocken, 1972), 19, 40.

20 Pope, "A Discourse on Pastoral Poetry" (which prefaces his own "Pastorals"), in idem, *Poetry and Prose*, 4–5.

21 Fraguier, "Dissertation concerning Pastoral Poetry" (excerpted and translated by Michael de la Roche in 1710), quoted in Congleton, *Theories of Pastoral Poetry in England, 1684–1798*, 158.

22 See Kermode, ed., *English Pastoral Poetry*, 14, 16.

23 In his subdivision of poetry into eight main denominations, for instance, Sir Philip Sidney (1554–86) ranks pastoral the last, calling it the "lowest hedge" which all "will soonest leape over." See his "An Apology for Poetry," in Kaplan, ed., *Criticism: Twenty Major Statements*, 110, 121.

24 In Barrell and Bull, eds., *English Pastoral Verse*, 78.

25 See Quixote's description of the golden age in Cervantes, *Don Quixote*, 85–86. Quixote constantly imagines life in terms of his readings: "Have you not read, sirs . . . ," ibid., 97.

26 Ibid., 902, referring back to 842–44, 847.

27 See *Genesis* 2.15, in May and Metzger, eds., *New Oxford Annotated Bible*, 3.

28 It was this flaw that eventually prompted a minor wave of antipastoral verse in the eighteenth century, as more poets turned away from nostalgia for a golden past to confront the harsh rural realities of their time.

29 See Liao, *Tao Yuanming*, 51–52; Zhong Youmin, *Tao Yuanming lunji*, 153–54; Kang-i Sun Chang, *Six Dynasties Poetry*, 22–23.

30 Cervantes, *Don Quixote*, 86, 902.

31 A. S. F. Gow, *The Greek Bucolic Poets* (Cambridge: Cambridge Univ. Press, 1953), xxiii.

32 Expression adapted from Bruno Snell, *The Discovery of the Mind: The Greek Origins of European Thought*, trans. T. G. Rosenmeyer (New York: Harper Torchbooks, 1960), 286.

33 Congleton, *Theories of Pastoral in England*, 298.

34 Kermode, ed., *English Pastoral Verse*, 11, quoting Puttenham.

35 This phrase is used by Zhong Hong in his *Poetry Ratings* in partial appraisal of Tao's language. See *H* 1:9; Guo Shaoyu, ed., *Zhongguo lidai wenlun xuan,* 1:322, entry on Tao Qian.

36 This is not to overlook the Jian'an poets' reflection of the hardships endured by the populace during the wars, famines, and disorder of the period.

37 From He Xiu's (129–80) commentary on *Gongyang zhuan*, Duke Xuan, 15th year (558 B.C.); in Guo Shaoyu, ed., *Zhongguo lidai wenlun xuan,* 1:5.

38 Among the early literati-farmer hermits were Jieyu, Changju, Jieni, and the anonymous old man mentioned in the *Analects* (18/5–7), whom Confucius (551–479 B.C.) and his disciple Zilu (542–480 B.C.) met in 487 B.C. For some idea of the line of literati-farmer recluses leading up to Tao, see for instance the biographies of Zheng Pu (first century B.C.), *HS* 72/10:3056; of Chunyu Gong (d. 80), Xu Zhi (c. 97–168), Xu Yin (c. 160–208), and "Recluses," in Fan Ye, *HouHan shu,* 39/5:1301, 53/6:1746–48, 83/10:2755–77; of "Recluses," *JS* 94/8:2425–63.

39 Attributed to a "fifty-year-old man," this song was first quoted (with a slightly different last line) by Wang Chong (27–97?) in his *Lun Heng,* ch. 27; see *Lunheng zhushi,* annot. Dept. of History, Beijing University, 4 vols. (Beijing: Zhonghua shuju, 1979), 2:491.

40 Two Han poems, Liu Zhang's (d. 178 B.C.) "Gengtian ge" and Yang Yun's (d. 54 B.C.) "Ge shi," read ostensibly like *tianyuan shi,* but actually use the farmstead subject allegorically; see respectively *XQH* 1:92–93 and *HS* 38/6:1991–96, *XQH* 1:112–13 and *HS* 66/9:2889–98. I have located only two other relevant but far less significant poems: Shu Xi's (264?–303?) "Blooming Millet," a song eulogizing rich harvests in the manner of precedents in the *Book of Poetry*; and Zhang Xie's (d. 307) "Miscellaneous Poems" #9, which mentions the poet ploughing but is really about the joy of reclusion and the beauty of the landscape; *XQH* 1:640, 747.

41 In point of fact, while "*tianyuan shi*" has become an established critical term among modern scholars, its origin remains somewhat obscure; none of the relevant works (histories, dictionaries, articles) I have come across discusses whether the term was used by premodern Chinese poets and critics. As far as I can trace, Zhang Jie (fl. 1130) has remarked how "later poets wrote on the farmstead theme [after Tao]" (*H* 1:59), while Zhong Xing (1547–1624) and Zha Shenxing (1650–1727) have

commented that the "farmstead" or "farmers' poetry" (*tianjia shi*) of Wang Wei and Chu Guangxi is derived from Tao (*H* 1:170–71, 2:56). Indeed without calling Tao a "farmstead poet," many High Tang poets clearly saw him as such—through their own lenses. Meng Haoran (689–740), for example, echoed Wang Ji (585–644) in admiring Tao's eremitic life when he wrote enviously of how Tao "daily indulges in the delights of the farmstead" (*QTS* 5:1619, 2:478). He and Wang Wei, Chu Guangxi, and others wrote poems whose titles or lines contain the words "farmers" or "farmstead" (*QTS* vols. 4–5, passim), even though what appeals to them about Tao's verse is not so much his sometimes harsh rural life as what they saw to be the self-contained freedom and casual content of a reclusive world.

42 Coleridge, *Biographia Literaria*, ch. 14, 2:6, 5.

43 Wordsworth, *The Prelude*, 2/272, 1/150, 11/348, in Wordsworth, *Poetical Works*, 506, 496, 573.

44 Coleridge, *Biographia Literaria*, ch. 14, 2:6.

Notes for Chapter 8: Crystallinity of Language and Style

1 For a succinct discussion of the aesthetics of the Six Dynasties, see Kao, "The Aesthetics of Regulated Verse," 346–51.

2 See *SS* 67/6:1754 and Shen Yue's postface to Xie's biography, *SS* 67/6:1778–79. For a discussion of Xie's literary influence, see Zhong Youmin, *Xie Lingyun lungao*, 237–40, 262–69; Kang-i Sun Chang, *Six Dynasties Poetry*, 79–80.

3 See Knechtges, *Han Rhapsody*, 42–43.

4 See for instance Mei Sheng's (d. 140 B.C.) "Qi fa" (Seven Incitements).

5 While open to various definitions, here the term *verisimilitude* refers to a way of presenting details in order to create a semblance of truth or reality. See Holman and Harmon, *Handbook to Literature*, 521.

6 自近代以來，文貴形似，窺情風景之上，鑽貌草木之中。…故巧言切狀，如印之印泥，不加雕削，而曲寫毫芥。

7 See Wu Feng et al., eds., *Jianming Zhongguo guji cidian* (Changchun: Jilin wenshi chubanshe, 1987), 433, entry on *Song shu*.

8 儷采百字之偶，爭價一句之奇；情必極貌以寫物，辭必窮力而追新。

9 In his "Wen fu," Lu Ji draws the distinction that while *shi* "follows the feelings" (*yuan qing*), *fu* is suitable for "describing things" (*ti wu*); in Guo Shaoyu, ed., *Zhongguo lidai wenlun xuan*, 1:171. To complete the picture, it may be recalled that since the end of the Han, expression of personal feelings and experience that is the defining quality of *shi* has also found a place in *fu*, resulting in a more lyrical kind of *fu* in contrast to the descriptive variety. See Watson, trans., *Chinese Rhyme-Prose*, 8–9.

10 Interestingly, Ye Xiaoxue has made a similar comment with reference to another example; see Xie, *Xie Lingyun shixuan*, 93, n.6.

11 *Shuitianju shifa*, quoted in Li Wenchu, *Tao Yuanming lunlüe*, 190.

12 Qian, *Guanzhui bian*, 4:1393.

13 See also Lin Wen-yüeh, "Zhongguo shanshui shi de tezhi," in *Shanshui yu gudian*, 41–46; Kang-i Sun Chang, *Six Dynasties Poetry*, 52–53. To give some more examples: of the twenty-two lines in "Ascending the Tower by the Pond" (*XLJ* 63–64), the first eighteen are done in full parallelisms except for the fifth couplet, while the last four are what may be called "half-baked" parallelisms, clearly intended to be parallel as shown by the marks of labor. Again, in "On the Way from South Mountain to North Mountain, Viewing the Scenery from the Lake" (*XLJ* 118), only the final couplet is not parallel; the sixth and tenth are half-baked, leaving sixteen out of twenty-two as fully parallel lines.

14 Seven-character verse became established in the fifth century. Most "ancient-style" verse and all "recent-style" verse use lines of either five or seven characters; the former may use both five- and seven-character lines.

15 Frankel, *Flowering Plum*, 146.

16 造化賦形，支體必雙；神理為用，事不孤立。夫心生文辭，運裁百慮，高下相須，自然成對。

17 In these two couplets the "both/and" formula has not been translated literally, for obvious reasons of awkwardness.

18 See for instance "Ascending the Tower by the Pond" and "Ascending Solitary Islet in the River," *XLJ* 63–64, 83–84.

19 Unless he is compelled by a specific occasion or purpose to write obscurely, as in "Shu jiu."

20 Conversely, simplicity of style may be a matter of artistic choice, without entailing a cosmological and existential vision of natural truth being immanent in the ordinary.

21 Wordsworth, "Goody Blake and Harry Gill," ll. 1–4, 13–16, in his *Poetical Works*, 420.

22 One of the most successful examples of reduplicating a polysyllabic word is Shakespeare's "Tomorrow, and tomorrow, and tomorrow, / Creeps in this petty pace from day to day, / To the last syllable of recorded time," where the repetition of "tomorrow" gives a graphic sense of the painful dragging of time. See *Macbeth* 5.5:19–21, in Shakespeare, *Complete Works*, 867.

23 故灼灼狀桃花之鮮，依依盡楊柳之貌，杲杲為出日之容，瀌瀌擬雨雪之狀，喈喈逐黃鳥之聲，喓喓學草虫之韻。雖復思經千載，將何易奪？

24 A full understanding of this issue would require a separate study of sound effects, involving linguistic, musical, psychological, and imaginative-associative dimensions which might combine to suggest some clue as regards the matching of sound and meaning.

25 Transcription follows Li Fang-kuei, "Shanggu yin yanjiu," 1–61. *Yiyi* first appeared in *Shijing* #167: "Long ago, when we set out, / The willows were light and tender." Hence the use of ancient Chinese pronunciation for explanation.

26 *Shuangshuang* is the name of a beast in *Shanhai jing* and a bird in *Gongyang zhuan*, but had not been used in the present sense before Tao.

27 Apart from the excerpts illustrating the use of reduplications, there are many examples of unobtrusive parallelisms (which should be read in context) forming part of Tao's natural poetic rhythm: "The departed swallows leave not a shadow; / The arriving geese raise lingering sounds" (*TYJ* 39); "Our clear singing diffuses fresh sounds; / Green wine unlocks pleasant faces" (*TYJ* 49); "A chill wind brushes the withered branches; / Fallen leaves cover the long path" (*TYJ* 119).

28 "Yu Xie Minshi tuiguan shu," in Su Shi, *Su Shi wenji*, 49/4:1418; *Su Shi xuanji*, ed. Wang Shuizhao (Shanghai: Guji chubanshe, 1984), 420.

29 An allusion to Z 6/25, signifying the natural process of change in time.

30 Tao's expression comes from *Huainanzi,* ch. 1: "The sage values not a foot of jade but an inch of shadow [i.e. time measured on a sundial], for time is hard to get and easy to lose." More immediately, his great-grandfather Tao Kan is quoted in his biography as having said this: "Even the great sage Yu values an inch of shadow; . . . how can one idle about in drunkenness? Not benefitting one's age in life nor being known to posterity after death is to relinquish oneself" (*JS* 66/6:1774).

31 Cf. Jane Austen's powerful description of the autumn scene, charged with the feelings of the heroine Anne Elliot, in *Persuasion*, ed. D. W. Harding (Harmondsworth: Penguin, 1965), 106–7.

32 The one parallelism (ll. 3–4) in the eight descriptive lines of the poem merges into its flow.

33 See Rickett, "Method and Intuition: The Poetic Theories of Huang T'ing-chien," in idem, *Chinese Approaches to Literature from Confucius to Liang Ch'i-ch'ao*, 97–119.

34 Jin, ed., *Song shi sanbai shou*, 169.

35 "Preface to *Lyrical Ballads*," in Kaplan, ed., *Criticism: Twenty Major Statements*, 281, 286.

36 Kang-i Sun Chang, *Six Dynasties Poetry*, 15.

Notes for Chapter 9: Neo-Daoist Aesthetics and the Art of Nature

1 Z 33/76; cf. also *Liezi* 4, "Confucius," in Yang Bojun, ed., *Liezi*, 141.

2 Predicated on distinctions with limited validity, specific meanings can be "removed" as contexts vary and so do not "reach" the absolute truth of Dao. This kind of witty, at times mystical, conversation had its precedent in *Zhuangzi*, and in turn became an inspiration for the technique of *gongan* in Chan Buddhism.

3 客問樂令「旨不至」者。樂亦不復剖析文句，直以麈尾柄确几曰：「至不？」客曰：「至。」樂因又舉麈尾曰：「若至者，那得去？」於是客乃悟服。樂辭約而旨達，皆此類。

4 Chen Shou, *Sanguo zhi, Wei shu* 29/3:821, quoting from "Guanlu biezhuan."

5 殷中軍問：「自然無心於稟受，何以正善人少，惡人多？」諸人莫有言者。劉尹答曰：「譬如瀉水著地，正自縱橫流漫，略無正方圓者。」一時絶歎，以爲名通。

6 Zhu Ziqing, *Biaozhun yu chidu*, "Richang shenghuo de shi," in his *Zhu Ziqing ji*, 680.

7 One of his more often used adjectives is "fair" *(jia)*, whose generality suggests a congenial quality without reducing it to specificity: "Today the weather is fair" (*TYJ* 49); "Spring and autumn give many fair days" (*TYJ* 57); "Autumn chrysanthemums have a fair hue" (*TYJ* 90).

8 According to Shen Zhenqi, there are in Tao's poetry 140 references to *Shijing*, 133 to *Zhuangzi*, 73 to *Shiji*, 70 to *Chuci*, and 67 to *Lunyu*. See his *Tao Xie shi zhi bijiao*, 152.

9 Liu Shao, *Renwu zhi*, 5 (ch. 1, "Jiu zheng"); emphasis mine.

10 Ibid., 4–5.

11 "Wanji lun," in *Yuhan shanfang ji yishu*, vol. 59, 4a.

12 四體姸蚩，本無關於妙處。傳神寫照，正在阿堵中。

13 *SunChuozi*, quoted in annotation of Lu Chui's (470–526) *Xin kelou ming*; in Xiao Tong (501–31), ed., *Wen xuan*, 6:2429.

14 Whose meaning differs from its uplifting import in the line "Abiding by rusticity (*zhuo*), I have returned to my farmland" (*TYJ* 40).

15 Song Qi (998–1061), *ci* to the tune "Yulouchun," in Tang Guizhang, ed., *Quan Song ci*, 1:116.

16 Zhang Xian (990–1078), *ci* to the tune "Tianxianzi," ibid., 1:70.

17 Wang Anshi, "Bochuan Guazhou," in *Wang Wengong wenji*, ed. Tang Wubiao, 2 vols. (Shanghai: Renmin chubanshe, 1974), 2:744. Emphases in these three excerpts are mine.

18 *Chuci*, "Yu fu," in Hawkes, trans., *Songs of the South*, 207. An identical version of the song is found in *M* 4A/8, but there the "moral" is that one is responsible for others' treatment of oneself.

19 One is reminded of the triumphant moment in "Mulan" when the heroine, home at last after her war service and bouncing about in

happiness, sings of her excitement in four lines each with the word *wo* in the second position:

> I open my east chamber door,
> Sit on my west chamber couch,
> Take off my wartime gown,
> And put on my old-time clothes.

20 See Wang Yunxi and Gu Yisheng, eds., *Zhongguo wenxue piping shi*, 1:89–118.

21 Frankel, review of *The Poetry of T'ao Ch'ien*, 314–15.

22 The cultivation of simplicity can be an equally drawn-out process, but I believe Tao is one of those few who write in a largely instinctive way, for whom craftsmanship is a secondary process.

23 "Preface to *Lyrical Ballads*," in Kaplan, ed., *Criticism: Twenty Major Statements*, 282, 293–94.

24 Another Daoist-Confucian amalgam.

25 此古人所以染翰慷慨，屢伸而不能已者也。夫導達意氣，其惟文乎？

26 Quoted in Hu Zi, ed., *Tiaoxi yuyin conghua*, 1:16.

27 See Hightower, "Allusion in the Poetry of T'ao Ch'ien," 108–32, esp. 109–21.

28 In a late Ming edition of *Wenxin diaolong* there is an added paragraph of about four hundred characters in ch. 40, "Yinxiu," in which Tao's name is mentioned. Most scholars since the time of Ji Yun (1724–1805) have considered it a forgery, and Zhan Ying's recent proposal that the Ming edition was based on a genuine Song edition does not resolve the issue. See Zhan Ying, *Wenxin diaolong de fengge xue*, 78–94.

29 Dong Zhongshu, *Chunqiu fanlu*, "Yubei pian;" Su Yu, *Yizheng*. Quoted in Zhu Ziqing, *Shiyanzhi bian*, 25.

Notes for Chapter 10: Luminosity of the Unconscious: The Ineffable Truth

1 "Appended Remarks" to *Yijing*, part 1, ch. 12, in Goa Heng, ed., *Zhouyi dazhuan*, 541–42; cf. Wilhelm, trans., *I Ching*, 322.

2 盡意莫若象，盡象莫若言。言生於象，故可尋言以觀象；象生於意，故可尋象以觀意。… 故言者所以明象，得象而忘言；象者所以存意，得意而忘象。

ZhouYi lüeli, "Ming xiang," in Wang Bi, *Wang Bi ji*, 2:609.

3 "Southern Mountains" has been used as a symbol of longevity since *Shijing* (#166), but here it refers to Lushan, situated southeast of Chaisang where Tao was living. (Both lie south of modern Jiujiang in Jiangxi province.)

4 Suzuki, *Tō Enmei shi kai*, 273.

5 *The Task*, IV/282, 291, 297; in Cowper, *Poetical Works*, 188, 189.

6 "Tintern Abbey," ll. 47–49; in Wordsworth, *Poetical Works*, 164.

7 See Frederick P. W. McDowell, "Aestheticism," in Preminger et al., eds., *Princeton Encyclopedia*, 6–7.

8 See Hsü, *Zhongguo yishu jingshen*, 45–143, esp. 48–56, 70–87, 132–36.

9 In much the same way as *ren* (humanity) is treated in the *Analects*, constantly elucidated but never completely definable.

10 "Wen fu," in Guo Shaoyu, ed., *Zhongguo lidai wenlun xuan*, 1:174, 170.

11 *Four Quartets*, "Burnt Norton," V, in T. S. Eliot, *Collected Poems*, 194.

12 It may be interesting to note that Tao is quoted in his biography as having said: "As long as I appreciate the relish of the lute, why bother with the sound of the strings?" See *JS* 94/8:2463; *H* 1:12.

13 Cowper, *The Task*, IV/240–46; Tennyson, "Flower in the crannied wall," ll. 4–6; Blake, "Auguries of Innocence," ll. 1–4. In Nicholson and Lee, eds., *Oxford Book of Mystical Verse*, 88, 162, 105.

14 Preminger et al., eds., *Classical Literary Criticism*, 117 (IX).

15 Wang Guowei, *Renjian cihua*, 1/3, 2/4; *H* 1:265.

16 Daisetz T. Suzuki, trans., *The Lankāvatāra Sūtra* (London: Routledge, 1932), 169 (3:76), 193 (6:82).

17 I have in mind Roman Jakobson's broad distinction (among others) between the referential and poetic functions of language. See his "Closing Statement: Linguistics and Poetics," esp. 353–57.

18 Yu-kung Kao characterizes the inner couplets of this poem as a "continuous sequence" rather than a "parallel pattern"; see his "The Aesthetics of Regulated Verse," 371.

Notes for Chapter 11: Art as Embodiment of Life: Naturalness and Truthfulness

1 Yuan Haowen, "Lunshi sanshi shou," in Yang Chunqiu et al., eds., *Lidai lunshi jueju xuan*, 158.

2 Xin Qiji, *ci* poem to the tune "Zhegutian;" Tang Guizhang, ed., *Quan Song ci*, 3:1963.

3 "On the Sublime," in Kaplan, ed., *Criticism: Twenty Major Statements*, 58.

4 *Memoirs*, quoted in Abrams, *The Mirror and the Lamp*, 231. See pp. 226–35 for a succinct discussion of Western views on this issue.

5 Arthur Schopenhauer, *The World as Will and Representation*, trans. E. F. J. Payne, 2 vols. (New York: Dover, 1969), 1:446.

6 Zhang Jie, *Suihantang shihua*, in Ding Fubao, ed., *Lidai shihua xubian*, 1:458–59.

7 Ye Xie, *Yuan shi*, "Waipian: shang," in Ding Fubao, ed., *Qing shihua*, 2:597.

8 Paz, *Sor Juana*, 5.

9 A more practical factor, of course, is that many literati did not need to concern themselves with earning a living.

10 陶公「飢來驅我去」，誤墮其中，杜陵不審，鼓其餘波，…學詩者一染此數家之習，白練受污，終不可復白。尚戒之哉！

11 This contrasts, for instance, with Sidney's view of a brazen Nature to be turned golden by poetry.

Notes for Epilogue: A Destiny between Fate, Nature, and Heaven's Decree

1 See "Miscellaneous Poems" #7 and "Elegy for Myself" (*TYJ* 119, 197).

2 "A slumber did my spirit seal," ll. 7–8; in Wordsworth, *Poetical Works,* 149.

3 See *SJ* 47/6:1947; the *Shijing* quotation is from #218.

4 詩曰：「高山仰止，景行行止。」雖不能爾，至心尚之。汝其慎哉！吾復何言。

5 歲云夕矣，慨然永懷，今我不述，後生何聞哉！
Though Tao did not write a history to set the record straight, nor would he presume to equate his role with that of the Master.

6 "Prospectus of *The Recluse,*" ll. 89–90, printed with the preface to *The Excursion* (1814); in Wordsworth, *Poetical Works,* 590.

7 Wang Guoying, *Zhongguo shanshui shi yanjiu,* 398.

Selected Bibliography

Abrams, M. H. *A Glossary of Literary Terms*, 5th ed. Fort Worth: Holt, Rinehart and Winston, 1988.

———. *The Mirror and the Lamp: Romantic Theory and the Critical Tradition*. Oxford: Oxford Univ. Press, 1953.

Balazs, Étienne. *Chinese Civilization and Bureaucracy*, trans. H. M. Wright. New Haven: Yale Univ. Press, 1964.

Ban Gu 班固. *Han shu* 漢書, 12 vols. Beijing: Zhonghua shuju, 1962.

Barnhart, Richard. *Peach Blossom Spring: Gardens and Flowers in Chinese Paintings*. New York: The Metropolitan Museum of Art, 1983.

Barrell, John and John Bull, eds. *The Penguin Book of English Pastoral Verse*. Harmondsworth: Penguin, 1982.

Bauer, Wolfgang. "The Hidden Hero: Creation and Disintegration of the Ideal of Eremitism." In Munro, ed., 157–97.

Birch, Cyril, ed. *Studies in Chinese Literary Genres*. Berkeley: Univ. of California Press, 1974.

Bloomfield, Morton W., ed. *Allegory, Myth, and Symbol*. Cambridge: Harvard Univ. Press, 1981.

Bodde, Derk. *Essays on Chinese Civilization*, ed. Charles Le Blanc and Dorothy Borei. Princeton: Princeton Univ. Press, 1981.

Bush, Susan. "Tsung Ping's Essay on Painting Landscape and the 'Landscape Buddhism' of Mount Lu." In *Theories of the Arts in China*, eds. Susan Bush and Christian Murck. Princeton: Princeton Univ. Press, 1983, 132–64.

Cervantes, *Don Quixote*, trans. J. M. Cohen. Harmondsworth: Penguin, 1950.

Chadwick, Charles. *Symbolism*. London: Methuen, 1971.

Chan, Wing-tsit, trans. and comp. *A Source Book in Chinese Philosophy*. Princeton: Princeton Univ. Press, 1963.

Chang, H. C. *Chinese Literature, Vol. 2: Nature Poetry*. Edinburgh: Edinburgh Univ. Press, 1977.

Chang, Kang-i Sun. "Description of Landscape in Early Six Dynasties Poetry." In Lin and Owen, eds., 105–29.

———. *The Evolution of Chinese Tz'u Poetry: From Late T'ang to Northern Sung*. Princeton: Princeton Univ. Press, 1980.

———. *Six Dynasties Poetry*. Princeton: Princeton Univ. Press, 1986.

———. "Symbolic and Allegorical Meanings in the *Yüeh-fu pu-t'i* Poem Series." *Harvard Journal of Asiatic Studies* 46.2 (1986): 353–85.

Chen Shou 陳壽. *Sanguo zhi* 三國志, 5 vols. Beijing: Zhonghua shuju, 1982.

Chen-Courtin, Dorothy. "The Literary Theme of 'Peach Blossom Spring' in Pre-Ming and Ming Painting." Diss. Columbia Univ. 1979.

Ch'en Yin-k'o 陳寅恪. *Chen Yinke xiansheng wenshi lunji* 陳寅恪先生文史論集, 2 vols. Hong Kong: Wenwen Publications, 1972.

———. "Taohuayuanji pangzheng" 桃花源記旁証. In his *Wenshi lunji*, 1: 183–93.

———. "Tao Yuanming zhi sixiang yu qingtan zhi guanxi" 陶淵明之思想與清談之關係. In his *Wenshi lunji*, 1: 381–407.

———. "Tianshi dao yu binhai diyu zhi guanxi" 天師道與濱海地域之關係. In his *Wenshi lunji*, 1: 141–81.

———. "*Weishu* Sima Rui zhuan Jiangdong minzu tiao shizheng ji tuilun" 魏書司馬叡傳江東民族條釋証及推論. In his *Wenshi lunji*, 2: 219–55.

Ch'ien Mu 錢穆. *Zhongguo xueshu sixiang shi luncong* 中國學術思想史論叢, vol. 3. Taipei: Dongda tushu gongsi, 1977.

Chuci (Songs of the South). See Qu Yuan et al.

———. See David Hawkes, trans.

Coleridge, Samuel T. *Biographia Literaria*, ed. J. Shawcross, 2 vols. Oxford: Oxford Univ. Press, 1968.

———. *Coleridge: Poems*, ed. John Beer. London: Dent, 1974.

———. *The Portable Coleridge*, ed. I. A. Richards. New York: Viking, 1950.

Confucius. See Yang Bojun, trans.

———. See Lau, D. C., trans.

Congleton, J. E. *Theories of Pastoral Poetry in England, 1684–1798*. Gainesville: Univ. of Florida Press, 1952.

Cowper, William. *Cowper: Poetical Works*, ed. H. S. Milford, 4th ed. London: Oxford Univ. Press, 1971.

Davis, A. R. *Tao Yüan-ming: His Works and Their Meaning*, 2 vols. Cambridge: Cambridge Univ. Press, 1983.

de Bary, William Theodore, et al., comp. *Sources of Chinese Tradition*. New York: Columbia Univ. Press, 1960, vol. 1.

de Man, Paul. *Blindness and Insight: Essays in the Rhetoric of Contemporary Criticism*, ed. Wlad Godzich, 2nd ed. Minneapolis: Univ. of Minnesota Press, 1983.

Demiéville, Paul. "Philosophy and Religion from Han to Sui." In *The Cambridge History of China*, vol. 1: The Ch'in and Han Empires, 221 B.C.–A.D. 220, eds. Denis Twitchett and Michael Loewe. Cambridge: Cambridge Univ. Press, 1986, 808–72.

Deng Shiliang 鄧仕樑. *Liang Jin shilun* 兩晉詩論. Hong Kong: Chinese Univ. of Hong Kong, 1972.

Ding Fubao 丁福保, ed. *Lidai shihua xubian* 歷代詩話續編, 3 vols. Beijing: Zhonghua shuju, 1983.

———. *Qing shihua* 清詩話, 2 vols. Beijing: Zhonghua shuju, 1963.

Eliot, George. *Essays of George Eliot*, ed. Thomas Pinney. London: Routledge & Kegan Paul, 1963.

Eliot, T. S. *Collected Poems*. London: Faber & Faber, 1974.

Eoyang, Eugene. "Moments in Chinese Poetry: Nature in the World and Nature in the Mind." In *Studies in Chinese Poetry and Poetics*, ed. Ronald C. Miao, vol. 1. San Francisco: Chinese Materials Center, 1978, 105–28.

———. "The Solitary Boat: Images of Self in Chinese Nature Poetry." *Journal of Asian Studies* 32.4 (1973): 593–621.

Fan Ye 范曄. *HouHan shu* 後漢書, 12 vols. Beijing: Zhonghua shuju, 1965.

Fang Xuanling 房玄齡 et al. *Jin shu* 晉書, 10 vols. Beijing: Zhonghua shuju, 1974.

Fellows, Otis E., and Stephen F. Milliken, *Buffon*. New York: Twayne, 1972.

Frankel, Hans H. *The Flowering Plum and the Palace Lady: Interpretations of Chinese Poetry*. New Haven: Yale Univ. Press, 1976.

———. Review of *The Poetry of T'ao Ch'ien*, trans. James R. Hightower. *Harvard Journal of Asiatic Studies* 31 (1971): 313–19.

Frodsham, J. D. *The Murmuring Stream: The Life and Works of the Chinese Nature Poet Hsieh Ling-yün (385–433), Duke of K'ang-lo*, 2 vols. Kuala Lumpur: Univ. of Malaya Press, 1967.

———. "The Origins of Chinese Nature Poetry." *Asia Major* (n.s.) 8.1 (1960): 68–104.

Frye, Northrop, Sheridan Baker, and George Perkins. *The Harper Handbook to Literature*. New York: Harper & Row, 1985.

Fukui Kōjun 福井康順. *Shinsen den* 神仙伝. Tokyo: Meitoku shuppansha, 1983.

Fukunaga Mitsuji 福永光司. "Sha Reiun no shisō" 謝靈運の思想. *Tōhō shūkyō* 東方宗教 13/14 (1958): 25–48.

———. "Tō Enmei no 'shin' ni tsuite" 陶淵明の真について. *Tōhōgakuhō* 東方學報 33 (1963): 1–80.

Funatsu Tomihiko 船津富彦. *Sha Reiun* 謝靈運. Tokyo: Shūeisha, 1983.

Fung Yu-lan. *A History of Chinese Philosophy*, trans. Derk Bodde, 2 vols. Princeton: Princeton Univ. Press, 1952–53.

Gadamer, Hans-Georg. *The Relevance of the Beautiful and Other Essays*, ed. Robert Bernasconi, trans. Nicholas Walker. Cambridge: Cambridge Univ. Press, 1986.

Gan Bao 干寶. *Soushen ji* 搜神記, ed. Hu Huaishen 胡懷琛. Beijing: Commercial Press, 1957.

Gao Dapeng 高大鵬. *Taoshi xinlun* 陶詩新論. Taipei: Shibao wenhua chuban shiye youxiangongsi, 1981.

Gao Heng 高亨, ed. *Zhouyi dazhuan* [jinzhu] 周易大傳[今注]. Jinan: Qilu shushe, 1979.

Ge Hong 葛洪. *Baopuzi nei wai pian* 抱朴子[內外篇], 4 vols. Taipei: Commercial Press, 1979.

———. *Baopuzi neipian* [jiaoshi] 抱朴子內篇[校釋], rev. ed., ed. Wang Ming 王明. Beijing: Zhonghua shuju, 1985.

Ge Xiaoyin 葛曉音. *Badai shishi* 八代詩史. Xi'an: Shaanxi renmin chubanshe, 1989.

Gernet, Jacques. *A History of Chinese Civilization*, trans. J. R. Foster. Cambridge: Cambridge Univ. Press, 1982.

Graham, A. C., trans. *Chuang-tzu: The Inner Chapters*. London: Unwin, 1986.

———. *The Book of Lieh-tzu*. (1960); rpt. New York: Columbia Univ. Press, 1990.

Guo Maoqian 郭茂倩, ed. *Yuefu shiji* 樂府詩集, 2 vols. Taipei: Liren shuju, 1984.

Guo Qingfan 郭慶藩, ed. *Zhuangzi* [jijie] 莊子[集解], 4 vols. Beijing: Zhonghua shuju, 1961.

Guo Shaoyu 郭紹虞. *Qing shihua xubian* 清詩話續編, 2 vols. Shanghai: Guji chubanshe, 1983.

———. *Zhongguo wenxue piping shi* 中國文學批評史, 3 vols. Shanghai: Commercial Press, 1947.

———, ed. *Zhongguo lidai wenlun xuan* 中國歷代文論選, 4 vols. Shanghai: Guji chubanshe, 1979–80.

Hawkes, David, trans. *The Songs of the South*, 2nd ed. Harmondsworth: Penguin, 1985.

He Wenhuan 何文煥 , ed. *Lidai shihua* 歷代詩話, 2 vols. Beijing: Zhonghua shuju, 1981.

Henricks, Robert G., trans. *Philosophy and Argumentation in Third-Century China: The Essays of Hsi K'ang*. Princeton: Princeton Univ. Press, 1983.

Hightower, James R. "Allusion in the Poetry of T'ao Ch'ien." *Harvard Journal of Asiatic Studies* 31 (1971): 5–27. Rpt. in Birch, ed., 108–32.

———. "The *Fu* of T'ao Ch'ien." In *Studies in Chinese Literature*, ed. John L. Bishop. Cambridge: Harvard Univ. Press, 1966, 45–106.

———. *The Poetry of T'ao Ch'ien*. Oxford: Oxford Univ. Press, 1970.

———. "T'ao Ch'ien's 'Drinking Wine' Poems." In *Wen-lin: Studies in the Chinese Humanities*, ed. Chow Tse-tsung. Madison: Univ. of Wisconsin Press, 1968, 3–44.

Hisayuki Miyakawa. "Local Cults around Mount Lu at the Time of Sun En's Rebellion," in Welch and Seidel, eds., 83–101.

Holman, C. Hugh, and William Harmon. *A Handbook to Literature*, 5th ed. New York: Macmillan, 1986.

Holzman, Donald. "Confucius and Ancient Chinese Criticism." In Rickett, ed., 21–41.

———. "Literary Criticism in China in the Early Third Century A.D." *Asiatische Studien* 28.2 (1974): 113–49.

———. *Poetry and Politics: The Life and Works of Juan Chi, A.D. 210–263*. Cambridge: Cambridge Univ. Press, 1976.

Hong Shunlong 洪順隆. *Liuchao shilun* 六朝詩論. Taipei: Wenjin chubanshe, 1978.

———. *You yinyi dao gongti* 由隱逸到宮體. Taipei: Heluo tushu chubanshe, 1980.

Horie Tadamichi 堀江忠道. *Tō Enmei shi bun sōgō sakuin* 陶淵明詩文綜合索引. Tokyo: Ibundō shoten, 1978.

Hsiao, Kung-chuan. *A History of Chinese Political Thought*, vol. 1, trans. Frederick W. Mote. Princeton: Princeton Univ. Press, 1979.

Hsü Fu-kuan 徐復觀. *Zhongguo wenxue lunji* 中國文學論集. Taipei: Student Book Co., 1974.

———. *Zhongguo yishu jingshen* 中國藝術精神, 3rd ed. Taipei: Student Book Co., 1974.

Hu Zi 胡仔, ed. *Tiaoxi yuyin conghua* 苕溪漁隱叢話, 2 vols. Beijing: Renmin wenxue chubanshe, 1981.

Hucker, Charles O. *A Dictionary of Official Titles in Imperial China*. Stanford: Stanford Univ. Press, 1985.

Ikkai Tomoyoshi 一海知義. *Tō Enmei* 陶淵明. Tokyo: Iwanami shoten, 1965.

Innes, Mary M., trans. *The "Metamorphoses" of Ovid.* Harmondsworth: Penguin, 1955.

Jakobson, Roman. "Closing Statement: Linguistics and Poetics." In *Style in Language*, ed. Thomas A. Sebeok. Cambridge: M.I.T. Press, 1960, 350–77.

Jin Xingyao 金性堯, ed. *Song shi sanbai shou* 宋詩三百首. Shanghai: Guji chubanshe, 1986.

Kao, Yu-kung. "The Aesthetics of Regulated Verse." In Lin and Owen, eds., 332–85.

———. "Lyric Vision in Chinese Narrative: A Reading of *Hung-lou Meng* and *Ju-lin Wai-shih*." In *Chinese Narrative: Critical and Theoretical Essays*, ed. Andrew H. Plaks. Princeton: Princeton Univ. Press, 1977, 227–43.

Kaplan, Charles, ed. *Criticism: Twenty Major Statements*. Scranton, PA: Chandler Publishing Co., 1964.

Keats, John. *Letters*, ed. Maurice B. Forman. London: Oxford Univ. Press, 1974.

Kermode, Frank, ed. *English Pastoral Poetry*. London: George G. Harrap, 1952.

Knechtges, David R. *The Han Rhapsody: A Study of the Fu of Yang Hsiung*. Cambridge: Cambridge Univ. Press, 1976.

Krieger, Murray. "A Waking Dream: The Symbolic Alternative to Allegory." In Bloomfield, ed., 1–22.

Kwong, Charles. "The Rural World of Chinese 'Farmstead Poetry' *(Tianyuan Shi):* How Far Is It Pastoral?" *Chinese Literature: Essays, Articles, Reviews* 15 (1993): 57–84.

Laozi. See Zhu Qianzhi, ed.

Laozi. See Lau, D. C., trans. *Tao Te Ching.*

Lau, D. C., trans. *The Analects*. Harmondsworth: Penguin, 1979.

———, *trans. Mencius*. Harmondsworth: Penguin, 1970.

———, *trans. Tao Te Ching*. Harmondsworth: Penguin, 1963.

Lee Chik-fong 李直方. *Han Wei Liuchao shi lungao*. 漢魏六朝詩論稿. Hong Kong: Longmen shudian, 1967.

Lee, Guy, trans. *Virgil: The Eclogues*. Harmondsworth: Penguin, 1984.

Li Chendong 李辰冬. *Tao Yuanming pinglun* 陶淵明評論. Taipei: Dongda tushu gongsi, 1978.

Li Ch'i. "The Changing Concept of the Recluse in Chinese Literature." *Harvard Journal of Asiatic Studies* 24 (1962–63): 234–47.

Li Fang-kuei 李方桂. "Shanggu yin yanjiu" 上古音研究. *Tsing Hua Journal of Chinese Studies* (n.s.) 9 (1971): 1–61.

Liji. See Wang Meng'ou, trans.

Li Jian 李健 and Kang Jinsheng 康金聲, eds. *Gudai tianyuanshi zhuxi* 古代田園詩注析. Taiyuan: Shanxi renmin chubanshe, 1989.

Li Wenchu 李文初. *Tao Yuanming lunlüe* 陶淵明論略. Guangdong: Renmin chubanshe, 1986.

Li Yanshou 李延壽. *Nan shi* 南史, 6 vols. Beijing: Zhonghua shuju, 1975.

Liao Zhongan 廖仲安. *Tao Yuanming* 陶淵明. Shanghai: Guji chubanshe, n.d.

Liezi. See Graham, A. C., trans.

Liezi. See Yang Bojun, ed.

Lin, Mao-sung. *A Comparative Study of Some Themes and Techniques in the Poetry of T'ao Ch'ien and Robert Frost*. Taipei: National Taiwan Normal Univ., 1976.

Lin, Shuen-fu. "Intrinsic Music in the Medieval Chinese Lyric." In *The Lyrical Arts: A Humanities Symposium*, eds. Erling B. Holstmark and Judith P. Aikin. Special Issue of *Journal Ars Lyrica*, 1988, 29–54.

Lin, Shuen-fu and Stephen Owen, eds. *The Vitality of the Lyric Voice*. Princeton: Princeton Univ. Press, 1986.

Lin Wen-yüeh 林文月. "The Decline and Revival of *Feng-ku* (Wind and Bone)." In Lin and Owen, eds., 130–66.

———. *Shanshui yu gudian* 山水與古典. Taipei: Chunwenxue chubanshe, 1976.

———. "'Southern Mountain' and 'Spring Grass,'" trans. Felicia Hecker. *Renditions* 16 (1981): 44–61.

Liu Dajie 劉大杰. *Zhongguo wenxue fazhan shi* 忠國文學發展史, 3 vols. Shanghai: Guji chubanshe, 1982.

Liu, James J. Y. *Chinese Theories of Literature*. Chicago: Univ. of Chicago Press, 1975.

———. *Language-Paradox-Poetics: A Chinese Perspective*, ed. Richard J. Lynn. Princeton: Princeton Univ. Press, 1988.

Liu Shao 劉邵. *Ren wu zhi* 人物志, ed. Ren Jiyu 任繼愈. Beijing: Wenxue guji kanxingshe, 1955.

Liu Xiangfei 劉翔飛. "Lun zhaoyin shi" 論招隱詩. *Zhongwai wenxue* 中外文學 7.12 (1979): 98–113.

Liu Xie 劉勰. *Wenxin diaolong* [yizhu] 文心雕龍[譯注], eds. Lu Kanru 陸侃如 and Mou Shijin 牟世金, 2 vols. Jinan: Qilu shushe, 1981–82.

———. *Wenxin diaolong* [zhu] 文心雕龍[注], ed. Fan Wenlan 范文瀾, 2 vols. Beijing: Renmin wenxue chubanshe, 1978.

———. *The Literary Mind and the Carving of Dragons*, trans. Vincent Yu-chung Shih, rev. ed. Hong Kong: Chinese Univ. Press, 1983.

Liu Yiqing 劉義慶. *Shishuo xinyu* [jiaojian] 世說新語[校箋], ed. Yang Yong 楊勇. Hong Kong: Dazhong shuju, 1969.

Lu Jianrong 盧建榮. *Wei Jin ziran sixiang* 魏晉自然思想. Taipei: Lianming wenhua youxiangongsi, n.d.

Lu Kanru 陸侃如 and Feng Yuanjun 馮沅君. *Zhongguo shishi* 中國詩史, 3 vols. Beijing: Zuojia chubanshe, 1957.

Lu Qinli 逯欽立. "Guanyu Tao Yuanming" 關於陶淵明. In *TYJ* 201–60.

———. *Han Wei Liuchao wenxue lunji* 漢魏六朝文學論集, ed. Wu Yun 吳雲. Xi'an: Shaanxi renmin chubanshe, 1984.

———. "Tao Yuanming shiji shiwen xinian" 陶淵明事跡詩文繫年. In *TYJ* 261–90.

———, ed. *XianQin Han Wei Jin Nanbeichao shi* 先秦漢魏晉南北朝詩, 3 vols. Beijing: Zhonghua shuju, 1983.

Lu Xun 魯迅. "Wei Jin fengdu ji wenzhang yu yao ji jiu zhi guanxi" 魏晉風度及文章與藥及酒之關係. In his *Eryi ji* 而已集, vol. 17 of *Lu Xun sanshi nienji* 魯迅三十年集. Hong Kong: Xinyi chubanshe, 1967.

Luo Genze 羅根澤. *Zhongguo wenxue piping shi* 中國文學批評史, 3 vols. Shanghai: Guji chubanshe, 1984.

Luo Liantian 羅聯添, ed. *Zhongguo wenxueshi lunwen xuanji* 中國文學史論文選集, vol. 2. Taipei: Student Book Co., 1978.

Mair, Victor H., and Tsu-lin Mei. "The Sanskrit Origins of Recent Style Prosody." *Harvard Journal of Asiatic Studies* 51 (1991): 375–470.

Marinelli, Peter V. *Pastoral*. London: Methuen, 1971.

Mather, Richard B. "The Controversy over Conformity and Naturalness during the Six Dynasties." *History of Religion* 9.2/3 (1969/70): 160–80.

———. "Individualist Expressions of the Outsiders during the Six Dynasties." In Munro, ed., 199–214.

———. "The Landscape Buddhism of the Fifth Century Poet Hsieh Ling-yün." *Journal of Asian Studies* 18.1 (1958): 67–79.

———, trans. *Shih-shuo Hsin-yü: A New Account of Tales of the World*. Minneapolis: Univ. of Minnesota Press, 1976.

May, Herbert G., and Bruce M. Metzger, eds. *The New Oxford Annotated Bible with the Apocrypha*, rev. ed. New York: Oxford Univ. Press, 1977.

Mencius. See Lau, D. C., trans.

———. See Yang Bojun, trans.

Moore, Charles, ed. *The Chinese Mind*. Honolulu: Univ. of Hawaii Press, 1967.

Mote, Frederick W. "Confucian Eremitism in the Yüan Period." In *Confucianism and Chinese Civilization*, ed. Arthur Wright. Stanford: Stanford Univ. Press, 1975, 252–90.

Mou Zongsan 牟宗三. *Zhongguo zhexue shijiu jiang* 中國哲學十九講. Taipei: Xuesheng shuju, 1983.

Munro, Donald J. *The Concept of Man in Early China*. Stanford: Stanford Univ. Press, 1969.

———, ed. *Individualism and Holism: Studies in Confucian and Taoist Values*. Ann Arbor: Center for Chinese Studies, Univ. of Michigan, 1985.

Murakami Yoshimi 村上嘉実. "In-itsu" 隱逸. *Shirin* 史林 39.6 (1956): 461–79.

Murck, Christian, ed. *Arts and Traditions: Uses of the Past in Chinese Culture*. Princeton: Princeton Univ. Press, 1976.

Nicholson, D. H. S. and A. H. E. Lee. *The Oxford Book of English Mystical Verse*. Oxford: Oxford Univ. Press, 1917.

Nienhauser, William H., et al., eds. *The Indiana Companion to Traditional Chinese Literature*. Bloomington: Indiana Univ. Press, 1986.

Obi, Kōichi 小尾郊一. *Chūgoku bungaku ni arawareta shizen to shizenkan—Chūsei bungaku o chūshin to shite* 中國文學に現われた自然と自然觀 中世文學を中心として. Tokyo: Iwanami, 1962.

Okamura Shigeru 岡村繁. *Tō Enmei* 陶淵明. Tokyo: Nippon hōsō shuppan kyōkai, 1974.

Ovid. See Innes, Mary M., trans.

Owen, Stephen. *Remembrances: The Experience of the Past in Classical Chinese Literature*. Cambridge: Harvard Univ. Press, 1986.

———. "The Self's Perfect Mirror: Poetry as Autobiography." In Lin and Owen, eds., 71–102.

———. *Traditional Chinese Poetry and Poetics: Omen of the World*. Madison: Univ. of Wisconsin Press, 1985.

Paz, Octavio. *Sor Juana*, trans. Margaret Sayers Peden. Cambridge: Harvard Univ. Press, 1988.

Peschel, Enid R. *Four French Symbolist Poets*. Athens: Ohio Univ. Press, 1981.

Poggioli, Renato. *The Oaten Flute: Essays on the Pastoral and the Pastoral Ideal*. Cambridge: Harvard Univ. Press, 1975.

Pope, Alexander. *Poetry and Prose of Alexander Pope*, ed. Aubrey Williams. Boston: Houghton Mifflin, 1969.

Preminger, Alex, et al., eds. *Classical Literary Criticism: Translations and Interpretations*. New York: Frederick Ungar, 1974.

——— et al., eds. *Princeton Encyclopedia of Poetry and Poetics*, enlarged ed. Princeton: Princeton Univ. Press, 1974.

Qian Zhongshu 錢鍾書. *Guanzhui pian* 管錐篇, 4 vols. Beijing: Zhonghua shuju, 1979.

———. *Tan yi lu* 談藝錄 (1937). Rpt. Hong Kong: Longmen shudian, 1965.

Qu Yuan 屈原 et al. *Chuci* [tongshi] 楚辭[通釋], ed. Wang Fuzhi 王夫之. Hong Kong: Zhonghua shuju, 1960.

Quan Tang shi 全唐詩, ed. Peng Dingqiu 彭定求 et al., 25 vols. Beijing: Zhonghua shuju, 1960.

Ren Jiyu 任繼愈, ed. *Zhongguo zhexue shi* 中國哲學史, vols. 1–2. Beijing: Renmin chubanshe, 1985.

Rickett, Adele A. *Wang Kuo-wei's "Jen-chien Tz'u-hua": A Study in Chinese Literary Criticism*. Hong Kong: Hong Kong Univ. Press, 1977.

———, ed. *Chinese Approaches to Literature from Confucius to Liang Ch'i-ch'ao*. Princeton: Princeton Univ. Press, 1978.

Rogers, Michael C., trans. *The Chronicle of Fu Chien*. Berkeley: Univ. of California Press, 1968.

Ruan Ji 阮籍. *Ruan Ji ji* [jiaozhu] 阮籍集[校注], annot. Chen Bojun 陳伯君. Beijing: Zhonghua shuju, 1987.

Rump, Ariane, and Wing-tsit Chan, trans. *Commentary on the "Lao Tzu" by Wang Pi*. Honolulu: Univ. of Hawaii Press, 1979.

Schwartz, Benjamin I. *The World of Thought in Ancient China*. Cambridge: Harvard Univ. Press, 1985.

Shakespeare, William. *Complete Works*, ed. W. J. Craig. Oxford: Oxford Univ. Press, 1943.

Shangshu 尚書. *Shangshu* [jijie] 尚書[集解], ed. Zhou Bingjun 周秉鈞. Changsha: Yuelu shushe, 1984.

Shen Deqian 沈德潛, ed. *Qing shi beicai* 清詩別裁. Hong Kong: Zhongguo shuju, 1977.

Shen Yue 沈約. *Song shu* 宋書, 8 vols. Beijing: Zhonghua shuju, 1974.

Shen Zhenqi 沈振奇, *Tao Xie shi zhi bijiao* 陶謝詩之比較. Taipei: Xuosheng shuju, 1986.

Shijing 詩經. *Shijing* [yizhu] 詩經[譯注], trans. Zhu Minche 祝敏徹 et al. Lanzhou: Gansu renmin chubanshe, 1984.

Sima Guang 司馬光. *Zizhi tongjian* 資治通鑒, 10 vols. Beijing: Guji chubanshe, 1956.

Sima Qian 司馬遷. *Shiji* 史記, 10 vols. Beijing: Zhonghua shuju, 1982.

Song Qiulong 宋丘龍. *Su Dungbo he Tao Yuanming zhi bijiao yanjiu*. 蘇東坡和陶淵明詩之比較研究 Taipei: Commercial Press, 1980.

Soushen houji 搜神後記. See Wang Shaoying, ed.

Strickmann, Michel. "On the Alchemy of T'ao Hung-ching." In Welch and Seidel, eds., 123–92.

Su Shi 蘇軾. *Su Shi shiji* 蘇軾詩集. ed. Wang Wen'gao 王文誥, 8 vols. Beijing: Zhonghua shuju, 1982.

———. *Su Shi wenji* 蘇軾文集. ed. Kong Fanli 孔凡禮, 6 vols. Beijing: Zhonghua shuju, 1986.

Sui Shusen 隋樹森, ed. *Gushi shijiu shou* [jishi] 古詩十九首[集釋]. Hong Kong: Zhonghua shuju, 1958.

Sullivan, Michael. *Symbols of Eternity: The Art of Landscape Painting in China*. Stanford: Stanford Univ. Press, 1979.

Suzuki Torao 鈴木虎雄. *Tō Enmei shi kai* 陶淵明詩解. Tokyo: Kōbundō shobō, 1968.

Tai Jingnong 臺靜農. "Wei Jin wenxue sixiang de shulun" 魏晉文學思想的述論. In Luo, ed., 449–60.

Tang Changru 唐長孺. "Du 'Taohuayuanji pangzheng' zhiyi" 讀桃花源記旁証質疑. In his *Wei Jin Nanbeichaoshi luncong xubian* 魏晉南北朝史論叢續編. Beijing: Joint Publishing Co., 1959, 163–74.

———. "Wei Jin xuanxue zhi xingcheng ji qi fazhan" 魏晉玄學之形成及其發展. In his *Wei Jin Nanbeichao shi luncong* 魏晉南北朝史論叢. Beijing: Joint Publishing Co., 1955, 311–50.

Tang Guizhang 唐圭璋, ed. *Quan Song ci* 全宋詞, 5 vols. Beijing: Zhonghua shuju, 1980.

Tang Yongtong 湯用彤. *Han Wei Liang Jin Nanbeichao fojiao shi* 漢魏兩晉南北朝佛教史. Beijing: Zhonghua shuju, 1963.

———. *Wei Jin xuanxue lungao* 魏晉玄學論稿. In his *Tang Yongtong xueshu lunwen ji* 湯用彤學術論文集. Beijing: Zhonghua shuju, 1983.

Tao Qian. See Tao Yuanming.

Tao Yuanming 陶淵明. [Jianzhu] *Tao Yuanming ji* [箋注]陶淵明集, ed. Li Gonghuan 李公煥. SPTK edition.

———. *Jingjie xiansheng ji* 靖節先生集, ed. Tao Shu 陶澍. SPPY edition.

———. *Tao Jingjie shi* [jian] 陶靖節詩[箋], ed. Gu Zhi 古直. Taipei: Guangwen shuju, 1964.

———. *Tao Yuanming ji* 陶淵明集, ed. Lu Qinli 逯欽立. Beijing: Zhonghua shuju, 1979.

———. *Tao Yuanming ji* 陶淵明集, ed. Wang Yao 王瑤. Beijing: Zuojia chubanshe, 1956.

———. *Tao Yuanming ji* [jiaojian] 陶淵明集[校箋], ed. Yang Yong 楊勇. Hong Kong: Wuxingji shuju, 1971.

———. *Tao Yuanming ji* [jiaozhu] 陶淵明集[校注], ed. Sun Junxi 孫鈞錫. n.p.: Zhongzhou guji chubanshe, 1986.

Tao Yuanming yanjiu 陶淵明研究, ed. Jiusi Congshu Editorial Board 九思叢書編輯部, vol. 2. Taipei: Jiusi chubanshe, 1977.

Tao Yuanming yanjiu ziliao huibian 陶淵明研究資料彙編, ed. Dept. of Chinese, Beijing Univ. and Beijing Teachers' Univ. 北京大學北京師範大學中文系, 2 vols. Beijing: Zhonghua shuju, 1962.

Theocritus. See Wells, Robert, trans.

Todorov, Tzvetan. *Symbolism and Interpretation*, trans. Catherine Porter. Ithaca: Cornell Univ. Press, 1982.

Tu, Wei-ming. *Confucian Thought: Selfhood as Creative Transformation*. Albany: State Univ. of New York Press, 1985.

———. "Profound Learning, Personal Knowledge, and Poetic Vision." In Lin and Owen, eds., 3–31.

Vervoorn, Aat. *Men of the Cliffs and Caves: The Development of the Chinese Eremitic Tradition to the End of the Han Dynasty*. Hong Kong: The Chinese Univ. Press, 1990.

Virgil. See Lee, Guy, trans.

Wang Bi 王弼. *Wang Bi ji* [jiaoshi] 王弼集[校釋], ed. Lou Yulie 樓玉烈, 2 vols. Beijing: Zhonghua shuju, 1980.

———. See Rump and Chan, trans.

Wang Guowei 王國維. *Renjian cihua* 人間詞話, ed. Xu Diaofu 徐調孚. Hong Kong: Zhonghua shuju, 1961.

Wang Guoying 王國瓔. *Zhongguo shanshui shi yanjiu* 中國山水詩研究. Taipei: Linking Publishing Co., 1986.

Wang Meng'ou 王夢鷗, trans. *Liji* [jinzhu jinyi] 禮記[今注今譯], 2 vols. Taipei: Commercial Press, 1972.

Wang Shaoying 汪紹楹, ed. *Soushen houji* 搜神後記. Beijing: Zhonghua shuju, 1981.

Wang Shumin 王叔岷. *Tao Yuanming shijian zhenggao* 陶淵明詩箋証稿. Taipei: Yiwen yinshuguan, 1975.

Wang Yao 王瑤. *Zhonggu wenren shenghuo* 中古文人生活. Shanghai: Tangdi chubanshe, 1951.

———. *Zhonggu wenxue fengmao* 中古文學風貌. Shanghai: Tangdi chubanshe, 1951.

———. *Zhonggu wenxue sixiang* 中古文學思想 (1951). Rpt. Hong Kong: Zhongliu chubanshe, 1973.

Wang Yi-t'ung 王伊同. *Wuchao mendi* 五朝門第, rev. ed., 2 vols. Hong Kong: Chinese Univ. Press, 1978.

Wang Yunxi 王運熙. *Han Wei Liuchao Tang dai wenxue luncong* 漢魏六朝唐代文學論叢. Shanghai: Guji chubanshe, 1981.

Wang Yunxi 王運熙 and Gu Yisheng 顧易生, eds. *Zhongguo wenxue piping shi* 中國文學批評史, 3 vols. Shanghai: Guji chubanshe, 1981–85.

Wang Zhongling 王鍾陵. *Zhongguo zhonggu shige shi* 中國中古詩歌史. n.p.: Jiangsu jiaoyu chubanshe, 1988.

Wang Zhongluo 王仲犖. *Wei Jin Nanbeichao shi* 魏晉南北朝史, 2 vols. Shanghai: Renmin chubanshe, 1979–80.

Watson, Burton. *Chinese Lyricism*. New York: Columbia Univ. Press, 1971.

———, trans. *Chinese Rhyme-Prose*. New York: Columbia Univ. Press, 1971.

———, trans. *Complete Works of Chuang Tzu*. New York: Columbia Univ. Press, 1968.

Wei Jin Liuchao shi yanjiu lunwen ji 魏晉六朝詩研究論文集, ed. Zhongguo yuwen xueshe 中國語文學社. Hong Kong: Zhongguo yuwen xueshe, 1969.

Wei Jin Nanbeichao wenxueshi cankao ziliao 魏晉南北朝文學史參考資料, comp. Beijing daxue Zhongguo wenxueshi jiaoyanshi 北京大學中國文學史教研室. Hong Kong: Zhonghua shuju, 1986.

Wei Qingzhi 魏慶之, ed. *Shiren yuxie* 詩人玉屑, 2 vols. Shanghai: Guji chubanshe, 1978.

Welch, Holmes. *Taoism: The Parting of the Way*, rev. ed. Boston: Beacon Press, 1965.

Welch, Holmes, and Anna Seidel, eds. *Facets of Taoism*. New Haven: Yale Univ. Press, 1979.

Wells, Robert, trans. *The Idylls of Theocritus*. Harmondsworth: Penguin, 1989.

Wender, Dorothea, trans. *Hesiod and Theognis*. Harmondsworth: Penguin, 1973.

Westbrook, Francis A. "Landscape Transformation in the Poetry of Hsieh Lingyün." *Journal of the American Oriental Society* 100 (1980): 237–54.

Wilhelm, Richard, trans. *The I Ching or Book of Changes*, rendered into English by Cary F. Baynes. Princeton: Princeton Univ. Press, 1967.

Wilson, Edmund. *Axel's Castle: A Study in the Imaginative Literature of 1870–1930*. New York: Charles Scribner's Sons, 1931.

Wixted, John T. "The Nature of Evaluation in the *Shipin* by Zhong Hong (A.D. 459–518)." In Bush and Murck, eds., 225–64.

Wordsworth, William. *Poetical Works*, ed. Thomas Hutchinson, new ed., rev. Ernest de Selincourt. Oxford: Oxford Univ. Press, 1969.

———. *The Prelude*, eds. Jonathan Wordsworth et al. New York: Norton, 1979.

Wu Lifu 伍蠡甫, ed. *Shanshui yu meixue* 山水與美學. Shanghai: Wenyi chubanshe, 1985.

Xi Kang 嵇康. *Xi Kang ji* [jiaozhu] 嵇康集[校注], ed. Dai Mingyang 戴明揚. Beijing: Renmin wenxue chubanshe, 1962.

Xiao Tong 蕭統, ed. *Wen xuan* 文選, 6 vols. Shanghai: Guji chubanshe, 1986.

Xiao Zixian 蕭子顯. *Nan Qi shu* 南齊書, 3 vols. Beijing: Zhonghua shuju, 1972.

Xie Lingyun 謝靈運. *Xie Lingyun ji* [jiaozhu] 謝靈運集[校注], ed. Gu Shaobai 顧紹柏. Henan: Zhongzhou guji chubanshe, 1987.

———. *Xie Lingyun shixuan* 謝靈運詩選, ed. Ye Xiaoxue 葉笑雪. Shanghai: Gudian wenxue chubanshe, 1957.

Xu Yimin 許逸民, ed. *Tao Yuanming nianpu* 陶淵明年譜. Beijing: Zhonghua shuju, 1986.

Xunzi 荀子. *Xunzi* [jijie] 荀子[集解], ed. Wang Xianqian 王先謙. Taipei: Shijie shuju, 1967.

Yang Bojun 楊伯峻, ed. *Chunqiu Zuozhuan* [zhu] 春秋左傳[注], 4 vols. Beijing: Zhonghua shuju, 1981.

———, ed. *Liezi* [jishi] 列子[集釋]. Beijing: Zhonghua shuju, 1979.

———, trans. *Lunyu* [yizhu] 論語[譯注]. Hong Kong: Zhonghua shuju, 1984.

———, trans. *Mengzi* [yizhu] 孟子[譯注], 2 vols. Beijing: Zhonghua shuju, 1960.

Yang Chunqiu 羊春秋 et al., eds. *Lidai lunshi jueju xuan* 歷代論詩絕句選. Changsha: Hunan renmin chubanshe, 1981.

Ye Lang 葉朗. *Zhongguo meixueshi dagang* 中國美學史大綱. Shanghai: Renmin chubanshe, 1985.

Yeh Chia-ying 葉嘉瑩. *Jialing lunci conggao* 迦陵論詞叢稿. Shanghai: Guji chubanshe, 1980.

———. *Jialing lunshi conggao* 迦陵論詩叢稿. Beijing: Zhonghua shuju, 1984.

———. *Zhongguo gudian shige pinglun ji* 中國古典詩歌評論集. Hong Kong: Zhonghua shuju, 1977.

Yijing. See Gao Heng, ed.

Yijing. See Wilhelm, Richard, trans.

Yoshikawa Kōjirō 吉川幸次郎. *Chūgoku shishi* 中國詩史, 2 vols. Tokyo: Chikuma shobō, 1967.

Yu, Pauline R. *The Reading of Imagery in the Chinese Poetic Tradition*. Princeton: Princeton Univ. Press, 1987.

Yü, Ying-shih 余英時. "Individualism and the Neo-Taoist Movement in Wei-Chin China." In Munro, ed., 121–55.

———. "Life and Immortality in the Mind of Han China." *Harvard Journal of Asiatic Studies* 25 (1964–65): 80–122.

———. *Shi yu Zhongguo wenhua* 士與中國文化. Shanghai: Renmin chubanshe, 1987.

———. *Zhongguo sixiang chuantong de xiandai quanshi* 中國思想傳統的現代詮釋. Taipei: Linking Publishing Co., 1987.

Yuan Ke 袁珂. *Zhongguo shenhua chuanshuo* 中國神話傳說. Beijing: Zhongguo wenjian wenyi chubanshe, 1984.

———. *Zhongguo shenhua chuanshuo cidian* 中國神話傳說辭典. Hong Kong: Commercial Press, 1986.

———, ed. *Shanhai jing* [jiaozhu] 山海經[校注]. Shanghai Guji chubanshe, 1980.

Yuan Xingpei 袁行霈. *Zhongguo shige yishu yanjiu* 中國詩歌藝術研究. Beijing: Beijing Univ. Press, 1987.

Zhan Ying 詹瑛. *Wenxin diaolong de fengge xue* 文心雕龍的風格學. Beijing: Renmin wenxue chubanshe, 1982.

Zhang Longxi. *The Tao and the Logos: Literary Hermeneutics, East and West*. Durham: Duke Univ. Press, 1992.

Zhao Yi 趙翼. *Oubei shihua* 甌北詩話. Taipei: Guangwen shuju, 1962.

Zhong Hong 鍾嶸. *Shipin* [zhu] 詩品[注], ed. Chen Yanjie 陳延傑. Beijing: Renmin wenxue chubanshe, 1980.

Zhong Qi 鍾祺. *Zhonggu shige luncong* 中古詩歌論叢. Hong Kong: Shanghai Book Co., 1965.

Zhong Youmin 鍾優民. *Tao Yuanming lunji* 陶淵明論集. Hunan: Renmin chubanshe, 1981.

———. *Xie Lingyun lungao* 謝靈運論稿. Jinan: Qilu shushe, 1985.

———. *Zhongguo shige shi: Wei Jin Nanbeichao* 中國詩歌史魏晉南北朝. Changchun: Jilin Univ. Press, 1989.

Zhongguo meixueshi ziliao xuanbian 中國美學史資料選編, comp. Beijing daxue zhexuexi meixue jiaoyanshi 北京大學哲學系美學教研室, 2 vols. Beijing: Zhonghua shuju, 1980–81.

Zhongguo zhexueshi ziliao xuanji—LiangHan zhibu 中國哲學史資料選輯：兩漢之部, comp. Zhongguo shehuikexueyuan zhexue yanjiusuo Zhongguo zhexueshi yanjiushi 中國社會科學院哲學研究所中國哲學史研究室, 2 vols. Beijing: Zhonghua shuju, 1982.

Zhu Qianzhi 朱謙之, ed. *Laozi* [jiaoshi] 老子[校釋]. Beijing: Zhonghua shuju, 1984.

Zhu Xi 朱熹, ed. *Sishu* [zhangju jizhu] 四書[章句集注]. Beijing: Zhonghua shuju, 1983.

Zhu Ziqing 朱自清. *Shiyanzhi bian* 詩言志辨. Taipei: Wuzhou chubanshe, 1964.

———. *Zhu Ziqing ji* 朱自清集. Taipei: Heluo tushu chubanshe, 1977.

Zhuangzi. See Guo Qingfan, ed.

Zhuangzi. See Watson, Burton, trans.

Zuozhuan. See Yang Bojun, ed.

Zürcher, E. *The Buddhist Conquest of China: The Spread and Adaptation of Buddhism in Early Medieval China*, 2 vols. Leiden: Brill, 1959.

Glossary

anshen liming	安身立命
Anshen lun	安身論
ba da	八達
Bai Juyi	白居易
Bao Jingyan	鮑敬言
Bao Zhao	鮑照
Baopuzi	抱朴子
Baxian lun	八賢論
bi	比
Bo Yi	伯夷
Cai Yong	蔡邕
Canglang shihua	滄浪詩話
Cao Cao	曹操
Cao Pi	曹丕
Cao Zhi	曹植
Chaisang	柴桑
chan	禪
Changju	長沮
Changsha	長沙
chaoyin	朝隱
Chen	陳
Chen Shidao	陳師道
Chen Zuoming	陳祚明
Chi Chao	郗超
Chu	楚
Chu Guangxi	儲光羲
chuanshen	傳神
Chuci	楚辭
ci	辭
cida	辭達
cixing	辭興
Da zhao	大招
Dan	丹
danggu	黨錮
Dao	道
Dao de lun	道德論
daoli	道理
de	德
Deng Can	鄧粲
diezi	疊字
dingzhen	頂針
Dong Zhongshu	董仲舒
Dongfang Shuo	東方朔
du	獨
Du Fu	杜甫

Duan Yucai	段玉裁
dun	遁
Fa yan	法言
Fang Dongshu	方東樹
feidun	肥遁
fen	分
fengli	風力
fu	賦
Fu Jia	傅嘏
Fu Jian	苻堅
Fu Xuan	傅玄
Fu Yuan	傅瑗
Fuxi	伏羲
Gan Bao	干寶
ganying	感應
Gong di	恭帝
Gong Sheng	龔勝
gongti shi	宮體詩
gu	蠱
Gu Kaizhi	顧愷之
Gu Yanwu	顧炎武
Guan Lu	管輅
Guo Pu	郭璞
Guo Wen	郭文
Guo Xiang	郭象
Han	漢
Han Wu gushi	漢武故事
Han Wudi neizhuan	漢武帝內傳
Han Yu	韓愈
He Long	郝隆
He Yan	何晏
He Yisun	賀貽孫
Houhan ji	後漢紀
Huan Wen	桓溫
Huan Xuan	桓玄
Huang Tingjian	黃庭堅
Huangfu Xizhi	皇甫希之
hundun	渾沌
jia	佳
Jia Mi	賈謐
Jia Yi	賈誼
jian	見
Jian'an	建安
Jiang Ji	蔣濟
jiang wu tong	將無同
Jiangzhou	江州
Jianwen di	簡文帝
Jieni	桀溺
Jin	晉
Jing Ke	荊軻
jingjie	境界
Jingjie	靖節
jingshen	精神
Jingu	金谷
Jingwei	精衛
jingxue	經學
Jingyuan	敬遠
jirang	擊壤
Jiu ge	九歌
ju	菊
junzi	君子
Kang Sengyuan	康僧淵
Lanting	蘭亭
Laozi	老子
li	理
Li Bai	李白
Li sao	離騷
li shan	立善
Li Ying	李膺

Liang	梁
Liang Ch'i-ch'ao	梁啟超
Liezi	列子
Liji	禮記
liqu mei	理趣美
Liu Bei	劉備
Liu Shao	劉邵
(Liu) Song	劉宋
Liu Xie	劉勰
Liu Yi	劉毅
Liu Yu	劉裕
Liu Yuxi	劉禹錫
Liu Ziji	劉子驥
Liu Zongyuan	柳宗元
Liuxia Hui	柳下惠
Lu	魯
Lu Ji	陸機
Lu Xun	魯迅
Mao Xianshu	毛先舒
Meng Haoran	孟浩然
Ming	明
ming (name)	名
ming (destiny)	命
mingjiao	名教
mingshi	名士
mu	畝
Ouyang Xiu	歐陽修
Pan Ni	潘尼
Pan Yue	潘岳
Pei Kai	裴楷
Pei Xisheng	裴希聲
Penglai	蓬萊
Pengze	彭澤
pu	樸
Qian Lou	黔婁
Qin	秦
Qing	清
qingjing jiaorong	情景交融
qingli	情理
qingtan	清談
qingyi	清議
qiqi	凄凄
Qiyuan	漆園
Qu Yuan	屈原
Renwu zhi	人物志
Ruan Ji	阮籍
Ruan Xiu	阮修
Ruan Zhan	阮瞻
rushen	入神
shan	善
Shan Tao	山濤
Shang	商
Shanhai jing	山海經
Shanju fu	山居賦
shanshui	山水
Shanyang gong	山陽公
shen	神
Shen Deqian	沈德潛
Shen Yue	沈約
Shennong	神農
shensi	神似
shenwu jiaorong	神物交融
shenxian zhuan	神仙傳
shi (literatus)	士
shi (poetry)	詩
shi (service)	仕
Shi Chong	石崇
Shi Decao	施德藻
Shi pin	詩品
Shi si lun	釋私論

shi yan zhi	詩言志
Shijing	詩經
shili	事理
Shishuo xinyu	世說新語
shizu	世族
Shu	疏
Shu Qi	叔齊
Shujiu	述酒
Shun	舜
Sima Jizhu	司馬季主
Sima Qian	司馬遷
Sima Xiangru	司馬相如
Sima Yan	司馬炎
Sima Yu	司馬昱
Sima Zhao	司馬昭
Song	宋
Song Lian	宋濂
Song shu	宋書
Soushen houji	搜神後記
Soushen ji	搜神記
Su Shi	蘇軾
Su Yu	蘇輿
Sun Chuo	孫綽
Sun Deng	孫登
Sun En	孫恩
Sun Sheng	孫盛
Sun Si	孫嗣
Sun Tong	孫統
Taikang	太康
Taiyuan	太元
Tan Daoluan	檀道鸞
Tang	唐
Tao Kan	陶侃
Tao Qian	陶潛
Tao Yuanming	陶淵明
Tian Chou	田疇
tian ming	天命
Tianshi dao	天師道
tianyuan shi	田園詩
tiwu	體物
tongda	通達
tongshi	通識
wang	望
Wang Anshi	王安石
Wang Bi	王弼
Wang Changling	王昌齡
Wang Cheng	王澄
Wang Dao	王導
Wang Fuzhi	王夫之
Wang Guowei	王國維
Wang Kangju	王康琚
Wang Meng	王濛
Wang Wei	王維
Wang Xizhi	王羲之
Wang Xuanzhi	王玄之
Wang Yan	王衍
Wei	魏
Wei Yingwu	韋應物
Wen Qiao	溫嶠
Wen xuan	文選
wu	無
wu wei	無為
wu wo	無我
wuwo liangwang	物我兩忘
Xi Kang	嵇康
Xi Shao	嵇紹
Xi Xi	嵇喜
Xia	夏
Xiahou Xuan	夏侯玄
xian	仙
Xiang jun	湘君

Xiang Xiu	向秀
xiao kang	小康
Xiao Tong	蕭統
Xiao Zixian	蕭子顯
xiaocao	小草
Xiaowu di	孝武帝
xiaoyao	逍遙
Xie An	謝安
Xie Lingyun	謝靈運
Xie Tiao	謝脁
Xie Wan	謝萬
Xie Xuan	謝玄
Xin Mi	辛謐
Xin Qiji	辛棄疾
xing	興
xingsi	形似
xingyun liushui	行雲流水
Xu Xun	許詢
xuan	玄
xuanxu	玄虛
xuanxue	玄學
xuanyan shi	玄言詩
Xunzi	荀子
Yan He	顏闔
Yan Hui	顏回
Yan Yanzhi	顏延之
Yan Yu	嚴羽
yang	陽
Yang Xiong	揚雄
Yang Xiuzhi	陽休之
Yang Zhu	楊朱
Yao	堯
Ye Xie	葉燮
Yijing	易經
yijing	意境
yili	義理
yiyi	依依
yin	陰
yin	隱
Yin Jingren	殷景仁
Ying Zhan	應詹
yonghuai shi	詠懷詩
Yongjia	永嘉
yongshi shi	詠史詩
you wo	有我
youxian shi	遊仙詩
Yu	禹
Yu Bing	庾冰
Yu Jun	庾峻
Yu Liang	庾亮
Yu You	庾友
yuanzhi	遠志
Yue Guang	樂廣
yuefu	樂府
Yun Jing	惲敬
zan	贊
zashi	雜詩
Zha	蚱
Zhai Tang	翟湯
Zhang Heng	張衡
Zhang Hua	張華
Zhang Jie	張戒
Zhang Wei	張偉
Zhang Xie	張協
Zhang Zhan	張湛
Zhangye	張掖
Zhao yinshi	招隱士
zhaohun	招魂
zhaoyin shi	招隱詩
zhen	真
Zhen Dexiu	真德秀
zheng	正
zheng	政
Zhengshi	正始

zhi 志
Zhi Dun 支遁
zhi ming 知命
zhida 指達
zhiguai 志怪
zhiyin 知音
zhizhi 質直
Zhong Hong 鍾嶸
Zhong Hui 鍾會
Zhou 周
Zhu Fashen 竺法深
Zhu Xi 朱熹
Zhu Ziqing 朱自清
Zhuang Zhou 莊周
Zhuangzi 莊子
Zhuangzi zhu 莊子注
Zhuge Liang 諸葛亮
zhuo 拙
Zilu 子路
ziran 自然
Zong Bing 宗炳
Zuo Si 左思
Zuozhuan 左傳

Index